D1523262

# SETTING
# NATIONAL
# PRIORITIES
*The 1983 Budget*

JOSEPH A. PECHMAN *Editor*

# SETTING NATIONAL PRIORITIES
## *The 1983 Budget*

Henry J. Aaron
Barry P. Bosworth
Edward M. Gramlich
Robert W. Hartman
William W. Kaufmann
Deborah S. Laren
Charles L. Schultze

**THE BROOKINGS INSTITUTION**
*Washington, D.C.*

# Foreword

THE BUDGET proposed by President Reagan for fiscal year 1983 raises numerous important and difficult issues. But the overriding question is whether the nation can have sustained economic growth and lower inflation with rising budget deficits and a tight monetary policy. The question arises because the president insists that the tax cuts enacted in 1981 and a sharply growing national defense budget should not be altered even though planned federal outlays will greatly exceed expected receipts for several years ahead. This volume, the thirteenth in an annual series since 1970, explains why the president's budget will produce widening deficits, examines alternative policies, and evaluates the implications of the various options for the short and long run.

The book first describes recent budget developments that led to the present unsatisfactory state of the budget. It then explains the president's proposals for fiscal 1983 and evaluates the prospects for achieving his budgetary and economic goals in the years ahead. Separate chapters devoted to the defense and nondefense budgets are followed by a chapter that analyzes the administration's new federalism, which proposes a major realignment of government responsibilities among the three levels of government. Various options to reach a satisfactory budget compromise are then presented, and the procedures by which the Congress reaches budget decisions are critically analyzed.

The first of two appendixes provides estimates for different income classes of the individual income tax cuts scheduled for the years 1982–84. The second lists the special income tax provisions that are in many ways equivalent to direct federal expenditures and compares their magnitudes.

Preparation of this volume was undertaken jointly by the Brookings Economic Studies and Foreign Policy Studies programs. Joseph A. Pechman is director, Barry P. Bosworth, Henry J. Aaron, Robert W. Hartman, and Charles L. Schultze are senior fellows, and Julie A. Carr and John Karl Scholz are research assistants, in the Economic Studies program. William W. Kaufmann, a consultant to the Foreign Policy Studies program, is a member of the faculty of the Massachusetts Institute of Technology. Edward M. Gramlich is director, and Deborah S. Laren is a research associate, of the Institute of Public Policy Studies of the University of Michigan.

The risk of factual error in this book was minimized by the work of Penelope Harpold and Ellen W. Smith. Elizabeth H. Cross, Nancy D. Davidson, and Caroline Lalire edited the manuscript.

The views expressed in this volume are solely those of the authors and should not be attributed to the trustees, officers, or other staff members of the Brookings Institution.

BRUCE K. MACLAURY  
*President*

*March 1982*  
*Washington, D.C.*

# Contents

Contents

# Appendix Tables

CHAPTER ONE

# Introduction and Summary

JOSEPH A. PECHMAN

PRESIDENT REAGAN's budget proposals for fiscal year 1983 continue the thrust of his policies to cut the growth of federal spending and taxes. During his first year in office he persuaded Congress to increase defense outlays, sharply reduce spending on domestic programs, and phase in a large tax cut over three years. These actions were expected to reduce inflation, promote economic growth through the stimulation of economic incentives, and eliminate the budget deficit by 1984. However, economic developments in 1981 did not unfold as the administration had hoped: the rate of inflation was cut by a third, but a deep recession began in midyear and budget estimates for the future suggested that federal spending will greatly exceed revenues under the new tax law, even after the economy recovers from the recession.

Despite the gloomy outlook, President Reagan stuck to his guns in the budget he submitted for 1983. He proposed further increases in defense outlays and additional large cuts in nondefense spending but insisted that the tax cuts enacted in 1981 be kept intact. He also proposed a major new initiative to shift governmental functions from the federal level to state and local levels. The president acknowledged that his proposals would postpone the achievement

Henry J. Aaron, Edward M. Gramlich, and William W. Kaufmann assisted in the preparation of this chapter. Ralph C. Bryant, Robert W. Hartman, and Charles L. Schultze made numerous helpful suggestions. Allan M. Rivlin provided research assistance, and Evelyn M. E. Taylor typed the manuscript.

of a balanced budget at least until 1987, but even this projection was regarded by congressional and private experts as too sanguine. Most budget forecasters predicted large and widening deficits in the years ahead under the administration's program.

The impending deficits are only symptoms of the major issues raised by the 1983 budget. The capital markets are concerned about the impact of the deficits on interest rates and on the rate of capital formation, which in turn will have significant effects on the growth and stability of the economy. The administration's defense plans are being scrutinized carefully to see whether the nation's defense needs can be met at a lower cost. Coming on top of last year's budget decisions, the new cuts in nondefense spending may be especially burdensome to disadvantaged groups in society and to state and local governments. The new federalism raises fundamental questions about the allocation of responsibilities among the various levels of government and how government services will be financed. And the long-run mismatch of budget outlays and receipts can be corrected only by making large additional cuts in spending and raising a substantial amount of new revenue as well. The congressional budgetary procedures were not designed to resolve such difficult issues, yet the condition of the economy in the years ahead depends heavily on the way Congress responds to the challenge.

## The Budget

The 1983 budget calls for outlays of $758 billion and receipts of $666 billion, leaving a deficit of $92 billion (table 1-1).

In preparing the 1983 budget, President Reagan was confronted with alarming estimates of the trend in the budget deficit. Starting with outlays and receipts on the assumption that current services would be unchanged and adding the cost of his defense program, he found that the deficits would amount to $101 billion in fiscal 1982, $146 billion in 1983, $165 billion in 1984, and $168 billion in 1985 (table 1-1). These estimates assumed that the economy would recover quickly from the 1981–82 recession and that in 1982–87 real gross national product would grow at a rate almost matching that of the early 1960s, which is the highest rate achieved during any five-year period since 1950.

Introduction and Summary 3

**Table 1-1. The Federal Budget in Fiscal Year 1981 and Alternative Projections for 1982–85**

Billions of dollars

| | | Projected | | | |
|---|---|---|---|---|---|
| Item | 1981 | 1982 | 1983 | 1984 | 1985 |
| *Current services with proposed defense outlays*[a] | | | | | |
| Outlays | 657.2 | 727.7 | 799.0 | 868.6 | 946.3 |
| Receipts | 599.3 | 626.4 | 653.3 | 703.8 | 778.3 |
| Deficit | − 57.9 | − 101.2 | − 145.6 | − 164.8 | − 168.0 |
| *Reagan budget estimates*[a] | | | | | |
| Outlays | 657.2 | 725.3 | 757.6 | 805.9 | 868.5 |
| Receipts | 599.3 | 626.8 | 666.1 | 723.0 | 796.6 |
| Deficit | − 57.9 | − 98.6 | − 91.5 | − 82.9 | − 71.9 |
| *Reagan budget proposals and alternative assumptions*[b] | | | | | |
| Outlays | 657.2 | 735.4 | 782.1 | 847.0 | 920.4 |
| Receipts | 599.3 | 627.1 | 657.3 | 711.3 | 776.0 |
| Deficit | − 57.9 | − 108.2 | − 124.8 | − 135.7 | − 144.4 |

Sources: Tables 2-2, 2-5, and 2-9. Figures are rounded.
a. Based on the administration's economic assumptions.
b. Based on alternative economic assumptions that give two-thirds weight to the projections of the Congressional Budget Office and one-third to those of the administration, and assuming that only half the savings projected in the budget for management initiatives and 80 percent of the proposed outlay cuts and tax revision measures will be realized.

To bring the deficits down, the president proposed sharp cuts in spending on some entitlements and other nondefense programs (including grants in aid to state and local governments), higher user fees for federal services that provide benefits for easily identifiable groups, adoption of management initiatives to improve the efficiency of federal operations, and elimination of unintended and obsolete tax benefits. The proposed cuts in outlays would apply to practically every nondefense program except social security, which would not be touched until a special commission makes its report after the 1982 elections. In total, fiscal 1983 nondefense outlays other than for social security and interest payments would be cut 13 percent in nominal terms and 20 percent in real terms below current services.

The president's budget would reduce the growth of total real federal spending from 4 percent a year in 1975–81 to 1 percent in 1981–87. However, spending for national defense would increase by almost 8 percent a year in real terms while real nondefense spending would decline by almost 2 percent a year. The decline

**4**                                                Joseph A. Pechman

in discretionary nondefense spending (that is, outlays other than entitlements and interest) would be even sharper, averaging about 8 percent a year in real terms. As a result of the nondefense cuts, total budget outlays would decline from the peak of 23.5 percent of GNP in 1982 to 21 percent in 1985; receipts would decline from the 1981 peak of 21 percent to about 19 percent in 1984 and 1985.

Full implementation of the president's budget recommendations would reduce outlays and increase receipts by $54 billion in 1983 and by rising amounts thereafter. If his economic assumptions are realized, the remaining deficits will decline from $99 billion in 1982 to $92 billion in 1983, $83 billion in 1984, and $72 billion in 1985. The president specifically rejected advice to delay the recently enacted income tax cuts or to increase excise taxes on alcohol, tobacco, and gasoline as a way of bringing the deficits down more quickly.

The administration's economic projections are widely regarded as optimistic and some allowance must be made for the inevitable slippage resulting from congressional action on the budget savings proposed by the president. As table 1-1 shows, an entirely different picture of budget prospects emerges when the Reagan budget is priced out on more realistic assumptions.[1] Instead of declining from $99 billion to $72 billion, the deficits could rise from $108 billion in 1982 to almost $145 billion in 1985. Despite differences in methodology and assumptions, most congressional and private projections agree that deficits this large or larger are likely unless spending is cut even more than the president proposes or taxes are increased, or both.

### The Economy

The effect of the projected deficits on the economy is the major issue raised by the 1983 budget. Although almost everyone agrees that the deficits must be reduced, the discussion often does not distinguish between the intermediate and longer-run consequences of such action. Deficit reduction during the current recession would reduce total demand for goods and services and

1. The major difference between the two sets of estimates results from differences in economic assumptions and the translation of these assumptions into estimated outlays and receipts. For details, see table 1-1, footnote b.

thus aggravate the contraction and slow the subsequent expansion. Reduction of the large and widening deficits that are in prospect for later years could improve economic prospects—if the reductions were accompanied by an easier monetary policy or if inflationary expectations were reduced enough so that the currently scheduled growth in the money supply could support a higher rate of economic growth.

Fiscal and monetary policies appear to be on a collision course in the years immediately ahead. The budget implies large and increasing deficits while the monetary authorities, who have the full support of the administration, are determined to slow inflation further by maintaining a policy of restraint. If the Federal Reserve holds to its announced targets for the money stock, the economy will be able to grow only if there is a large increase—well above the trend increases typical of recent history—in the velocity of money (that is, the rate at which money is used). But unusually large increases in velocity normally occur when high interest rates provide greater than normal incentives to businesses and households to economize on their monetary balances. In circumstances such as those now prevailing in the economy, output and employment may grow for brief periods. But any sustained expansion is likely to be choked off by rising interest rates, as increasing credit demands run up against the tight monetary targets. This is what happened in the aftermath of the 1980 recession, and the experience is likely to be repeated in the coming years unless the mix of fiscal and monetary policies is significantly altered.

It would be irresponsible for Congress, therefore, to proceed on the assumption that the administration's proposals will bring the deficits down below $100 billion in 1983–85, when the likelihood, even with optimistic assumptions, is that they will exceed $140 billion. But the task of doing something about these deficits is monumental. President Reagan has already recommended large cuts in outlays and modest tax increases that would reduce the 1985 deficit by almost $100 billion. To reduce the deficit even more, Congress would have to approve these deficit-reducing measures or their equivalent and add further reductions of its own. This would require a political consensus to reconsider budget options that the president has specifically rejected.

Keeping current monetary policy unchanged over the next

several years while accepting the large spending cuts and tax increases needed to reduce the deficit below the current projections might weaken the economy more than is intended. But if monetary policy was eased as the deficit was reduced, the change in policy mix would lower interest rates and shift spending away from consumption toward business investment; total output, employment, and productive capacity would then grow at modest rates. Only after the underlying inflation rate has been brought down still further will it be possible for the economy to experience vigorous growth simultaneously with moderate growth in the stock of money.

The period during which the nation will have to accept relatively slow economic growth in order to bring down inflation could be shortened, and the anti-inflation effectiveness of monetary and fiscal policies strengthened, by the adoption of some kind of incomes policy, such as tax incentives, voluntary guidelines, or more formal controls, to slow the growth of prices and wages directly. However, the administration has ruled out the use of incomes policy in any form. In this situation, even with an improved mix of fiscal and monetary policies, further reduction of the underlying inflation rate will require the continuation of slow growth and high unemployment for a number of years.

### The Defense Budget

A striking feature of the proposed budget is its generosity to the Department of Defense. The president proposes total obligational authority of $258 billion in fiscal 1983 for defense, 20 percent more than was appropriated in 1982 (13 percent more in real terms). Outlays would amount to $216 billion, an increase of 18 percent over the previous year (10.5 percent in real terms). This rate of growth would decline somewhat during the next four years, but the cumulative totals for the five-year defense plan would amount to $1.6 trillion in obligational authority and $1.4 trillion in outlays. From 1981 through 1987 outlays would increase in real terms by more than 61 percent, or over one-tenth of all the growth in national output projected for this period.

The Reagan defense plan has been criticized on a number of grounds. It is said to be unfair because its increases will be at the expense of major social programs. It is accused of being potentially inflationary because the defense goods and services required by it will, in the near term, exceed the ability of the economy to supply them. It is charged with being more generally counterproductive because it will continue to keep the federal deficit at an unacceptably high level in the years ahead. However, all these sacrifices would probably be accepted if national security were considered to be in jeopardy. Thus the central issue is whether external threats justify as large an increase in defense spending as President Reagan has requested.

There are ample grounds for considering more modest rates of growth. The president and his advisers have expressed concern about windows of vulnerability and dangers in the immediate future, but they have not proposed funding the crash programs that would close the windows or meet the dangers. A reasonable inference to be drawn from the long-term nature of the programs being undertaken—most of which will not increase U.S. military capabilities before the late 1980s or early 1990s—is that the emphasis has been placed as much on escalating defense spending and satisfying traditional service preferences as on the acquisition of the military output needed to deal with major U.S. vulnerabilities.

There has been a remarkable continuity in what constitute the fundamental conditions of American security in the current age. For most of the years since World War II, the United States has followed a defense policy with two major components: the deterrence of nuclear attack on the United States and its allies by means of second-strike strategic and theater nuclear capabilities designed to cover a wide range of military, economic, and urban targets primarily in the Soviet Union; and the containment of Soviet and satellite conventional power by means of U.S. and allied land, sea, and air forces with the intercontinental mobility to deal with one major and one lesser attack, wherever they might occur.

For all practical purposes, the administration has accepted this policy. However, two modifications in it are being proposed. Whereas previous administrations have concentrated on achieving the ability to outlast the enemy in short conventional wars, the current objective seems to be to prepare for nonnuclear conflicts of much longer duration. Furthermore, the administration plans to acquire the additional capabilities required for what it calls horizontal escalation. Thus any potential attacker must expect to be met not only with a direct defense in a given theater, but also with U.S. assaults on the attacker's own areas of vulnerability.

Despite the arguments about the relative strength of the U.S. and Soviet nuclear forces, a nuclear stalemate exists and is likely to continue for the foreseeable future. U.S. strategic nuclear forces can deliver at least 3,000 warheads on targets in the Soviet Union at the present time, and that number will rise as air-launched cruise missiles are deployed. However, the intercontinental ballistic missile leg of the strategic triad (whose three components are bombers, ICBMs, and submarine-launched ballistic missiles) has become vulnerable, and the ability of bombers to penetrate Soviet air defenses in the late 1980s may become increasingly questionable.

The nonnuclear balance continues to be more precarious. Conventional land forces in the continental United States are deficient in the intercontinental mobility needed to deploy them to distant theaters in sufficient time to meet realistic threats; they would also derive greater benefit from increased training than from more modern equipment. Naval forces, while fully capable of controlling essential sea lines of communication, are supported by an aging fleet of auxiliary vessels and are deficient in the frigates and destroyers required for convoy duty in a worldwide conflict. Should the Soviet Union engage in slower but more powerful buildups in Europe and the Caucasus than are currently anticipated, the United States and its allies could find themselves deficient in the active-duty land and tactical air forces to counterbalance these buildups.

The defense program of the Reagan administration only partly addresses such problems. The deployment of mobile (MX) missiles, planned by the Carter administration to reduce the vulnerability of the ICBM force, has been canceled. The administration still proposes to fund as much as $20 billion for the MX during the coming five years. But the deployment of the first forty missiles will leave them as vulnerable as the existing ICBM force. Another $35 billion will probably be required for the acquisition of 100 B-1B bombers to replace the B-52Hs, a substitution that will mean a small increase in the number of weapons that can be delivered to the Soviet Union on a second strike. Although it remains unclear what role continental air defenses should play beyond warning and peacetime surveillance, more than $5 billion is being programmed to modernize the existing system.

In fiscal 1983 alone, cancellations of some of the nuclear force programs (such as the B-1) and reductions in others (such as the MX and conventional air defense) would save about $3.5 billion in outlays. Total savings in outlays for the five-year plan could amount to as much as $42 billion in current dollars.

Nearly 90 percent of the resources the administration is programming for the conventional forces over the next five years are intended to modernize and increase the readiness and sustainability of existing capabilities. The remaining 10 percent, or approximately $115 billion, will go to six programs, of which the largest are the construction of thirty-six more ships for the Navy and the stockpiling of modern munitions for forty-five more days of intense combat.

Improvements in the baseline conventional forces of the United States—19 divisions, 29 tactical air wings, and a general purpose fleet of 535 ships—have much to be said for them in principle. It remains questionable, however, whether the large and rapid investments that are being planned should be made simply because they are high on the services' list of priorities. Over five years, the savings of more than $20 billion from cancellations of or reductions in a number of such programs could be more productively used elsewhere. One possibility would be to improve the equipment and training of the National Guard and Reserve land and tactical air forces, for which more than $14 billion will be appropriated in 1983. In time, these forces could provide the capabilities needed to hedge against unanticipated Soviet deployments into Eastern Europe and on the border of Iran.

It is by no means clear that the increments to the baseline force proposed by the administration would be worth the cost. The expansion in conventional naval forces, centering on three carrier battle groups and a 35 percent increase in amphibious lift, is more a satisfaction of the Navy's desire for a 600-ship fleet than it is the creation of a powerful instrument for the dubious strategy of horizontal escalation. For the latter purpose, an even larger fleet and still other forces would almost certainly be required. By the same token, the proposed large investment in chemical bombs and projectiles can only be described as premature. And the rapid acquisition of sufficient "smart" munitions for several months of intense conventional combat seems an excessive hedge against future uncertainties about the nature and duration of nonnuclear conflict. Indeed, since haste does not seem to be of the essence, a more sustainable approach to the modernization, readiness, and expansion of the conventional forces has much to recommend it. Such an approach, while allowing for substantial increases in capability during the coming five years, would result in spending $86 billion less, in current dollars, than is being proposed by the administration.

The forces authorized in the mid-1970s to carry out the traditional U.S. nuclear and nonnuclear defense policy would require appropriations of almost $213 billion in fiscal 1983 and outlays of $197 billion. An intermediate defense budget designed to underwrite the same policy and also to take account of continued increases in the capability of the Soviet Union to execute certain specific attacks would increase appropriations to $226 billion and outlays to approximately $205 billion. The Reagan request, by contrast, proposes appropriations of $258 billion and outlays of $216 billion.

Realistically, defense outlays in the president's budget could be reduced by $11 billion in 1983, $28 billion in 1984, and $29 billion in 1985. Cumulative outlays from the intermediate defense option could amount to as much as $1.3 trillion by 1987, nearly $130 billion, or 10 percent, less than the cumulative outlays that would be incurred by the Reagan five-year defense plan. A serious and systematic case for going beyond a buildup of this magnitude remains to be made.

### The Nondefense Budget

If Congress were to accept all the president's budget recommendations, virtually every domestic program would be cut by proposals approved last year and advanced this year. Most nondefense expenditures result from programs designed to help vulnerable groups. For that reason a large part of the sweeping reductions affect these vulnerable groups—the aged, disabled, handicapped, and poor.

The budget proposes large reductions in income security programs, especially in aid to families with dependent children (AFDC) and food stamps, which would be cut by $3.6 billion in fiscal 1983. The president also proposes to shift responsibility for AFDC and food stamps to the states in exchange for federal assumption of responsibility for medicaid. This swap would occur in 1984 if Congress agrees to it.

The 1983 budget is silent on the largest income security programs, retirement, survivors, and disability insurance under the social security system. After declaring that basic social security benefits are part of the social safety net, a group of programs that he indicated would not suffer major reductions, President Reagan in May 1981 submitted proposals to cut the long-run cost of social security by more than 22 percent. Opposition to these proposals led him to create a commission to make recommendations for changes in social security. The president announced that he would wait until after submission of that report, due December 31, 1982, before again proposing changes in the system.

Most programs to aid cities and to subsidize housing will be either severely cut or dismantled by the actions taken last year and the proposals in the 1983 budget. The Appalachian Regional Commission and the Economic Development Administration are being abolished. Community development block grants, created on the recommendation of President Nixon, and urban development action grants, created at the urging of President Carter, are being allowed to shrink. The budget sharply reduces authorization of new units for housing assistance, although outlays continue to rise as units already authorized are added to the stock of units the government is contractually obligated to subsidize. The administration proposes to drastically reduce subsidies for constructing new housing units. It plans to cancel some commitments made in previous years, but it would establish a new program of housing vouchers. Outlays for urban transportation will also be curtailed. Operating subsidies for urban mass transit will be eliminated. Some capital subsidies will be continued, but not for fixed rail systems.

Outlays under health programs will continue to rise, despite cutbacks in both medicare and medicaid. The reason for this growth is that the cost of medical services continues to rise much faster than output or the general price level. To deal with this problem, which affects not only federal health programs but private payers as well, the administration has promised an initiative to promote competition in the health sector. The administration claims this initiative will lead to large savings in future years, though not in 1983; the details of the plan remain to be worked out. Meanwhile, a long list of reductions in medicaid and medicare will save $4.5 billion in 1983 if all are adopted. The administration also seeks to extend the consolidation of health grant programs into block grants. Last year Congress refused to include some of the programs whose separate status the president wished to end, including family planning, migrant health centers, childhood immunization, and venereal disease control. That Congress will agree to the president's second request for consolidation is doubtful.

The 1983 budget proposes to cut by nearly half programs supporting elementary, secondary, and higher education. Most outlays under these programs date from the 1960s and 1970s, when successive administrations undertook to supplement the resources of states and localities for the elementary and secondary education of disadvantaged and handicapped children and to assist students attending colleges and universities. The 1983 budget would curtail grants to school districts for the education of disadvantaged and handicapped children. It would reduce the number of college and university students who could receive assistance, especially graduate and professional students, who would be eliminated from the guaranteed student loan program, and it would reduce the amounts that the remaining aided students could receive.

Job and training programs would also be slashed. The public service employment program has already been phased out. The administration proposes to restructure the Comprehensive Employment and Training Act, which expires this year, and to reduce outlays for it. The changes sought by the administration, such as termination of the payment of stipends to trainees, will exclude from training most welfare recipients and other potential trainees who lack resources on which to subsist. The administration also proposes to eliminate the work experience program under CETA on the ground that this program has been ineffective, but it will authorize community work and training programs under AFDC on the ground that they will help welfare recipients become self-sufficient.

The 1983 budget continues President Reagan's effort to cut spending on the social and economic programs built up over the preceding decades. It reflects his belief that government programs are ineffective in achieving their stated objectives and that the taxes necessary to pay for them hinder economic growth and development. The immediate effect, however, is to reduce the degree to which the federal government provides income support for the needy, job and training opportunities for the untrained and unemployed, health care for those unable to pay for it themselves, and aid for states and localities in serving the disadvantaged and the handicapped. Some of the savings from the proposed defense budget outlined above could usefully be employed to moderate these cuts.

**Federalism**

The 1983 budget also continues the administration's policy, established last year, of making significant changes in federal grant policy. Last year the president recommended consolidating categorical grants into block grants, proposals that culminated in the consolidation of fifty-seven categorical programs into nine new block grants. Total grants also were cut from $95 billion to $91 billion between fiscal years 1981 and 1982. The president now proposes consolidating another forty-one grants into seven new block grants and cutting total grants to $81 billion in 1983, or 15 percent below 1981 in nominal terms and 25 percent in real terms.

The president recommends a sweeping rearrangement of grant programs, to begin in fiscal 1984. As one part of his new federalism program—the "swap"—the federal government would assume sole responsibility for medicaid and turn over sole responsibility for the AFDC and food stamp programs to state governments. In fiscal 1984 this change would save the states an estimated $2 billion. Then, as part of what is known as the "turnback" portion of the program, the federal government would give the responsibility for operating forty-four other grant programs, totaling $30 billion, to state governments. Funds to finance this package, $28 billion in fiscal 1984, would come from a special trust fund consisting of earmarked alcohol, tobacco, and telephone excise taxes, two cents of the four-cent-per-gallon gasoline tax, and a portion of the windfall profits tax on oil.

This swap and turnback arrangement is to last four years, from fiscal 1984 to 1987. During that time states would receive amounts based on their 1979–81 share of grants, with an adjustment for gains or losses resulting from the medicaid-AFDC–food stamps swap, to continue the federal programs that have been turned back to them. If a state chooses to terminate some programs, the resulting surplus in its account would be paid to it as a "super revenue sharing" payment. Federal mandates will ensure that some funds are passed through to local governments, since some of the grants now going to local governments (general revenue sharing and community development block grants) are among those to be turned back.

Beginning in 1988 federal financial support is gradually withdrawn. The federal trust fund declines 25 percent a year and entirely disappears by 1991. At this point states must finance all the programs—the forty-four to be turned back, food stamps, and AFDC—themselves or eliminate them. There is no assurance that local governments will receive their share of the funds that were folded in. Indeed, there is no assurance, and no reason to expect, that any particular program included in the present grant system will be continued. These programs have been supported by federal matching arrangements (the federal government now pays for all food stamp benefits, about 60 percent of AFDC benefits, and about 80 percent of the other categorical programs), and if states have to raise their own taxes to continue the programs, they may be cut back sharply.

The combined effect of all these changes, if adopted, would be a massive unwinding of the federal grant system. As early as 1984 only $74 billion of federal grants would remain, including the $47 billion for programs to be turned back to the states. When the swap and the turnback arrangements are complete and the trust fund runs out at the end of the 1980s, federal grants will amount to $27 billion in 1984 dollars.

The objective of the new federalism plan is to separate clearly the roles of the federal, state, and local governments. The administration argues that the federal grant-making system is a "confused mess," usurps state-local functions, and distorts state-local decisions. It holds that the time has come to sort out federal and state-local responsibilities and to reduce the federal presence and intervention in state-local affairs. In this way, it argues, the efficiency of government decisions would be improved and the waste of overlapping bureaucracies at the various levels of government would be eliminated.

A major concern expressed by critics regarding these changes is that they would cut out numerous federal grants for services and activities that should remain a federal responsibility. They are particularly concerned about the large reduction in support for people with low incomes and for states and localities with low fiscal capacities. In the case of AFDC and food stamps, the change seems likely to lower public assistance benefits across the country, widen state disparities in benefits, and increase migration incentives.

At a time when the economy is depressed and interest rates are high, the cuts in federal grants will create new fiscal problems for many states and localities. The spread of tax limitation amendments will also make it difficult for many of them to adapt to the cuts and to the new responsibilities they are invited to assume. The efficiency objectives of the program could be realized without imposing a fiscal squeeze on the states and local governments by retaining the block grant consolidations (where appropriate) at or near current funding levels. Alternatively, the funds released by the proposed cuts could be allocated to general revenue sharing grants, and the state share of the grants that was eliminated last year might be restored.

If the federal government decides to pull back support for certain state-local services, the functions to be eliminated need not be those proposed by the administration. To avoid burdening communities with heavy concentrations of poor people, grants going directly to local governments could be kept out of the turnback programs. To avoid widening statewide disparities in income support for low-income people, cash and in-kind assistance might be fully financed and operated by the federal government or financed by the federal government and operated by the states under its direction. On this basis, the forty-four grant programs would be turned back to the states, but AFDC, food stamps, and medicaid would be a federal responsibility.

A final option is to adjust federal matching shares in grant programs so as to properly reflect the balance of interests between the federal government and the state and local governments. This change would reduce federal outlays and would maintain the decentralization of management decisions on federally supported activities, without eliminating desirable government services.

**Budget Options**

The administration's approach to deficit reduction exempts defense and social security and precludes any large tax increases. As a result, its cuts in outlays are concentrated in other entitlement programs and the same small part of the budget that was cut about 11 percent in real terms last year. Coming on top of these cuts, the new proposals would severely limit the scope of federal activities. As a share of GNP, outlays for the nonentitlement programs—covering such diverse activities as support for housing, education, health, highways, and law enforcement—would fall to levels below any reached in the last forty years.

The administration's program appears to be unacceptable for political as well as economic reasons. First, concentrating budget reductions in the very narrow area proposed by the administration makes it difficult to secure the social and political consensus needed to reduce the deficit by the needed amounts. Second, even complete enactment of the administration's program will still leave excessive deficits in fiscal years 1983–85 (see table 1-1). In this situation, defense and social security, as well as other entitlement programs, cannot remain immune from budget cuts, and some sacrifice will be required from those who received the bulk of the benefits of the 1981 tax cuts.

The defense buildup proposed by the administration would increase real defense outlays by almost 9 percent a year between 1981 and 1985. As indicated above, this buildup is unnecessarily ambitious. A more realistic target would be to cut back the rise in defense outlays to 6 or 7 percent a year from 1981 to 1985. As already noted, because of the lead time involved, the reduction in actual spending would amount to only $11 billion in 1983, but would build up to almost $30 billion in 1985.

While structural changes in social security must be postponed until the newly constituted National Commission on Social Security submits its report after the 1982 elections, short-term savings could be made in the entitlement programs by modifying the automatic adjustment in benefits for inflation. Between 1977 and 1980 the increase in the consumer price index overstated the true rise in the cost of living by some 5 to 6 percent and exceeded the average growth of wages by about 8 percent. Thus a reduction of the automatic inflation adjustment in the next few years can be defended. A reduction of 2.5 percentage points in the indexation factors for all entitlement programs except food stamps and SSI in 1983 and again in 1984 would reduce fiscal 1985 outlays by $13 billion, while a reduction of 4 percentage points each year would cut these outlays by $21 billion. Additional cuts could be made in the benefits under the means-tested programs, but these would place heavy burdens on the poor and the near-poor.

The major options for increasing taxes are to raise personal income taxes, to broaden the base of the income tax by eliminating unnecessary and inequitable perferences, and to raise federal taxes on consumption.

An increase in 1985 budget receipts of $54 billion could be obtained by delaying the July 1983 personal income tax cut and by postponing the introduction of income tax indexation, which is scheduled to begin in 1985. Since high-income taxpayers have already benefited from the cut in the top-bracket rate from 70 to 50 percent (which goes into effect in 1982), a surcharge of 12 percent might be imposed instead of delaying the 1983 tax cut. This would avoid the charge that high-income taxpayers will have benefited most from the 1981 tax cut and the subsequent delay in the final installment scheduled for 1983.

Broadening the base of the income tax by eliminating tax preferences is particularly relevant to today's problem because reforms could be selected to reward saving, provide incentives to hold down costs, and address some of the problems of the entitlement programs from the tax side. The total value of all tax preferences under the income tax exceeds $300 billion; it should be possible to reduce this total by 5 to 10 percent as part of a comprehensive program to bring the budget into better balance by 1985. For example, elimination of the deduction for interest on consumer installment borrowing would reduce consumption and increase personal saving. Limiting the tax-free portion of employer contributions to medical care plans to $120 a month would encourage the use of more efficient and lower-cost medical care by employees. Full taxation of unemployment benefits (they are now taxed only if the recipient has other income of $25,000 if married or $20,000 if single) and taxation of one-half of social security benefits (which are now tax-exempt) would provide urgently needed revenues.

The alternatives for increasing taxes on consumption include the adoption of a value-added tax, the imposition of an oil import fee or a windfall tax as natural gas is decontrolled, and increases in the excises on alcohol, tobacco, and gasoline, which have remained unchanged for many years. A 4 percent value-added tax would raise $50 billion in 1985; an oil import fee of $5 a barrel, $15 billion to $20 billion; natural gas decontrol combined with a windfall tax, $5 billion to $15 billion; and doubling the excises, over $10 billion. These tax increases, however, would increase consumer prices and would be regarded as unfair to those at the lower end of the income scale, who did not benefit from the 1981 tax cut. On the other hand, raising the prices of oil and natural gas would increase economic efficiency and encourage conservation.

The various options just enumerated on both the spending and tax sides of the budget are more than enough to eliminate the deficit remaining in the Reagan budget for fiscal 1985. While it is probably unnecessary to eliminate the deficit entirely, a program that cuts the 1985 deficit by a significant amount would relieve the pressure of credit demands in the capital markets and greatly improve the nation's economic prospects. This will require an agreement by the Congress and the administration on a selection among the options that will clearly bring the deficits under control.

### Making Budget Decisions

Congressional budget decisions are now made through a set of procedures that were created by the Budget Control and Impoundment Act of 1974. The act created a budget committee in each house of Congress to coordinate budget policy and a Congressional Budget Office to provide the two committees and other members of Congress with expert advice and assistance. It established a timetable for the enactment of two concurrent resolutions (the first on May 15, the second on September 15), which set targets for the key amounts in the budget and a reconciliation process to enforce these decisions. In principle, the procedures are flexible enough to accommodate any set of budget decisions; in practice, the procedures were strained in 1981 and will be strained to the limit in 1982 because of the wide-ranging decisions expected from Congress in response to President Reagan's budget proposals.

The procedures worked fairly well for the three years following enactment of the budget act, largely because there was little disagreement between Congress and the administration on budget matters. In 1979 President Carter's budget called for large spending cuts in order to keep the fiscal 1980 deficit under $30 billion. The reconciliation procedure was invoked in the Senate to reach this objective, but it could not be implemented in the House. The actual deficit for 1980 greatly exceeded the original estimates, but only partly as a result of the failure of the reconciliation process. Somewhat the same experience was repeated in 1980, but this time the Budget Committees succeeded in making a major procedural breakthrough by incorporating reconciliation instructions in the first concurrent resolution. In the end, the results of the reconciliation were disappointing, but the stage had been set for the Reagan budget triumphs in 1981.

The first concurrent resolution on the 1982 budget, which was passed by both houses in late May 1981, approved President Reagan's targets for outlays and receipts. It also contained instructions for budget reductions addressed to the various House and Senate committees that have spending responsibilities. The committees responded by submitting legislation affecting 250 different federal programs, which were then brought together in one large reconciliation bill. The bill was amended on the floor of the House to meet the administration's specifications; shortly thereafter, a similar version of the bill was approved by the Senate. The Omnibus Budget Reconciliation Act of 1981, which was finally approved on July 31, 1981, changed entitlement rules, reduced appropriations and authorizations in scores of nondefense programs, and even rewrote major parts of substantive law having no significant impact on the budget.

Despite this major administration victory, the remainder of the legislative process on the 1982 budget stalled. No appropriations bills had been passed by the time the fiscal year began on October 1, and most of the major bills were still bottled up at the year's end. During this period the government was able to function by the passage of continuing resolutions that permitted spending to continue at various rates depending on the stage a particular bill had reached in the appropriations process. (For example, if only one house of Congress had acted, spending would continue at the lesser of the appropriated amounts and the rate of the previous fiscal year.) The impasse occurred partly because the budget cuts demanded by the Reagan administration were so stringent and partly because the Appropriations Committees resisted the erosion of their prerogatives by the reconciliation process.

Operating a large part of the government under continuing appropriations is clearly an unsatisfactory way to conduct the public's business. It tends to perpetuate spending practices that conform to no one's preferences and leads to managerial inefficiencies as a result of the uncertain levels of funding for so many agencies. Thus superimposing the difficult policy issues for fiscal 1983, an election year, on the budgetary process as it has recently developed seems to invite inaction on the budget and continued unsatisfactory economic performance. The only hope of a better outcome depends on working out a political compromise on the 1983 budget.

When the current crisis subsides, attention will turn to methods of improving the congressional budgetary process. One approach would be to restore the power of the appropriations and authorization committees to originate substantive legislation affecting the budget. The role of the Budget Committees in this traditional arrangement would be to set fiscal policy and broad program limits. The specialized committees would conduct full reviews of existing and proposed programs, consider legislative alternatives, and ascertain the views of the various constituencies on key policy issues. To improve coordination, the congressional calendar might be revised to allow more time for work on the budget resolutions, the Budget Committees and the administration should be required to use the same set of economic assumptions, and the specialized committees should be given incentives to keep within the established budgetary limits. Essentially, the budgetary process would revert to what it was when it operated effectively in 1976–79.

An alternative approach is to strengthen the control of the Budget Committees over the budgetary process. The crucial procedural change in this approach would be to move reconciliation up to the first concurrent resolution and make the dollar limits in the resolution mandatory for the specialized committees. The budget resolution might also spell out in greater detail the kind of tax changes expected from the tax committees and impose tight limits on federal credit activities as well as budget outlays.

The most radical approach to the issue of budgetary procedures would be to enact a constitutional amendment requiring that the budget be balanced each year. Such an amendment would severely limit the flexibility of the administration and the Congress in fiscal matters (the result sought by its supporters) and would focus more attention on budget targets than on substantive policy issues. It would also require a whole new set of procedures to alert the administration and Congress to the possibility that a deficit was likely to be incurred and to modify spending or tax decisions during the course of a fiscal year in order to achieve a budget balance. If the budget balance directive is to mean anything, more authority will have to be given to the president to impound funds, subject perhaps to limits on how much particular programs could be cut. Such a shift in power over budget policies would be a significant departure from the division of responsibilities between the executive and legislative branches of government.

No budgetary process or constitutional amendment can make tough decisions easy. The present budgetary procedures have proved flexible enough to accommodate a variety of economic circumstances. They could readily provide a legislative vehicle for any grand compromise on the 1983 budget without impairing the government's ability to manage its fiscal affairs.

CHAPTER TWO

# The Budget and the Economy

JOSEPH A. PECHMAN *and* BARRY P. BOSWORTH

PRESIDENT Ronald Reagan submitted his budget for fiscal year 1982 to the Congress in February and March 1981, a few weeks after his inauguration. It called for a large increase in defense outlays, a drastic cut in federal nondefense spending, a three-stage cut in federal income taxes, and a balanced budget by fiscal 1984. As a result of these policies, the administration anticipated rapid economic growth in the next five years, a big drop in the rate of inflation, and an even bigger decline in interest rates. To the surprise of many, Congress went along with virtually all the recommendations of the new president. Yet even before fiscal 1982 began, it became evident that economic events were not unfolding as the administration had hoped, and that the plan to balance the budget by 1984 would be frustrated.

The budget for fiscal 1983, submitted on February 8, 1982, proposes additional increases in defense spending, even larger cuts in nondefense spending than Congress enacted last year, and an increase in taxes beginning in 1983. The deficit for fiscal 1982, which had been projected at $45 billion a year earlier, is now estimated by the administration to amount to $98.6 billion. The budget forecasts reduced deficits in the three years after 1982; but

We are grateful to Henry J. Aaron, Ralph C. Bryant, Robert W. Hartman, Darwin G. Johnson, George L. Perry, and Charles L. Schultze, who made numerous helpful comments and suggestions. Allan M. Rivlin provided research assistance, and Evelyn M. E. Taylor typed the manuscript.

**23**

by 1985 a deficit of $71.9 billion is still projected, even though the economy is expected to recover from the recession that began late in 1981.

This chapter explains why these developments occurred and evaluates future budget and economic prospects. The first section is concerned with budget developments in fiscal years 1980 through 1982. The second section examines President Reagan's budget proposals for fiscal 1983. The final section discusses the impact of the new budget plans on the economy.

### Recent Budget Developments

The year 1981 was the most remarkable budget year in recent memory. After several confrontations, Congress approved President Reagan's proposed spending and tax cuts with relatively minor modifications. But the year ended with the budget deficit much larger than it was at the beginning, and new measures were needed to prevent runaway deficits in fiscal 1983 and later years.

### The Fiscal 1982 Budget

President Reagan's budget plans were the centerpiece of his policies to solve the nation's economic problems. During his campaign for office, he argued that excessive government spending was the major cause of the high rates of inflation in recent years, and that high marginal tax rates were impairing productivity. Thus his budget for fiscal 1982 called for large domestic spending cuts, a reduction in individual income tax rates of 30 percent spread over three years beginning July 1, 1981, and liberalization of depreciation allowances retroactive to January 1, 1981.

OUTLAYS. The first action taken in Congress on these proposals was to adopt a budget resolution on May 21, 1981, which accepted virtually all the president's budget proposals for fiscal 1982. By law, this resolution provides the guidelines for action on the president's budget by the congressional appropriations and tax committees. In 1981, however, the first budget resolution also contained specific outlay reduction targets for action by the authorizing committees (those responsible for substantive law rather than pure money bills) through the device of "reconciliation" instructions. On July 31, 1981, Congress implemented these directives in the Omnibus Budget Reconciliation Act of 1981, which changed many basic laws and forced the appropriations committees to work within prescribed budget totals that conformed with the May budget resolution. At the same time, Congress also finished action on the huge tax reduction bill proposed by the administration.

By late summer, it became apparent that Congress would not be able to clear most of the appropriations bills before the beginning of the fiscal year on October 1. To keep the government operating, Congress adopted a continuing resolution on September 30, 1981, which permitted federal agencies to spend at the lower of the rates already approved by the House and Senate or, if one house had not acted, at the lower of the rates of the previous year or those approved by the one house.

Still unable to pass all the appropriations bills before it went home for the Christmas adjournment, Congress passed another continuing resolution on November 23, 1981. The first version of this resolution, which did not conform precisely with the president's request for a minimum cut of 4 percent in almost all nondiscretionary nondefense programs (on top of the cuts previously directed in the reconciliation bill), was vetoed after the spending authority of the September continuing resolution ran out, and nonessential government agencies were required to close for a day for the lack of funds. Congress immediately enacted a second resolution providing spending authority for a few weeks, and ultimately approved a resolution on December 11, 1981, which gave the president enough of the cuts he wanted to secure his agreement.[1]

The major changes in outlays for fiscal 1982 resulting from these decisions were increases of $2.8 billion in defense spending and reductions of $27.1 billion, largely in nondefense spending. Because defense spending involves long lead times, most of the new administration's ambitious plans in this sector will affect outlays in later years.[2] There were, however, significant changes in the

1. This series of episodes has been interpreted by congressional leaders and budget experts as both a success and a failure of the congressional budgetary process. See chapter 7 for a discussion of the issues.
2. The approved fiscal 1982 budget provided for the development of a new bomber, three more new ships and the reactivation of three older ones, more aircraft and helicopters,

composition and magnitude of the nondefense budget for 1982 and later years.

The nondefense budget cuts affected practically every major category of federal spending in fiscal 1982. President Reagan identified a number of "social safety net" programs that he promised to preserve, but even these programs were not immune from cuts.[3] The major outlay cuts ultimately approved by Congress included substantial reductions in the safety net programs;[4] a cut of about 10 percent in outlays for welfare programs (aid to families with dependent children, medicaid, food stamps, and school lunches); a reduction of over 10 percent in grants in aid to state and local governments; some reductions (but not as much as the cuts originally requested) in subsidy programs for agriculture, energy, transportation, natural resources and environment, and higher education; and a cut of about 40 percent in the annual adjustment of federal pay for comparability with pay in the private sector.

In total, Congress approved almost four-fifths of the cuts in 1982 nondefense outlays requested by the administration ($27.1 billion out of $34.8 billion) and reduced the trend of real nondefense outlays substantially below what it would otherwise have been. Outlays generated by continued high interest rates and the onset of recession offset some of these cuts, however, and caused total spending to continue rising.

TAXES. The tax bill also demonstrated President Reagan's persuasive powers with Congress. The House passed a bill on July 29, 1981, that cut taxes almost as much as the president had asked, but it delayed the income tax cut from July 1 to October 1,

---

increased military pay, and other increases in appropriations associated with better preparedness. These increases were a selection from what the military services had on their priority lists and did not obtain in the Carter budgets for 1981 and 1982. Only the increased military pay had a significant effect on outlays for fiscal 1982.

3. The safety net programs included social security benefits (retirement and disability benefits and medicare); unemployment benefits other than trade-adjustment assistance; cash benefits for dependent families, the elderly, and the disabled; and income support and medical benefits for veterans. In addition, the president proposed that outlays for Head Start, summer youth employment, and subsidized nutrition programs for low-income children and the elderly be maintained.

4. The minimum and student social security benefits were reduced, eligibility requirements for disability benefits were tightened, and unemployment compensation benefits for people unemployed for more than twenty-six weeks were cut. Benefits provided by the trade-adjustment assistance program were also cut.

1981. The House bill also contained a number of structural changes the president had not proposed, reduced the proposed income tax rate cuts and gave larger reductions to the lower- and middle-income brackets, and substituted an immediate deduction for the entire cost of capital equipment (expensing) in place of the administration's depreciation proposal. The president accepted the delay and reduction in the income tax rate cuts and most of the structural changes, but insisted on across-the-board rate cuts and the depreciation changes he had originally recommended. These changes were approved by the Senate and ultimately by the House in a final showdown on August 4, 1981, and the bill was signed by the president on August 13, 1981.

The Economic Recovery Tax Act of 1981 cut individual income tax rates 5 percent across the board on October 1, 1981, 10 percent on July 1, 1982, and another 8 percent on July 1, 1983, with the cumulative reduction amounting to 23 percent.[5] The top rate on unearned income was reduced from 70 percent to 50 percent (previously the top rate for only earned income), effective in 1982. To moderate the so-called marriage penalty, working couples were allowed a deduction of 10 percent of the first $30,000 of earned income of the spouse with lower earnings, beginning in 1983 (5 percent for 1982). Several new deductions for saving were added to the tax code.[6] The child and dependent care tax credit was increased, charitable contributions made by taxpayers who do not itemize their deductions will be deductible after a gradual five-year phase-in period, and the exclusion for capital gains on residences of persons over fifty-five years of age was increased

5. This translates into a reduction in marginal tax rates of 1.25 percent for calendar year 1981, 10 percent for 1982, 19 percent for 1983, and 23 percent for 1984 and subsequent years.
6. The new saving provisions were a one-time exclusion of $1,000 ($2,000 on joint returns) for interest received on "all savers" certificates issued by banks, thrift institutions, and credit unions in the period October 1, 1981, to December 31, 1982; deductions of up to the first $2,000 in earnings per person annually for voluntary contributions by employees to an individual retirement account (IRA), whether or not they are already covered by a pension plan; an increase in the IRA deduction for employees with nonworking spouses from $1,750 to $2,250; an increase in the limit on the deductions for contributions to retirement accounts by the self-employed (Keogh plans) from $7,500 to $15,000; and an exclusion up to $750 ($1,500 on joint returns) for dividends reinvested in a domestic public utility. The IRA, Keogh, and dividend reinvestment provisions became effective in 1982. In addition, the $200 ($400 on joint returns) exclusion of dividends and interest received in 1981 was eliminated and the $100 ($200 on joint returns) dividend exclusion of prior law was restored, beginning in 1982.

from $100,000 to $125,000. The estate and gift tax exemptions were increased over a period of five years from $175,000 to $600,000, and the top-bracket estate tax rate was reduced from 70 percent to 50 percent over a four-year period. Finally, the individual income tax rates, exemptions, and standard deduction (or zero bracket amount) will be "indexed" for increases in consumer prices beginning in 1985.

The effect of all these changes will be to reduce individual income tax liabilities in 1984 by an average of about 26 percent below what they otherwise would have been (see table A-2). The percentage reduction is nearly uniform throughout the scale of incomes, ranging from 24 to 27 percent in all classes. Because the tax burden rises with income, the cut increases sharply as a percentage of income both before and after taxes as income rises. For example, the after-tax income of a $20,000 taxpayer will go up by an average of 4 percent, in contrast to a 14 percent increase for a $100,000 taxpayer. When inflation is taken into account, effective income tax rates in 1984 will be higher than they were under the 1980 law for incomes below $15,000, slightly lower for those with incomes between $15,000 and $100,000, and substantially lower for only the small number of taxpayers with incomes above $100,000 (table A-3).

Marginal individual income tax rates under the new tax law will be lower in 1984 than they were for the same real incomes in 1980. For incomes up to about $100,000, the reductions merely offset the "bracket creep" that occurred as a result of inflation in the latter half of the 1970s; for incomes above $100,000, the marginal rates will be lower than they have been since the early 1940s (table 2-1).[7]

For businesses, the major change was the liberalization of allowances for depreciation for business investment. During the presidential campaign, candidate Reagan endorsed the so-called 10-5-3 proposal, which would have shortened the period for tax write-offs to ten years for structures, five years for equipment, and three years for vehicles. The final bill retained the original five- and three-year periods for equipment and vehicles, but limited the ten-year write-off to public utility property and mobile

7. For more details on the effects of the 1981 income tax reductions, see appendix A.

**Table 2-1. Marginal Federal Income Tax Rates under the Laws for 1970, 1975, 1980, and 1984, Indexed for Inflation**[a]
Percent

| Adjusted gross income class, 1981 (dollars) | Marginal rates | | | |
|---|---|---|---|---|
| | 1970 law | 1975 law | 1980 law | 1984 law |
| 5,000–10,000 | 16.3 | 15.4 | 14.5 | 13.4 |
| 10,000–15,000 | 18.7 | 19.3 | 19.0 | 17.0 |
| 15,000–20,000 | 20.4 | 21.3 | 22.4 | 20.0 |
| 20,000–25,000 | 21.4 | 22.8 | 24.7 | 22.4 |
| 25,000–50,000 | 24.1 | 27.0 | 30.2 | 27.8 |
| 50,000–100,000 | 34.7 | 41.3 | 45.5 | 39.0 |
| 100,000–200,000 | 51.0 | 55.8 | 57.2 | 43.9 |
| 200,000–500,000 | 61.1 | 64.6 | 63.3 | 44.9 |
| 500,000–1,000,000 | 66.2 | 66.7 | 64.0 | 42.3 |
| 1,000,000 and over | 63.9 | 64.8 | 60.2 | 39.3 |
| All classes[b] | 18.0 | 18.8 | 19.6 | 18.0 |

Source: Calculations based on the Brookings 1977 income tax file projected to 1981.
a. Under the indexed laws, the limits of the rate brackets, personal exemptions, and the standard deductions are adjusted for the estimated change in the GNP deflator to 1981. Marginal rates are averages of the tax rates applied to the last dollar of income on each tax return.
b. Includes income below $5,000 and negative incomes.

homes. Other structures can be written off over a fifteen-year period. In addition, business firms with little or no tax liability were allowed to transfer their unused investment credits and depreciation deductions to other firms through liberal leasing arrangements that do not require that the ownership of the assets be relinquished.

The total reduction in tax receipts under the 1981 act rises from $38.3 billion in fiscal 1982 to $139.0 billion in 1984 and $286.5 billion in 1987. This is by far the largest tax reduction in history, and the first to put into place a long-range tax cut without reference to future spending commitments.

### Condition of the Budget

The budgets for fiscal years 1980, 1981, and 1982 were originally planned by President Jimmy Carter. Although the Reagan administration took office three months after the beginning of fiscal 1981, its decisions had only a marginal effect on the year's fiscal outcome. Carter submitted a complete budget for fiscal 1982 before he left office, but it was substantially revised by the new

Table 2-2.  The Federal Budget, Fiscal Years 1980–82
Billions of dollars

|  | 1980ᵃ | | 1981ᵃ | | 1982 | |
|---|---|---|---|---|---|---|
| Item | January 1979 estimate | Actual | January 1980 estimate | Actual | February 1981 estimate | February 1982 estimate |
| Outlays | 528.7 | 576.7 | 612.4 | 657.2 | 691.6 | 725.3 |
| Receipts | 499.7 | 517.1 | 596.7 | 599.3 | 646.6 | 626.8 |
| Deficit | − 29.0 | − 59.6 | − 15.8 | − 57.9 | − 45.0 | − 98.6 |

Sources: *The Budget of the United States Government, Fiscal Year 1980*, p. 576; *Fiscal Year 1981*, p. 614; *Fiscal Year 1982*, p. 613; *Fiscal Year 1983*, p. 9-62; and The White House, "America's New Beginning, A Program for Economic Recovery," February 18, 1981, p. 12. Figures are rounded.
   a. Some items formerly classified as budget receipts are now classified as outlays. To be consistent with the new 1983 figures, the original estimates of receipts and outlays have been reduced by $2.9 billion in 1980, $3.3 billion in 1981, and $3.9 billion in 1982, but the deficit figures were not affected.

administration. Yet the budgets for all three years have one thing in common: in each case, the original estimates called for relatively modest deficits and projected a budget balance within three years. In each case, the original estimates erred by large amounts, primarily because of economic surprises. The effect of inflation on outlays was greatly underestimated in 1980 and 1981; interest rates rose to unprecedented levels; and the real growth of the economy, which was interrupted by severe recessions in 1980 and 1981, was far less than was anticipated. The result was that outlays exceeded expectations and the deficits turned out to be far higher than originally estimated.

Table 2-2 summarizes budget developments in this period. Originally, the budget projected deficits of $29.0 billion, $15.8 billion, and $45.0 billion for fiscal years 1980, 1981, and 1982, respectively.[8] Actual deficits were $59.6 billion in 1980 and $57.9 billion in 1981, while the deficit for 1982 was estimated at $98.6 billion in the 1983 budget. Most of the increase in the deficits resulted from higher outlays; receipts were higher than originally estimated in 1980 and 1981, but lower in 1982.

The major factors accounting for this outcome are summarized in table 2-3. On the outlay side, the largest source of the higher spending was the disappointing economic performance, which

8. The outgoing Carter administration submitted a budget that called for a 1982 deficit of $27.5 billion, but this amount was almost immediately raised to $45 billion by the incoming Reagan administration, largely as a result of the tax program that was planned for fiscal 1982.

**Table 2-3. Major Changes in Outlays and Receipts from Original Estimates, Fiscal Years 1980–82**

Billions of dollars

| Item | 1980 | 1981 | 1982 (projected) |
|---|---|---|---|
| *Outlays* | | | |
| Changes in economic conditions | 27.1 | 32.3 | 25.9 |
| Inflation | 12.0 | 14.8 | 1.5 |
| Unemployment | 6.5 | . . . | 7.9 |
| Interest rates and increased borrowing | 6.8 | 14.5 | 16.6 |
| Support for financial institutions | 1.8 | 3.0 | . . . |
| Policy changes | 9.3 | 5.7 | 7.7 |
| Unforeseen events | 1.8 | 0.6 | a |
| Estimating differences and other changes | 9.8 | 6.2 | 0.2 |
| Total change from original estimates | 48.0 | 44.8 | 33.8 |
| *Receipts* | | | |
| Changes in economic conditions | 13.5 | 4.6 | −31.0 |
| Legislative changes | 3.9 | −2.0 | 11.2 |
| Total change from original estimate | 17.4 | 2.6 | −19.8 |

Sources: *The Budget of the United States Government, Fiscal Year 1980*, p. 25; *Fiscal Year 1981*, p. 71; *Fiscal Year 1982*, p. 83; *Fiscal Year 1983*, pp. 2-14, 6-27; Office of Management and Budget, "The Dramatic Increases in 1980 and 1981 Outlays," internal document; and authors' estimates. Figures are rounded.
a. Included in estimating differences.

raised outlays by $27.1 billion in 1980, $32.3 billion in 1981, and $25.9 billion in 1982. These enlarged outlays reflected increases caused by a combination of inflation, unemployment, and high interest rates. Policy changes also increased outlays significantly during 1980 and 1981, as did natural disasters and errors in estimation. In 1982, $7.7 billion of the outlay increases were the result of congressional modifications of the original cuts proposed by President Reagan. On the receipts side, growth in nominal incomes as a result of inflation raised tax receipts in 1980 and 1981; legislative changes were relatively small on balance, so that receipts were higher than originally estimated. For 1982, the delay in the tax cut from July 1 to October 1, 1981, and other changes made by Congress raised receipts by $11.2 billion, but this gain was more than offset by the $31 billion reduction in receipts resulting from the 1981–82 recession.

Thus, in planning his budget for fiscal 1983, President Reagan was faced with a budget deficit that continued to rise—despite unprecedented cuts in nondefense spending—because of economic decline, tax cuts, and growing defense outlays. Preliminary estimates by his own administration made in December 1981 indicated that, without further action, the deficits for 1983 and 1984 would exceed $150 billion;[9] estimates by the Congressional Budget Office and private forecasters were even higher.[10] This was the setting for the planning and preparation of the fiscal 1983 budget.

### The Fiscal 1983 Budget

In making his decisions on the budget for fiscal 1983, President Reagan was forced to choose between accepting continued high deficits or cutting them by a combination of tax increases and cuts in outlays for defense and nondefense programs. He early ruled out cutting planned increases in defense outlays and concentrated his spending cuts in the nondefense programs. Thus much of the debate among his advisers before he made his final decision concerned increases in taxes for 1983 and later years. The president refused to consider any rollback of the recently enacted cuts in income taxes and eventually rejected advice to impose higher excises on alcohol, tobacco, and gasoline or any other major tax increases. Instead he opted for further large cuts in nondefense spending, modest reforms in income taxes, and improvements in collection and enforcement procedures. The result was a budget that projected large, but slowly declining, deficits over the period 1983–87.

### Current Services

Budget planning begins with current services estimates, which project outlays and receipts on the assumption that policy remains unchanged. These estimates allow for anticipated changes of a relatively uncontrollable nature (such as increases in the number of social security retirees), but omit all proposed or pending new initiatives either by the president or by Congress. Temporary programs are assumed to expire, but those that are routinely renewed are assumed to be renewed. The outlay estimates reflect the effect of inflation on most spending, so as to provide a constant real program base for comparison with the president's budget.

9. *Wall Street Journal*, December 10, 1981, p. 1.
10. *New York Times*, December 19, 1981, p. 1.

**Table 2-4.  Changes in the Current Services Budget, Fiscal Year 1983**
Billions of dollars

| Item | Amount |
|---|---|
| *Outlays* | |
| 1982 current services estimate | 726.4 |
| 1982–83 changes | 52.9 |
| Income security | 19.9 |
| Social security | 15.3 |
| Unemployment compensation | − 2.5 |
| Other | 7.1 |
| National defense | 16.1 |
| Net interest | 16.0 |
| Health | 8.5 |
| Farm income stabilization | − 4.1 |
| Energy and natural resources | − 2.9 |
| Community and regional development | − 1.1 |
| Education, training, and employment | − 1.1 |
| Other (net) | 1.6 |
| 1983 current services estimate | 779.3 |
| *Receipts* | |
| 1982 current services estimate | 626.4 |
| 1982–83 changes | 26.9 |
| Effect of inflation and growth | 78.2 |
| Payroll tax | 2.0 |
| Economic Recovery Tax Act of 1981 | − 53.3 |
| 1983 current services estimate | 653.3 |

Sources: *Budget of the United States Government, Fiscal Year 1983*, pp. 3-20, 4-18; *Budget of the United States Government, Fiscal Year 1983, Special Analysis A: Current Services Estimates*, pp. 7, 10: and authors' estimates.

The receipts estimates are based on current law, including any tax changes scheduled for the future, under the economic assumptions made by the administration.[11]

In February 1982 the current services estimate of outlays in fiscal 1982 was $726.4 billion. To continue ongoing federal programs and activities at the 1982 levels, total outlays would have to reach $779.3 billion in 1983—$52.9 billion more than in 1982. Most of this increase is accounted for by increases in outlays for national defense, income security, interest on the national debt, and health programs, and is largely a result of the effect of continued inflation and high interest rates (table 2-4).

Current services receipts increase from $626.4 billion in fiscal

11. However, the highway trust fund taxes, which are scheduled to expire in October 1984, are assumed to be extended.

**Table 2-5. Current Services and Proposed Reagan Budget, Fiscal Years 1982–85**
Billions of dollars

| Item | 1982 | 1983 | 1984 | 1985 |
|---|---|---|---|---|
| *Outlays* | | | | |
| Current services | 726.4 | 779.3 | 853.7 | 917.3 |
| Current services with proposed | | | | |
| defense outlays | 727.7 | 799.0 | 868.6 | 946.3 |
| Proposed budget | 725.3 | 757.6 | 805.9 | 868.5 |
| *Receipts* | | | | |
| Current services | 626.4 | 653.3 | 703.8 | 778.3 |
| Proposed budget | 626.8 | 666.1 | 723.0 | 796.6 |
| *Deficit* | | | | |
| Current services | − 100.0 | − 126.0 | − 149.9 | − 139.0 |
| Current services with proposed | | | | |
| defense outlays | − 101.2 | − 145.6 | − 164.8 | − 168.0 |
| Proposed budget | − 98.6 | − 91.5 | − 82.9 | − 71.9 |

Sources: *Budget of the United States Government, Fiscal Year 1983*, p. 3-8; and authors' estimates. Figures are rounded.

1982 to $653.3 billion in 1983. Increased tax receipts from projected real growth and inflation under the old law were expected to amount to $78.2 billion, and scheduled increases in the payroll tax for social security will raise receipts by $2 billion. But the 1981 tax bill cut 1983 receipts by an estimated $53.3 billion, which will reduce the increase in receipts to $26.9 billion (table 2-4).

With receipts rising by $26.9 billion and outlays by $52.9 billion, the current services deficit will increase from $100 billion in fiscal 1982 to $126 billion in 1983.[12] The current services deficit was then projected to increase to $149.9 billion in 1984 and to decline to $139.0 billion in 1985 (table 2-5). Thus, largely as a result of the 1981 tax cut, receipts were not expected to rise enough in 1983–85 to offset the projected increases in outlays under existing programs. New initiatives were clearly needed on both the outlay and receipts sides of the budget to bring the prospective deficits down.

### The Reagan Budget

The current services deficits estimated for fiscal years 1983–85 understate the fiscal problem faced by the president because they

12. The current services deficit for fiscal 1982 is slightly higher than the projected deficit ($100.0 billion versus $98.6 billion) because the administration submitted proposals in the 1983 budget that are not counted in current services but would reduce the 1982 deficit by $1.4 billion.

**Table 2-6. President Reagan's Budget Program, Fiscal Years 1983–85**
Billions of dollars

| Item | 1983 | 1984 | 1985 |
|---|---|---|---|
| Current services deficit with proposed defense outlays | − 145.6 | − 164.8 | − 168.0 |
| Proposed changes | | | |
| Savings in entitlement programs | 11.7 | 17.1 | 22.8 |
| Savings in discretionary programs | 14.2 | 26.1 | 35.3 |
| User fee increases | 2.5 | 3.5 | 3.8 |
| Management initiatives | 20.3 | 24.0 | 23.9 |
| Tax revisions | 7.2 | 13.4 | 13.0 |
| Proposed outlay increases | − 1.8 | − 2.1 | − 2.7 |
| Total | 54.1 | 82.0 | 96.1 |
| Proposed budget deficit | − 91.5 | − 82.9 | − 71.9 |

Source: *Budget of the United States Government, Fiscal Year 1983*, p. 3-8. Figures are rounded.

do not allow for the increases he proposes in defense outlays. The deficits on what he calls "current services with an adequate defense" amount to $146 billion in 1983, $165 billion in 1984, and $168 billion in 1985 (table 2-5). The plan he submitted to Congress proposes to bring these deficits below $100 billion by a combination of outlay cuts in nondefense programs, increases in user fees, initiatives to improve the management of the federal government, and tax revisions (table 2-6).

The proposed outlay cuts would affect the so-called entitlement programs as well as the discretionary programs. The major changes in entitlements, which would reduce the fiscal 1983 deficit by $11.7 billion, include curtailments in medicare and medicaid benefits, cuts in cash public assistance and food stamps, reductions in the cost-of-living increases for federal civilian and military retirees, and restrictions on the use of guaranteed student loans, grants, and work programs by college students. No changes were proposed in the social security program, pending the report of a bipartisan National Commission on Social Security, which is due by January 1983.

The cuts in discretionary programs would apply to virtually every agency of government. Cuts are proposed in housing and employment programs, assistance for highway construction, funds for mass transit and railroads, discretionary health and income security programs, low-income energy assistance, social services, and grants for elementary and secondary education. In total, the cuts in the discretionary programs would amount to $14.2 billion in fiscal 1983, including a reduction of $2.7 billion in interest outlays to reflect the lower federal borrowing requirements resulting from the deficit reduction measures.

Congress was asked last year to raise user fees for federal programs that provide benefits to easily identifiable groups, but no action was taken on these proposals. The 1983 budget renews the recommendation that user fees be increased substantially. The proposals, which would reduce the deficit by $2.5 billion in 1983, would increase fees at federal recreation areas, charge boat and yacht owners for special services provided by the Coast Guard, institute new fees for airlines and general aviation to pay for the nation's airport and air navigation system, and recover the costs of constructing and maintaining commercial water navigation projects and disposal facilities for nuclear wastes.

The budget contains a large number of management initiatives to improve the efficiency of federal operations. These include plans to accelerate leasing of outer continental shelf (OCS) lands for private oil and gas development, increase the sales of federal lands and surplus property, reduce federal pay raises, and prevent fraud, waste, and abuse. In addition, tax collections would be accelerated by speeding up corporate tax payments, and tax enforcement would be improved by increasing the number of Internal Revenue Service auditors and expanding withholding to interest and dividend income. If fully effective, the management initiatives would decrease outlays by $14.8 billion and increase receipts by $5.5 billion, thus reducing the prospective deficit for fiscal 1983 by $20.3 billion.

Finally, the president also proposed a variety of tax changes designed to eliminate unintended tax benefits and obsolete incentives.[13] The proposals would deny contractors the privilege of deferring income on long-term contracts until the contract is completed, introduce a new minimum tax that would apply to corporations paying little or no tax, remove a provision under which life insurance companies escape tax through modified coinsurance arrangements, require the amortization of interest and taxes incurred during the construction of commercial buildings (instead of immediate write-offs), repeal all business energy

13. These proposals are largely a renewal of the proposals that were made by the administration in September 1981, but not acted on by Congress.

Table 2-7. Size of the Budget and Its Composition, Fiscal Years 1979 and 1981–85
Percent

| | | | | Projected | | |
|---|---|---|---|---|---|---|
| Budget component | 1979 | 1981 | 1982 | 1983 | 1984 | 1985 |
| Share of GNP | | | | | | |
| National defense | 5.0 | 5.6 | 6.1 | 6.4 | 6.7 | 7.0 |
| Entitlements | 9.4 | 10.2 | 10.5 | 9.9 | 9.5 | 9.3 |
| Net interest | 1.8 | 2.4 | 2.7 | 2.8 | 2.6 | 2.4 |
| Discretionary nondefense outlays | 5.1 | 5.4 | 5.1 | 3.8 | 3.2 | 2.9 |
| Offsetting undistributed receipts[a] | −0.4 | −0.6 | −0.9 | −0.9 | −0.8 | −0.8 |
| Total outlays | 20.9 | 23.0 | 23.5 | 22.1 | 21.3 | 20.9 |
| Total receipts | 19.7 | 21.0 | 20.3 | 19.4 | 19.1 | 19.1 |
| Deficit | −1.2 | −2.0 | −3.2 | −2.7 | −2.2 | −1.7 |
| Share of total outlays | | | | | | |
| National defense | 24.0 | 24.3 | 25.8 | 29.2 | 31.4 | 33.6 |
| Entitlements | 45.1 | 44.4 | 44.8 | 45.0 | 44.9 | 44.5 |
| Net interest | 8.7 | 10.5 | 11.4 | 12.7 | 12.2 | 11.6 |
| Discretionary nondefense outlays | 24.0 | 23.5 | 22.3 | 17.6 | 15.8 | 14.4 |
| Offsetting undistributed receipts[a] | −1.8 | −2.7 | −4.4 | −4.6 | −4.3 | −4.1 |
| Total outlays | 100.0 | 100.0 | 100.0 | 100.0 | 100.0 | 100.0 |

Source: *Budget of the United States Government, Fiscal Year 1983*, pp. 3-21, 9-60, 9-61. Figures are rounded.
a. Includes the following receipts which are not distributed by function in the budget: the federal contribution to the employee retirement fund, rents and royalties on the outer continental shelf lands, and receipts from disposition of federal surplus property.

tax credits, and limit the use of tax-exempt industrial development bonds. These tax reforms would raise fiscal 1983 tax receipts by $7.2 billion, and would offset about half the 1981 reductions in corporate income taxes for 1983–85.[14]

The effect of this long list of proposals for the next three years is summarized in table 2-6. The 1983 current services deficit with the administration's proposed defense spending is reduced from $145.6 billion to $91.5 billion, or by $54.1 billion. In the next two years, the cuts would be even greater, but the remaining deficits would still be large: $82.9 billion in 1984 and $71.9 billion in 1985.

If realized, the Reagan program would greatly reduce the budget in relation to the size of the economy and radically alter the composition of the budget (table 2-7). Total budget outlays amounted to 23.0 percent of GNP in fiscal 1981 and are expected to reach 23.5 percent in 1982, the highest percentage since the end of World

14. President Reagan also endorsed the idea of providing special tax incentives and relief from regulation for businesses locating in "enterprise zones," but this proposal will not affect the budget significantly until fiscal 1985, when receipts would be reduced by $500 million.

War II. By 1985 this ratio would decline to 20.9 percent, the same level as in 1979. During the same period, receipts would decline from the postwar peak of 21.0 percent of GNP reached in 1981 to 19.1 percent in 1985, the same level as in 1977. The share of outlays for national defense in the budget would increase from 24.0 percent in 1979 to 33.6 percent, while the share of the entitlement programs (such as social security, medicare, and medicaid) would remain roughly unchanged at about 45 percent. Net interest payments would rise from 8.7 percent to 11.6 percent, but receipts from the sale of land, oil leases, and surplus federal property (which are counted as reductions in outlays) would rise from 1.8 percent to 4.1 percent. Thus the brunt of the large increase in defense outlays would be borne by the discretionary nondefense programs, which would be cut from 24.0 percent of the budget in 1979 to 14.4 percent in 1985. These programs include grants to states and local governments, farm price supports, research support, pay of employees in nondefense agencies, and the basic overhead costs of government.

*The New Federalism*

A major feature of President Reagan's 1983 program is the inclusion of a new initiative to transfer forty-four federal programs to the states and localities and to provide revenue resources to fund these programs during the period when the transfer is made. In addition, the federal government would transfer the public assistance and food stamp programs to state and local governments, and in return would accept full responsibility for the medicaid program, which finances medical care for the poor.

The administration proposes that the states should have four years to decide whether to maintain the forty-four programs transferred to them. A special transition trust fund would be established to assist in the financing of the transferred programs. This fund would receive approximately $28 billion a year from existing federal excise taxes. Between 1984 and 1987, the states could use their transition accounts to continue the federal programs that are to be turned back to them. If a state chooses to terminate some of the designated federal programs before 1987, the resulting surplus in its transition account would be available as a "super revenue sharing" payment.

Beginning in 1988, the programs designed for turnback would no longer be operated by the federal government, and the federal taxes dedicated to the fund would be reduced by one-quarter of the initial amount each year. By 1991, all the federal excise taxes allocated to the fund would expire, and the states would be able, at their own option, to replace these taxes by their own taxes or to let them expire. This complicated procedure is equivalent to a simple phasing out of federal support and a reduction of federal excise taxes, with interim (but declining) financing for the states.

The transfer of medicaid to the federal level and of public assistance and food stamps to the state and local levels would involve a swap of about $20 billion in outlays in 1984. Similarly, the $28 billion trust fund would be sufficient to pay for the forty-four programs designated to be transferred to the states. Hence the new federalism proposals do not affect the official estimates of the budget deficits in 1984 and 1985. It should be emphasized, however, that these arrangements are an even exchange only *after* the cuts proposed in the 1983 budget.[15]

*Reliability of the Estimates*

Every budget contains estimates that are based exclusively on the administration's economic forecast and assume that the president's program will be enacted without change. As experience in recent years suggests (see table 2-3), presidential expectations for the economy are frequently too optimistic.

President Reagan expects the recession that began in July 1981 to end by mid-1982 and that strong economic growth will be resumed in the last half of 1982. Real gross national product is projected to increase 3.0 percent from the fourth quarter of 1981 to the fourth quarter of 1982, with even higher growth rates during the last two quarters of the year. Because of the economic decline in the first half of the year, real GNP will increase only 0.2 percent from the 1981 average to the 1982 average. The expansion is expected to continue without interruption for at least five years, with real GNP growth averaging 4.7 percent from mid-1982 to mid-1987. If achieved, this growth rate would exceed the average of 3.5 percent for the period from 1947 to 1981, but would be somewhat lower than the 5.4 percent average from 1961 to 1966.

15. For an analysis of the new federalism proposal, see chapter 5.

Table 2-8. Economic Assumptions of the Reagan Administration and the Congressional Budget Office, Calendar Years 1981–85

| Economic indicator | 1981 | Projected | | | |
|---|---|---|---|---|---|
| | | 1982 | 1983 | 1984 | 1985 |
| | *Percent change, year to year* | | | | |
| *GNP in current dollars* | | | | | |
| Reagan administration | 11.3 | 8.1 | 11.5 | 10.2 | 9.7 |
| Congressional Budget Office | 11.3 | 7.5 | 11.9 | 10.4 | 9.7 |
| *GNP in constant 1972 dollars* | | | | | |
| Reagan administration | 2.0 | 0.2 | 5.2 | 5.0 | 4.7 |
| Congressional Budget Office | 2.0 | −0.1 | 4.4 | 3.6 | 3.5 |
| *GNP deflator* | | | | | |
| Reagan administration | 9.1 | 7.9 | 6.0 | 5.0 | 4.7 |
| Congressional Budget Office | 9.1 | 7.5 | 7.3 | 6.6 | 6.0 |
| *Consumer price index* | | | | | |
| Reagan administration | 10.3 | 7.3 | 6.0 | 4.6 | 4.8 |
| Congressional Budget Office | 10.3 | 7.5 | 6.9 | 6.9 | 6.4 |
| | *Percent, annual average* | | | | |
| *Unemployment rate* | | | | | |
| Reagan administration | 7.6 | 8.9 | 7.9 | 7.1 | 6.4 |
| Congressional Budget Office | 7.6 | 8.9 | 8.0 | 7.4 | 7.2 |
| *Treasury bill rate* | | | | | |
| Reagan administration | 14.1 | 11.7 | 10.5 | 9.5 | 8.5 |
| Congressional Budget Office | 14.1 | 12.0 | 13.2 | 11.3 | 9.4 |

Source: *Budget of the United States Government, Fiscal Year 1983*, pp. 2-5, 2-7; and Congressional Budget Office, *The Prospects for Economic Recovery*, report to the Senate and House Committees on the Budget, part 1 (Government Printing Office, 1982), p. xviii.

Inflation is expected to recede from the 1982 rate of 7 to 8 percent to 4.5 percent in 1987; in these circumstances, interest rates are expected to decline substantially (table 2-8).

The administration's economic projection for 1982 and 1983 is at the optimistic end of the range of estimates circulating at the beginning of 1982. Most forecasters expect the recovery from the recession to begin in late 1982 at or near the rate projected by the administration, but to proceed at a much lower rate in 1983 and later years.[16] They also expect a higher rate of inflation and higher interest rates. A set of budget projections along these lines has been provided by the Congressional Budget Office (table 2-8).

The CBO projections are in close agreement with those of the

16. A growing number are even gloomier. Some believe that the recovery will be weak or will be aborted—as was the case with the recovery from the 1980 recession—because of the clash between fiscal and monetary policies.

Table 2-9. Effect of Alternative Assumptions on the Projected Budget Deficits, Fiscal
Years 1982–85
Billions of dollars

| Item | 1982 | 1983 | 1984 | 1985 |
|------|------|------|------|------|
| Budget deficit, Reagan assumptions | −98.6 | −91.5 | −82.9 | −71.9 |
| Effect of alternative economic assumptions and technical reestimates[a,b] | −8.4 | −19.2 | −29.4 | −43.1 |
| Overestimate of management savings[b,c] | −0.7 | −6.5 | −9.6 | −11.3 |
| Congressional action on proposed outlay cuts and tax revision measures[b,d] | −0.4 | −7.6 | −13.8 | −18.1 |
| Adjusted deficit | −108.1 | −124.8 | −135.7 | −144.4 |
| Deficit as a percent of GNP | −3.5 | −3.6 | −3.6 | −3.5 |

Sources: *Budget of the United States Government, Fiscal Year 1983*, pp. 3-8, 3-12; Congressional Budget Office,
*An Analysis of the President's Budgetary Proposals for Fiscal Year 1983* (GPO, 1982), p. 21; and authors' estimates.
Figures are rounded.
a. Based on a weighted average of receipts and outlays as estimated by the administration and CBO, with one-
third weight to the former and two-thirds weight to the latter.
b. Includes effect on interest payments.
c. Assumes that the savings will be only half those projected in the budget for management initiatives other than
accelerated leasing of OCS lands, which is allowed for in the technical reestimates.
d. Assumes that Congress will approve 80 percent of the outlay cuts and the tax revision measures (aside from
those included in management savings) proposed in the budget.

administration for 1982. However, they assume that the annual
rates of growth of real GNP (in 1972 dollars) will average about
1.1 percentage points less in 1983–85 and that there will be roughly
corresponding increases in the inflation rate (GNP deflator). These
changes, which reduce the real growth rate for 1982–87 to slightly
above the average rate in 1947–81, would increase budget outlays
for unemployment compensation and other entitlement programs
and for interest payments on the national debt. In addition, the
CBO also made adjustments in the administration's figures for
outlays for farm price support programs, the rate of spending on
defense procurement and interest payments, and for estimated
offsetting receipts from leasing of OCS lands (which enter into the
budget as reductions in outlays). As a compromise between the
two sets of estimates, we reestimated outlays and receipts by
taking a weighted average of the administration's estimates and
the CBO estimates.[17] This would raise the budget deficits by $8.4
billion in fiscal 1982, $19.2 billion in 1983, $29.4 billion in 1984,
and $43.1 billion in 1985 (table 2-9).
   Another source of uncertainty in the budget for fiscal 1983 is

17. The weights were one-third for the administration's estimate and two-thirds for
the CBO estimates.

the savings expected from the management initiatives proposed by the administration. Generous estimates were made of deficit reductions from sales of assets; prevention of fraud, waste, and abuse; improved debt collection; and better enforcement of the tax laws. The budget also projects increased tax receipts averaging $1.6 billion in 1983–85 from the extension of withholding to interest and dividends, a reform that has been rejected by Congress several times.

The total savings from the management initiatives proposed by the administration (other than from accelerated leasing of OCS lands) were estimated in the budget to amount to $1.2 billion in fiscal 1982 and from $12 billion in 1983 to $18 billion in 1985. It is impossible to predict how much of these savings will actually materialize, but it is likely that there will be considerable slippage. If the savings were only half the amounts expected by the administration and an adjustment is made for the additional interest payments on the national debt, the deficits would be understated by $0.7 billion in 1982, $6.5 billion in 1983, $9.6 billion in 1984, and $11.3 billion in 1985.

Finally, the administration's estimates presume that the proposed cuts in nondefense outlays and increased receipts from the proposed tax revision measures are all acceptable to the Congress. Even in 1981, when the president was so successful in putting his budget program across, the outlay cuts actually made represented about 80 percent of the cuts he originally proposed. Assuming he is equally successful in 1982, the deficits would be raised above those he projected by $0.4 billion in fiscal 1982, $7.6 billion in 1983, $13.8 billion in 1984, and $18.1 billion in 1985 (including the adjustment for interest payments).

These adjustments to the official budget figures do not exhaust all the possibilities. Instead of growing at the average rate for 1947–81, the economy could repeat the experience of 1979–81, when real GNP rose at an average annual rate of only 0.9 percent. The effect of the management initiatives could be overestimated even more seriously than the 50 percent assumed above. And Congress could find more than 20 percent of the proposed nondefense outlay cuts and tax revision measures unacceptable. Even without these more pessimistic assumptions, however, the budget problem is much more serious than the picture that emerges from

President Reagan's budget. Instead of deficits that decline from $98.6 billion to $71.9 billion in the next three years, the deficits may well be rising—from over $108 billion in 1982 to $145 billion in 1985 (table 2-9).[18] The 1985 deficit would amount to 3.5 percent of the GNP, an unprecedented figure for a period of expansion.

## The Budget and the Economy

Budget deficits have become the focal point of the discussion of economic policy. Yet the discussion often fails to distinguish between the short- and long-run consequences of the deficits. Today's economic difficulties will not be solved by simple reductions of budget deficits. In fact, increases in taxes or reductions in spending, without offsetting monetary policy adjustments, could make the recession worse by further reducing total demand. Monetary restraint, undertaken to counter persistent inflation, has caused the current recession, and a sustained recovery is unlikely without a substantial reduction in interest rates.

Driven by a deep concern about inflation, the monetary authorities are pursuing a policy that emphasizes slow growth of the money supply, with resulting restraint on demand, production, and employment. In effect, it is a policy of refusing to finance a strong economic expansion until inflation recedes to substantially lower levels.

Beyond 1982, the key to an improved economic situation must lie in a realignment of economic policy—a shift in the mix of fiscal and monetary policy, by matching reductions of future budget deficits with an easier monetary policy. As presently constituted, fiscal and monetary policies appear to be on a collision course: the monetary authorities clearly intend to hold to a policy of restraint, while fiscal policy threatens to become highly expansionary. The money supply targets for 1982 and 1983 place a low ceiling on the economy's growth of nominal GNP. Unless inflation should decline with unusual rapidity, such a policy implies slow growth in real output and continuation of high levels of unemployment. These are costs that the monetary authorities believe the country has no choice but to pay in the absence of other policies for reducing inflation.

18. Alternative methods of reducing these deficits and those in later years are discussed in chapter 6.

The administration has assigned principal responsibility for controlling inflation to the Federal Reserve System, and has announced its support for the policy of sharply limiting the growth of money and credit. It is, however, unwilling to recognize that the policy of monetary restraint is not compatible with its own desire for a rapid economic expansion. Believing instead that the announcement of a tough monetary policy and the provision of supply-side incentives will reduce inflation without major losses in real output or jobs, the administration has moved forward with a budget policy that presumes the economy will be growing rapidly through the mid-1980s. Large tax rate reductions and major increases in defense spending have created expectations that fiscal policy will be even more stimulative than intended in future years (that is, the deficits will be large and rising).[19] The two major elements of economic policy appear to be hopelessly at odds, and there are few signs of a willingness to compromise on either side.

*Monetary Policy*

Over the last decade monetary policy has become an increasingly important means of controlling economic activity. In part, this was a natural result of the shifting objectives of policy. In the 1960s government was strongly committed to an acceleration of economic growth, and fiscal measures seemed the more direct policy tool; the monetary authorities played primarily an accommodative role.[20] In the 1970s the growing concern with inflation shifted the primary objectives of government policy in the direction of restraint on economic activity, and it has been easier to achieve that restraint on the monetary side.[21]

19. See the discussion of table 2-9 above.

20. For a brief period in 1966, the Federal Reserve pursued an independent policy of restraint because of the failure of the administration and the Congress to raise taxes to pay for the Vietnam War expenditures. That policy was short-lived, however, and the Federal Reserve backed down in late 1966 when the economy appeared to be sliding into a recession. The event did mark the beginning of the gradual shift of emphasis in policy, however, and the reference above to the last decade implies an unduly sharp line of demarcation in policy.

21. Monetary policy has long been viewed as more effective in restraining the economy than providing for expansion because the availability of credit is often a necessary but not a sufficient condition for new investment projects. There are also important political reasons why monetary policy is likely to be used when restraint is needed. It is easier to obtain popular support for tax cuts and the expansion of spending programs than for a shift toward fiscal restraint. While fiscal policy is set in a public forum subject to review by voters and the pressures that that implies, monetary policy is determined by an independent agency in private and explained in terms that are difficult for the average person to understand.

The emphasis on monetary policy has also been accompanied by a change in the procedures under which it operates. The goals of policy are to reduce inflation and increase output and employment. But because of the lag between a change in policy and its effect on the economy, the tendency is to use an intermediate target to guide the conduct of policy in the short run. Over the last decade there has been a shift from relying on interest rates or credit conditions to using the money supply as the intermediate target.[22] The use of interest rates was criticized because of the ambiguities of interpreting interest rate movements during periods of significant changes in inflation expectations, and because holding interest rates stable implies that unforeseen surges in economic activity and credit demands will be accommodated rather than resisted by the monetary authorities.[23]

In October 1979 the Federal Reserve changed its operating procedures, which provide the link between its policy tools (adjustments in reserve requirements, security purchases, or loans to member banks) and the monetary growth targets. Previously, the Federal Reserve evaluated its progress toward the money supply targets on the basis of short-run interest rate movements. Given the interest rates set by the Federal Reserve, unforeseen changes in credit demands led to accommodative changes in bank reserves and the supplies of money and credit outstanding. Since 1979 the Federal Reserve has used the quantity of bank reserves as the primary short-term guide to control the money supply; thus, given the quantity of reserves made available by the Federal Reserve, unforeseen changes in credit demand now lead to greater interest rate variability.

Quite apart from the change in operating procedures, monetary policy also became more restrictive after 1979 in the effort to reduce the surge in inflation that accompanied the second oil shock. The tightening of policy is evident in the reduction in the

22. Some advocates of monetary policy have called for the adoption of a rigid rule for money supply growth regardless of developments in the economy. There is disagreement as to the extent to which the current monetary targets reflect such a policy.

23. The Federal Reserve has left itself a considerable range of flexibility in that: (1) the monetary growth targets are specified as a range rather than a single value; (2) targets are established for several alternative definitions of the money supply, and the emphasis in public discussions shifts among them; and (3) the Federal Reserve varies the speed with which it moves to correct for deviations of the actual rate from the target path. The emphasis on aggregates can also be viewed as a means of avoiding political responsibility for the high level of interest rates that accompany a restrictive monetary policy.

Table 2-10. **Alternative Measures of Inflation, Calendar Years 1977–81**
Percent

| Measure | 1977 | 1978 | 1979 | 1980 | 1981 |
|---|---|---|---|---|---|
| | *Annual change*[a] | | | | |
| Consumer price index | 6.7 | 9.0 | 12.7 | 12.5 | 9.5 |
| Selected components | | | | | |
| Food | 7.7 | 11.5 | 9.9 | 10.3 | 5.0 |
| Energy | 8.2 | 7.5 | 36.5 | 18.9 | 12.6 |
| Home purchases | 7.9 | 11.0 | 15.5 | 12.6 | 2.0 |
| Home financing | 9.7 | 15.9 | 24.2 | 22.8 | 21.0 |
| Used cars | −2.5 | 11.5 | 2.1 | 15.3 | 22.3 |
| Other components | 5.9 | 6.5 | 7.6 | 9.6 | 8.8 |
| Average hourly earning index | 7.4 | 8.5 | 8.0 | 9.6 | 8.3 |
| Employment cost index | 7.0 | 7.7 | 8.7 | 9.0 | 8.8 |

Source: Department of Labor, Bureau of Labor Statistics.
a. Percentage change from fourth quarter of prior year to fourth quarter of current year.

money supply growth targets since 1979 and the sharp rise of 4 to 5 percentage points in interest rates on securities of all maturities. While the interpretation of interest rate movements is complicated by uncertainty about inflation expectations, real interest rates (the difference between interest rates and expected inflation) have increased substantially.

Monetary restraint since 1979 has slowed inflation by reducing sales, production, and employment. In addition, higher domestic interest rates, by attracting foreign capital, have led to a rise in the value of the dollar and a decline in the price of imported goods. The high cost of borrowing has also forced many holders of primary commodities to unload their inventory stocks, further depressing prices. Favorable developments in world energy and grain markets have also been important factors. While the overall inflation rate has declined by 3 percentage points during 1981, much of the price deceleration has been the result of these special factors (see table 2-10). The underlying rate of wage and price inflation within the domestic industrial sectors has declined by only about 1 percentage point. Future gains in reducing inflation are likely to come more slowly.

Meanwhile, unemployment has increased from 6 percent in 1979 to almost 9 percent in early 1982; total output has not grown; and capital formation has fallen below the level of 1979. As in past recessions, the reduction in inflation has been achieved at substantial costs.

The Federal Reserve's money growth targets—2.5 to 5.5 per-cent for the M1 definition of the money stock for 1982, and lower in subsequent years—implies that monetary policy will continue to limit future economic growth severely. By definition, nominal GNP growth is equal to the sum of the rates of growth of money and its velocity of circulation (the ratio of GNP to the money stock). Thus, if velocity grows at the 3.5 percent annual average of the 1970s, nominal GNP growth could be no more than 6 to 9 percent. If inflation declines to 7 percent, as forecast by the administration, the upper range of nominal GNP growth would allow for real GNP growth of only 2 percent.

In practice, the velocity of money can fluctuate sharply over a period as short as a year, and higher velocity growth might be achieved. Ordinarily, higher velocity would require higher interest rates, as users are offered incentives to economize on money balances. But continuation of high interest rates would choke off economic expansion by limiting the growth in business invest-ment, housing, and other credit-sensitive sectors. Under current circumstances, however, given the rapid changes in financial institutions, the uncertainty about money supply measurement, and the possibility that interest rates are currently reflecting substantial risk premiums, there is a chance that velocity might rise even as nominal interest rates decline, as was the case in 1974–75.

### Fiscal Policy

The potential problems raised by large future budget deficits are quite different from the fiscal policy problems of the last three years. The large rise in the budget deficit from fiscal years 1979 to 1982 has resulted from monetary restraint and a sagging economy, not from explicit decisions to boost spending or reduce taxes. Monetary restraint has increased interest payments, and the two recessions of 1980 and 1981 lowered revenues and raised transfer payments. The fiscal 1980 and 1981 budgets contained very little in the way of new spending initiatives (except for defense), and the major tax changes were deferred to 1982 and 1983.

The prospect of large future increases in the deficit, however, suggests that fiscal policy will come into increasing conflict with the objectives of monetary policy. The combination of fiscal stimulus and monetary restraint could result in severe upward pressure on interest rates. Some observers go further and argue that anticipation of such a collision in the future—with the potential for some disruption of financial markets—has already contributed in a major way to the rise in interest rates in 1981 and early 1982. This lack of coordination of future fiscal and monetary actions is seen by many as the major weakness of current economic policy.

The administration has argued that future budget deficits could be financed by increasing private saving (reducing consumption) rather than by crowding out business investment, thus avoiding the problem of continued high interest rates. Certainly the 1981 tax bill significantly increased saving incentives, and the rise in interest rates, which reduces investment, has made saving more attractive. To date, empirical studies of the effect of these incentives have reached conflicting conclusions. If some of the more optimistic studies are correct, the private saving share of the GNP should rise by about 2 percentage points—roughly the magnitude of the future rise in the deficit. In any case, the tax rate reductions will initially be reflected in a change in saving, because consumption responds to income changes only with a substantial lag. Thus, during 1982 and early 1983, over half the 1982 tax cut may be absorbed by higher saving. But the effect of the new incentives is a longer-term phenomenon that will become visible only in 1983 and beyond.[24]

### Integrating Fiscal and Monetary Policies

Two separate issues dominate the discussion of future policy. How restrictive should overall policy be? What should be the balance between fiscal and monetary restraint? Clearly the monetary authorities are committed to continued slow growth in order to reduce inflation, and they believe that fiscal policy should be brought in line with that objective by actions to reduce the prospect for large budget deficits in the future. Such a policy implies slow future growth and the continuation of unemployment in the range of 8 to 9 percent. Public debate over this aspect of policy tends to be highly divisive because support for the policy is closely related

24. A relatively large change in saving is implied by studies such as that of Michael Boskin, "Taxation, Saving, and the Rate of Interest," *Journal of Political Economy,* vol. 86 (February 1978), pt. 2, pp. S3–S27. The outcome should be evaluated in terms of the total private saving rate rather than the personal saving rate, because the latter involves serious measurement and conceptual problems.

to one's own risk of being among the unemployed and one's concern for the social consequences of high unemployment. It is not a policy that is equally burdensome to all the groups in society.

Whatever overall growth of demand is permitted, the mix of fiscal and monetary policy will have important implications for capital formation and economic growth in the future. Increased reliance on fiscal restraint would promote a higher rate of future growth by reducing consumption and allowing a higher share of output to be allocated to capital formation.

Political conflict over whether fiscal restraint should be achieved by reducing expenditures or increasing taxes makes such a shift in policy difficult. The policy debate is also complicated by differing views about the magnitude of the deficit problem. Without dramatic action by the Congress, deficits could well rise to more than $200 billion by 1985 (see chapter 6). Deficits of that magnitude lie behind fears of a possible financial crisis. Such a fiscal policy is clearly too expansive, and restrictive actions are warranted even without an adjustment of monetary policy. On the other hand, if strong actions are taken by the administration and Congress to limit the deficit sharply, then the debate over the appropriate mix of fiscal and monetary policy becomes meaningful, because additional fiscal restraint could cause significantly lower than anticipated levels of total output.

Even if agreement can be reached on greatly reduced deficits and some easing of monetary restraint (with or without an explicit accord), one must expect slow economic growth and continued high unemployment for a number of years, unless some other way is found to bring down the underlying rate of inflation in the meantime. While incentives for saving and investment can bring about important and necessary structural realignments for the economy over the long term, so-called supply-side measures do not offer a painless path to disinflation in the short run.

It is for these reasons that some form of incomes policies— such as tax incentives, wage-price guidelines, or formal wage controls—continue to seem attractive. Such programs cannot substitute for fiscal and monetary restraint, but potentially they can speed up the process of moving to price stability. Incomes policies are difficult to operate and impose their own costs on the economy, but they must be evaluated against the cost of continued high unemployment. Certainly the administration is correct in its emphasis on faster economic growth as the basic solution to the nation's economic problems. That growth is not possible, however, without the support of monetary policy; and the barrier to the achievement of that accommodation is the fear of the inflationary consequences of a less restrictive policy.

# CHAPTER THREE

# The Defense Budget

WILLIAM W. KAUFMANN

TO THE PROVERBIAL MAN from Mars, American peacetime defense budgets must appear to be governed by some mysterious force, perhaps like the red tide that comes and goes along New England's shores. Spending ebbs under Eisenhower and flows under Kennedy. It ebbs again under Nixon, and begins once more to flow under Ford and Carter. Has the high-water mark been reached, or will the flow become a flood?

The answer is not yet clear. Carter, in his last budget (for fiscal 1982), unveiled a plan to increase defense spending over the coming five years at an average annual rate of nearly 5 percent in real terms. By March 1981 President Reagan, making more optimistic assumptions about inflation than his predecessor, proposed not only to increase the 1981 defense budget, but also to raise the rate of spending from 5 to 8.4 percent in real terms. The initial growth in total obligational authority intended to promote this surge amounted to $32.6 billion more than Carter had proposed in fiscal 1981 and 1982. It was to be used to speed completion of the Carter programs and items lower on the armed forces' list of priorities. Virtually no change was proposed in the size of the nuclear and nonnuclear forces or in the way these forces might be used.

I thank Henry J. Aaron, Nancy A. Ameen, Richard K. Betts, Martin Binkin, Bruce Blair, Robert W. Hartman, Michael K. MccGwire, and John D. Steinbruner for their advice, and Susan E. Nichols for her superior secretarial assistance.

Table 3-1. Defense Outlays Projected by the Carter and Reagan Administrations in 1981
Billions of dollars

| Administration and date of projection | Fiscal year | | | | | | |
|---|---|---|---|---|---|---|---|
| | 1981 | 1982 | 1983 | 1984 | 1985 | 1986 | Total |
| Current dollars | | | | | | | |
| Carter (January 1981) | 157.6 | 180.0 | 205.3 | 232.3 | 261.8 | 293.3 | 1,330.3 |
| Reagan (March 1981) | 158.6 | 184.8 | 221.1 | 249.8 | 297.3 | 336.0 | 1,447.6 |
| Reagan (September 1981) | 158.6 | 181.8 | 214.9 | 242.6 | 297.3 | 336.0 | 1,431.2 |
| Fiscal 1982 prices | | | | | | | |
| Carter (January 1981) | 172.5 | 180.0 | 188.2 | 197.1 | 207.0 | 217.5 | 1,162.3 |
| Reagan (March 1981) | 174.0 | 184.8 | 205.6 | 218.1 | 245.3 | 263.3 | 1,291.1 |
| Reagan (September 1981) | 174.0 | 181.8 | 199.8 | 211.8 | 245.3 | 263.3 | 1,276.0 |

Sources: *Department of Defense Annual Report, Fiscal Year 1982* (Government Printing Office, 1981), p. 10; press release, Office of Assistant Secretary of Defense (Public Affairs), "FY 1981 and FY 1982 Department of Defense Budget Revisions," no. 77-81, March 4, 1981; and Edward Cowan, "Reagan Reported Paring $30 Billion from 1983 Budget," *New York Times*, December 30, 1981.

Only six months later, concern about future budget deficits, doubts about the fairness of cutting social programs but not defense, and questions about the rationale for the proposed increases in defense spending became widespread. In September the president reluctantly agreed to slow the increase in defense outlays for the next three fiscal years (1982–84) by a total of $16 billion in current dollars. Table 3-1 shows the Carter defense spending plan of January 1981, the Reagan substitute of March, and the Reagan revision of September. For the six-year period fiscal 1981–86, the Carter plan entailed real outlays (in fiscal 1982 prices) of $1,162.3 billion. The revised Reagan plan proposed to increase that total by $113.7 billion, to $1,276 billion, for the same six years. Congress essentially accepted the Reagan proposals for 1981 and 1982.

## The New Defense Plan

The president's defense budget for 1983 and his five-year defense plan, which now runs through fiscal 1987, reflect his continued determination to increase defense spending. At the end of seven years, from fiscal 1981 to 1987, outlays will have increased, in real terms, by 59 percent. Table 3-2 shows actual and projected total obligational authority and outlays in current and 1983 prices from fiscal 1981 through 1987. Defense outlays, which ran at 5.6 percent of gross national product in fiscal 1981, will grow to 7.4 percent by 1987. These outlays rise each year on the average by 8.1 percent in real terms, but the growth is 10.5 percent in 1983 and 9.6 percent in 1985. The bills for most of the sharp increases in obligational authority in fiscal 1981 and 1982 are only now beginning to fall due.

This delayed effect will come as no surprise to observers of the federal budget. During fiscal 1981 and 1982 the Reagan administration increased by nearly $7 billion over the Carter estimates those appropriation accounts that fund the operations and support of the armed forces. The purpose of this increase was to improve the readiness of existing capabilities. But the administration also increased by more than $25 billion the key investment accounts—procurement and research, development, test, and evaluation—to accelerate the modernization of the existing force structure and also to take advantage of the economies to be achieved from buying new equipment in large orders.

Funding for operations and support constitutes "fast" money; budget authority and outlays are nearly identical in any fiscal year. Funding for investment is relatively "slow" money; budget authority committed in one fiscal year may not spend out for a number of years, depending on what is being acquired. For the most part, investment spending, once budget authority is obligated (and a contract is signed), is more difficult to control than spending for operations and support.

**Table 3-2. The Current Reagan Defense Plan, Fiscal Years 1981–87**
Billions of dollars unless otherwise specified

| Item | 1981 | 1982 | 1983 | 1984 | 1985 | 1986 | 1987 | Total |
|---|---|---|---|---|---|---|---|---|
| Total obligational authority | | | | | | | | |
| Current dollars | 176.1 | 214.2 | 258.0 | 285.5 | 331.7 | 367.6 | 400.8 | 2,033.9 |
| Fiscal 1983 prices | 202.2 | 227.8 | 258.0 | 269.8 | 297.8 | 314.0 | 325.9 | 1,895.5 |
| Percent increase | 10.9 | 12.7 | 13.2 | 4.6 | 10.4 | 5.4 | 3.8 | . . . |
| Outlays | | | | | | | | |
| Current dollars | 156.1 | 182.8 | 215.9 | 247.0 | 285.5 | 324.0 | 356.0 | 1,767.3 |
| Fiscal 1983 prices | 181.4 | 195.4 | 215.9 | 233.2 | 255.6 | 276.0 | 288.7 | 1,646.2 |
| Percent increase | 4.7 | 7.7 | 10.5 | 8.0 | 9.6 | 8.0 | 4.6 | . . . |
| *Addendum:* | | | | | | | | |
| Index of inflation | 0.861 | 0.936 | 1.00 | 1.059 | 1.117 | 1.174 | 1.233 | . . . |

Source: *Department of Defense Annual Report to the Congress, Fiscal Year 1983* (GPO, 1982), pp. B-1, B-3.

It is currently estimated that by the end of fiscal 1982 a backlog of $110 billion will be obligated but not spent (compared with $86 billion at the end of fiscal 1981). Another $34 billion in budget authority will remain to be obligated. These balances of budget authority come from appropriations of previous fiscal years and are in addition to the authority to be appropriated for 1983. If the president's defense budget is adopted, it is estimated that the balance of budget authority not spent or not even obligated will rise to about $185 billion. The potential surge in future defense outlays thus could be both large and uneven.

In light of the federal deficits that are projected for 1983 and subsequent years, the president's defense budget has come under critical scrutiny from a number of quarters. As in September 1981, the president will find himself pressed to consider reductions in budget authority and outlays. Cuts will almost certainly be debated in Congress, however much the president resists them. As these pressures mount, two basic questions will require consideration. Can restraint in defense increases be justified while Afghanistan is occupied by Soviet forces, Poland exists in a state of siege, and Soviet defense spending allegedly continues to rise? If so, where can that restraint be exercised without undue risk to the safety of the United States and its friends?

## The Issue of Restraint

It is difficult to identify a force that guarantees low risk in a dynamic and competitive world. However, as a point of reference, the force goals established in the mid-1970s were considered sufficient to underwrite U.S. foreign and defense policies. A budget for this baseline force, with its costs estimated in fiscal 1983 dollars, is compared with the Reagan defense budget for 1983 in table 3-3. Essentially, this force is designed to incorporate a reliable second-strike nuclear capability against a large variety of targets, the conventional capability to conduct simultaneously a major campaign and a minor campaign overseas in conjunction with allies, and enough nonnuclear war reserve stocks to last for forty-five days of intense combat. For costing purposes, it is assumed to have been "born" fully equipped and stocked, which is not an outrageous assumption considering the modern equip-

**Table 3-3. Baseline and Reagan Defense Budgets for Fiscal Year 1983**
Billions of dollars

| Category of expenditure | Baseline | Reagan |
|---|---|---|
| **Total obligational authority** | **212.5** | **258.0** |
| Strategic forces | 26.0 | 37.2 |
| Theater nuclear capabilities | 2.0 | 3.3 |
| Conventional forces | 141.8 | 174.8 |
| Intelligence and communications | 19.9 | 19.9 |
| Military construction | 5.4 | 5.4 |
| Revolving and management funds | 0.9 | 0.9 |
| Retired pay | 16.5 | 16.5 |
| **Outlays** | **196.9** | **215.9** |

Sources: Author's estimates in tables 3-6, 3-9, 3-16, 3-17; and *Department of Defense Annual Report to the Congress, Fiscal Year 1983*, p. B-7.

ment and stocks the armed forces inherited from the war in Vietnam.

It is no secret that the baseline force has been underfunded for the past eight years. A rough estimate suggests that to have fleshed it out with personnel, equipment, and supplies, operated and supported it, and modernized it in an orderly way—with due account taken of the inheritance from previous years—would have required nearly $1.8 trillion in fiscal 1983 dollars over the eight-year period. Instead, close to $1.6 trillion (also in fiscal 1983 dollars) was actually spent. The Carter administration tacitly acknowledged this underfunding in its farewell five-year defense plan, which proposed to begin making good many of the deficits as well as to launch a number of new and expensive modernization programs. The pace of change, however, was to be gradual.

A case can be made, quite apart from this underfunding, that the baseline force structure—and particularly the nonnuclear part of it—is no longer adequate to the dangers of the 1980s. With defense as with police departments, there is always a problem of determining how much to buy when uncertainty exists about both the probability of trouble and the relationship among forces, deterrence, and violence. However, the possibility cannot be precluded that more and greater troubles will arise in this than in the previous decade. To deal with this possibility, an expansion of U.S. capabilities and costs exceeding those of the baseline force might well seem prudent. The Reagan administration believes that at least some expansion is necessary.

Most such beliefs and the plans accompanying them have at least one thing in common. In none is it assumed that the United States will confront a major national emergency in the immediate future. The Carter five-year plan called for an average annual increase in real total obligational authority of nearly 5 percent over the period; President Reagan moves the average up to more than 8.1 percent a year for the next five years. The result in both cases is an augmentation of U.S. military power. But additions to the baseline capability do not begin to appear for another four or five years.

Comparable if not greater increases could be achieved in a shorter time. Existing nuclear forces, especially bombers and fleet ballistic missile submarines, could be placed on higher alerts and older bombers brought out of storage. About 1,600 relatively survivable warheads could be added to the U.S. second-strike capability in this way. Existing production facilities for conventional equipment could be put on three shifts and new facilities constructed. A national emergency could be declared. Some form of conscription could be introduced; the National Guard could be called to federal service; older ships and tactical aircraft could be taken out of mothballs. Within two years, land forces could be doubled in size, air forces increased by nearly 50 percent, and the fleet expanded by 10 percent. That no one in a position of responsibility has advocated such draconian and costly measures suggests, to the extent that a buildup in defense is justified, that it can proceed at a measured pace.

Other, equally important reasons could warrant a carefully controlled buildup. It is entirely understandable that senior officials of the armed forces, seeing the budgetary barriers lowered but remembering well the historical ebb and flow of funding for defense, seek to order as much equipment as they can while they can. It is equally comprehensible that they stress long-lead-time items even more than recruits, combat consumables, spare parts, and all the other items that will make the capital goods effective. In a developing emergency, it is too late to acquire new attack carriers and aircraft, but there is at least some chance that the shorter-lead-time items can be recovered before the emergency becomes acute. But understandable though such a strategy may be, a cost is attached to it. The inflation in the price of defense goods is already higher than for goods in the nondefense sector of the economy. A large surge in the demand for defense goods will drive the inflation higher still, even with the benefits of multiyear contracting. Whether the additional goods can be acquired in the shorter period of time—and whether they will be worth the increased prices, especially if time is not of the essence—certainly deserves consideration.

Haste can have another and hidden cost. The armed forces, in the rush to spend their newfound wealth, may not acquire the capabilities they really need to deal with the dangers and uncertainties of the future. It has become a commonplace in defense circles to argue that perceptions are at the heart of deterrence and political leverage. Thus, whatever the actual strength and skill of opposing capabilities, nuclear as well as nonnuclear, if observers judge one side to be superior to the other, political and military consequences are said to ensue. According to this argument, forces must be acquired to ensure the correct perceptions, even though the additional forces may be irrelevant to carefully formulated military objectives and cost billions in the bargain.

No doubt there is something to this argument, though not much. Buying to influence perceptions, however faulty those perceptions may be, more often than not requires attempts to achieve equality or superiority in some simple and easily identifiable measure, regardless of its military merit. If the Warsaw Pact countries can deploy 45,000 tanks and NATO only 17,000, the implication is that NATO must eliminate the tank deficit, even though the Western alliance may plan for an initial defensive battle and has acquired more than 6,000 antitank launchers for that purpose. If the Soviet strategic missiles can lift 23,000 tons of payload and comparable U.S. forces can lift only 9,000 tons, somehow this deficiency must be corrected, even though the difference may have no military significance.

Cheaper and equally efficacious ways of dealing with such misperceptions do exist. Carefully reasoned expositions by authoritative policymakers of expected outcomes of possible conflicts, and the probability of deterring such conflicts, constitute only one of these ways. Unfortunately, it seems to have gone out of fashion.

Perhaps as influential as the argument about perceptions is the

claim that the armed forces have become the captives of a baroque
technology and, like other American consumers, have fallen in
love with size, speed, ostentation, electronics, and all the other
supposed products of that technology. Here too there may be
something to the argument, but not a great deal. Like others
charged with providing public goods, military organizations may
be less sensitive to costs than those who must compete in the
private sector. But that is only a small part of the explanation for
*Nimitz* attack carriers and Aegis-equipped cruisers, F-15 and
F-16 aircraft, M-1 tanks, AH-64 attack helicopters, and the
DIVAD air defenses built into the Army's divisions. These large,
complex, and costly weapon systems are also the product of other
and more serious predispositions.

One of them is the assumption that the United States, if it ever
has to fight the Soviet Union, will go into battle badly outnumbered
in men and equipment. It must therefore compensate for numerical
inferiority with great qualitative superiority.

Another is the equally stubborn determination, regardless of
changes in technology and cost, to perform certain missions and
avoid others, particularly if they have a "defensive" connotation.
The Navy thus has a deep traditional commitment to seeking out
the enemy battle fleet and destroying it, even if it should be holed
up in Murmansk and Vladivostok under the umbrella of land-
based air defenses and fighter aircraft. But to get at those fleets
means large-deck carriers, high-performance naval aircraft, and
sophisticated seagoing air defenses such as are incorporated into
the Aegis cruiser. The Air Force, for its part, is wedded to the
missions of deep air superiority and interdiction as the way to
exert a decisive influence on the land battle, and doing so independently of the Army. But that inevitably means big, fast, long-
legged fighters with sophisticated avionics that can fly the necessary distances, fight through an environment dense with hostile
surface-to-air missiles and manned interceptors, and fire a significant amount of modern ordnance at vital targets. And if F-15s are
not provided in sufficient numbers for the mission, F-16s will be
upgraded in performance (and cost) as the next-best substitute.
Meanwhile, the Army would prefer to fight tanks with tanks and
concentrate on close air support of the ground forces and local air
defense. Outnumbered in tanks, it must be able to destroy four or
five of the enemy's for every one it loses: hence the M-1 with all

its advanced technology. And seeing the missions of close air support and local air defense once again take a back seat in the Air Force, yet limited by old interservice treaties on what kinds of aircraft it can own, it will try to make up for the neglect of the Air Force with complicated and fragile AH-64 attack helicopters, Patriot missiles, and costly DIVAD air defenses for its units. If the Marine Corps is counted, as indeed it should be, the United States thus has an Air Force air force, a Navy air force, an Army air force, and a Marine Corps air force.

It is by no means clear that the United States and its allies would be badly outnumbered in Central Europe, Korea, or the Persian Gulf. Nor is it evident that some of the current emphasis on traditional missions, high technology, and redundancy of tactical air forces is all that well placed. But the more important point is that these issues have not been seriously examined in some years. Accordingly, since the consensus seems to be that there is no rush to repair any weaknesses that may exist in the U.S. defense posture, there is much to be said for slowing, deferring, or even canceling certain programs until specific threats, missions, equipment, and forces have undergone a systematic assessment.

### The Problem of Budget Control

Regulating the investment in high-technology weapon systems is difficult and will in any event affect long-run rather than near-term outlays, as can be seen in table 3-4. This is true in part because these systems are paid for so slowly. But it may be equally true because once contracts are signed, budget authority obligated, and cancellation clauses incorporated into the contracts, it can become nearly as costly to terminate as to continue or stretch out a particular program, and the payments required by the cancellation clauses may have to be made at a fiscally awkward time. That is why, if the objective is to control outlays in the near term and if long-run budget authority has not been apportioned with great care and discipline by the Office of Management and Budget, the "fast" money associated primarily with minor procurement, operations, and support becomes the target of fiscal control.

The first-year costs of personnel reductions are usually higher

60                                                      William W. Kaufmann

Table 3-4. Outlays, by Appropriation Categories and Major Weapons, as a Percent
of First-Year Budget Authority Spent Each Year over a Six-Year Period

| | Year | | | | | |
|---|---|---|---|---|---|---|
| Category of expenditure | First | Second | Third | Fourth | Fifth | Sixth |
| Procurement | | | | | | |
| Ships | 2.0 | 14.0 | 18.0 | 18.0 | 18.0 | 18.0 |
| Aircraft | 10.1 | 44.3 | 35.9 | 6.0 | 3.7 | ... |
| Missiles | 19.1 | 49.1 | 27.6 | 4.2 | ... | ... |
| Tanks | 6.3 | 39.8 | 38.3 | 11.0 | 4.6 | ... |
| Ammunition | 12.1 | 52.2 | 28.4 | 7.3 | ... | ... |
| Research, development, test, | | | | | | |
| and evaluation | 56.4 | 35.8 | 5.6 | 2.2 | ... | ... |
| Operation and maintenance | 83.1 | 14.0 | 1.9 | 1.0 | ... | ... |
| Military construction | 7.7 | 36.4 | 30.4 | 12.7 | 6.5 | 6.3 |
| Personnel | 97.7 | 1.9 | 0.4 | ... | ... | ... |
| Family housing | 59.8 | 25.0 | 8.8 | 4.0 | 2.4 | ... |

Sources: Les Aspin, "Defense's Catch-22," *New Republic,* March 3, 1982, p. 12; Les Aspin, "The Defense Budget," memorandum, January 26, 1982; and author's estimates.

than the savings. However, pay increases and adjustments in retired pay can, in principle, be controlled. Flying and steaming hours can always be reduced to conserve fuel and minimize wear and tear on aircraft and ships. Acquisition of spare parts can be postponed and some first-line weapon systems cannibalized in order to keep others operating. Major repairs and overhauls of weapon systems can be deferred to save on labor and minor procurement. Training exercises can be curbed to conserve weapons, vehicles, and ammunition. Inventories of supplies and war reserves can be drawn down; upkeep on government property can be delayed. The only difficulty is that as postponements, delays, and drawdowns accumulate, the combat effectiveness of the affected forces begins to decay. As the process continues, the time and cost of repairing the damage becomes as long and large as would be needed to acquire new weapon systems.

If fiscal policy nonetheless dictates that, with no alternative, a tight rein be held on the fast money, a damage-limiting strategy can be instituted. The strategic offensive forces—bombers, intercontinental ballistic missiles (ICBMs), and submarine-launched ballistic missiles (SLBMs)—are already partially exempt from these periodic bouts with operating austerity on the assumption that a certain percentage of them must at all times be on alert and ready to launch. In an era of nuclear shadowboxing, cautious testing, and local conflicts carefully localized, as in Korea, Vietnam, and Afghanistan, a somewhat similar approach can, if essential, be used for the more expensive conventional forces. That is to say, certain ground, naval, air, and mobility units can be made exempt from reductions in fast money so that at least some portion of the force is immediately ready for action.

Admittedly, such an approach will mean that a substantial fraction of the conventional forces will fall on even more evil days than if cuts in fast money are allocated equally across the board. But if fiscal objectives have to be met in the short run and the flow of fast money has to be controlled, prudence may call for the preservation of 100 percent effectiveness in 30 percent of the force (and 70 percent effectiveness in the remainder) rather than an effectiveness of 80 percent across the entire force. And if such an option has to be exercised, it can at least be accompanied by a commitment to abolish those deficits in effectiveness once the period of austerity has passed.

### Choices

If in principle the case can be made for tightening control over the growth in defense budget authority and outlays during fiscal 1983 and the subsequent four years, where, practically speaking, do the opportunities for prudent discipline lie? What serious choices other than the Reagan five-year defense plan are available for rearming America? Is the case for the current plan and the pace of growth in the resources dedicated to it so watertight that no other possibilities are conceivable, or does some range of options exist?

### The Strategic Nuclear Forces

The U.S. defense capability that always attracts the greatest concern and publicity consists of the strategic nuclear forces. Made up of ICBMs, SLBMs, and heavy bombers, a network of surveillance and warning devices, continental air defenses (and one inactive, obsolete antiballistic missile site), a skeletal civil defense system (now administered by the Federal Emergency Management Agency), and a web of ground, airborne, and satellite command-control-communications capabilities, the strategic nuclear forces are correctly seen as the foundation on which all other U.S. and allied defenses rest. Without them, the United States and its friends would be vulnerable to coercion or destruction by hostile nuclear forces no matter how powerful they might otherwise be.

In the past the strategic nuclear forces have been considered capable of playing a wide range of roles: from deterrence of direct nuclear attacks on the United States and its allies to deterrence of large-scale conventional attacks and even of nuclear proliferation. Now and for the foreseeable future their main function will probably be confined to the second-strike deterrence of nuclear war and, if deterrence should somehow fail, to the earliest possible termination of such a disastrous conflict.

No doubt the existence of strategic nuclear forces will continue to induce a certain degree of caution in the use of other types of organized force and in the scale of that use, at least among the great powers. However, despite their potential for first use, the U.S. strategic nuclear forces (and for that matter their Soviet counterparts) were designed primarily with the objective of surviving a surprise nuclear attack and engaging in a deliberate and controlled retaliation against a number of enemy targets. Thus the central issues in the assessment and planning of these forces are (1) how much of the offensive force and associated capabilities can survive a surprise attack (however unrealistic such a contingency may be); (2) how many enemy targets of what kinds can be covered by a full U.S. retaliation; and (3) to what degree can the retaliatory forces actually be withheld from attacking certain classes of targets (such as cities) and kept for as long as necessary in reserve.

PERFORMANCE. Most planners would probably agree, in dealing with these issues, that neither the United States nor the Soviet Union now has or is likely to obtain in the foreseeable future the capability to deliver a full disarming first strike against the other. Because of the number, diversity, and alertness of the forces each side deploys, a knockout blow of this kind simply does not seem feasible.

For planning purposes, however, the U.S. ICBM force—currently consisting of 550 Minuteman III missiles with up to 1,650 warheads, 450 Minuteman II missiles with up to 450 warheads, and 52 Titan II missiles (shortly to be deactivated) with 52 high-yield warheads—has to be considered vulnerable. That is to say, given the warhead yield, accuracy, and reliability of the reentry vehicles on certain Soviet ICBMs, the coordinated firing of 2,106 of these reentry vehicles could be expected to destroy up to 95 percent of the U.S. ICBM silos. The Soviet ICBM force is already equipped with more than the requisite number of appropriate reentry vehicles.

U.S. planners also have to consider the possibility that their Soviet counterparts, having made the U.S. ICBMs at least nominally vulnerable, will now strive to put U.S. SLBMs and bombers similarly at risk by means of the capability not only to attack submarine ports and bombers but also to sink submarines at sea, intercept retaliating bombers with improved air defenses, and shoot down SLBM reentry vehicles with modern antiballistic missiles. Such a possibility may seem remote, but the Soviet Union is developing or improving capabilities in all these areas and attempting to provide some form of civil defense protection for as much as 15 percent of its urban population, including the top civilian and military leadership.

Despite these efforts, there are good grounds for believing that more than 3,500 U.S. nuclear warheads on alert bombers and SLBMs on station would survive a Soviet surprise attack and be available for retaliation. Even after losses inflicted by enemy defenses and failures in reliability, the retaliating warheads would be sufficient to cover a wide range of soft targets in the Soviet Union, including military targets, other installations, and a number of urban-industrial areas. Some of the warheads, particularly those on the SLBMs, could be withheld from attacks on the urban-industrial targets and kept in reserve, if believed desirable by the national command authorities; plans have existed for more than twenty years to permit this and certain other types of options. For even longer there has been, as there remains, doubt about the ability of the command-control-communications network to survive long enough to allow the president or his successors much time for deliberation and control. That is only one of several reasons why the discussions of highly selective, limited, and protracted nuclear exchanges are more academic than operational.

If this assessment is correct, it seems fair to say that the strategic nuclear forces of the United States and the Soviet Union are now and for many years have been locked in a military stalemate, regardless of the many asymmetries in their size, composition, basing, and performance. Unless one side or the other is extremely careless, that stalemate is likely to continue indefinitely. Despite possible developments in high-energy lasers, particle beams, and other exotic technologies, the probability remains low that either side will achieve the capability for a full disarming first strike, an impenetrable defense, or some workable combination of the two. Other strategies—which depend on achieving great asymmetries in target destruction and damage and contemplate several exchanges after which the side with the superior residual force coerces the side with fewer remaining weapons—are so high in risk and so lacking in operational detail that their implementation, even in a time of desperation, must be considered even less likely.

VULNERABILITIES. Despite the existing and prospective stalemate, the stakes are still so high in the strategic arena that there is an understandable tendency to adopt hedges against events of very low probability. On the same principle, measures can be justified to forestall the asymmetries that may arise when a portion of the deterrent is threatened with erosion. Reasonably prudent planners thus are bound to be concerned about both the weaknesses that already exist and those that are likely to appear in the U.S. strategic nuclear posture.

The potential vulnerability of the ICBM force is the most publicized of these weaknesses, but the fragility of the command-control-communications network is equally a problem. There is also the well-known possibility that the penetration of Soviet air defenses will become increasingly risky for bombers such as the B-52 during the late 1980s. Much has been made, moreover, of the growing age of the existing offensive and defensive forces, despite the backfitting of new Trident I missiles into twelve Poseidon boats, the commissioning of the first Trident submarine, and the beginning of cruise missile production.

The potential weaknesses are nonetheless troublesome. As a consequence of them, the most survivable of the U.S. strategic retaliatory forces—whether they are on their normal day-to-day alert or on a generated alert prompted by a crisis, when many more warheads would become survivable—are not able to cover all the highest-priority targets in the Soviet Union. Of these targets, which could easily amount to 5,000 or 6,000, perhaps as many as 2,000 might be classified as hard targets requiring, as one example, the delivery of warheads with accuracies of less than one-tenth of a nautical mile and yields in the hundreds of kilotons. The United States does not now deploy a ballistic missile or reentry vehicle with this or any other appropriate combination of yield and accuracy.

The strategic arms control agreements negotiated thus far have not compensated in any way for these weaknesses, although the basing mode proposed by the Carter administration for the MX ICBM could have made somewhat more sense with SALT II (and its constraints on numbers of warheads) than without it. It is unlikely, moreover, that future arms control negotiations and agreements will act as significant substitutes for unilateral U.S. strategic nuclear planning. What they can do instead, by reducing future uncertainties, controlling the growth in numbers of warheads, and removing exotic capabilities from the competition, is to make planners on both sides more confident and possibly more moderate in their demands. These are important and perhaps achievable objectives. But they will not relieve planners of the obligation to decide what to do next about the nuclear capabilities.

THE REAGAN PROGRAM. The Reagan planners, in recognition of this obligation, devised a program for the U.S. strategic nuclear forces, much of which the president made public in October 1981. Although the cost of the program was given as $180.3 billion over the six years from fiscal 1982 to 1987, the total apparently reflects the amount expected to be obligated to all strategic capabilities, old and new, for both investment and operations during those six fiscal years. The program would continue and expand the initiatives undertaken by previous administrations to equip a portion of the B-52 force (up to 151 B-52Gs) with air-launched cruise missiles; proceed with the development of the high-technology bomber known as Stealth; produce the Trident submarine and the Trident I missile; develop the higher-accuracy Trident II missile as a follow-on to the Trident I; proceed with the production of the MX missile; and accelerate research and development on ballistic missile defenses. The Reagan administration, however, would differ from the immediate past in five respects.

An advanced version of the B-1 bomber canceled by the Carter administration would be put into production with the aim of achieving an initial operating capability by fiscal 1986, perhaps four or five years before the Stealth bomber could become available. To supplement or replace the B-52H, currently the backbone of the penetrating bomber force, 100 B-1Bs would be acquired.

The MX program would be drastically reoriented. The multiple-protective-shelter basing mode planned for Nevada and Utah has been canceled, and 100 rather than 200 MX missiles would be acquired. The first 40 would be installed in existing Minuteman silos. The basing mode for the remainder, as yet undecided, would be announced by 1983. Basing options currently under consideration include an airborne patrol, deep basing possibly in the south side of mountains, and some form of deceptive (or shell-game) basing, to be supplemented later, if necessary, by a new type of ballistic missile defense.

A substantially expanded civil defense program would be inaugurated, intended to protect a large percentage of the population from nuclear fallout. The effectiveness of the system would depend on a combination of evacuation and fallout shelters. Funding for this program, which has been doubled for fiscal 1983, now appears in the budget of the Federal Emergency Management Agency.

The aging continental air defense system, with its 312 old interceptors, costly distant early warning line, and obsolete ground-control centers, would be modernized by an automated early warning line, additional AWACS (airborne warning and control system) aircraft capable of detecting and tracking intruders at low altitude, and 90 to 120 F-15 aircraft with lookdown and shootdown capabilities. This modernized air defense system would presumably be capable of intercepting the new Soviet long-range bomber, which conceivably could be deployed in meaningful numbers by the late 1980s.

Finally, national command-control-communications would be upgraded by a series of measures. The ELF (extremely low frequency) system for communicating with ballistic missile submarines would be completed. Additional satellite channels would become available for communications to and from the strategic

**Table 3-5. Potential Reductions or Cancellations in Major Strategic Nuclear Programs, Selected Fiscal Years, 1983–87**
Billions of dollars

| Program | Action | Reduction in total obligational authority, 1983–87 | Reduction in outlays | | |
|---|---|---|---|---|---|
| | | | 1983[a] | 1985 | 1983–87 |
| **Intermediate budget** | | | | | |
| 100 MX missiles | Cancel procurement | 11.9 | 1.5 | 1.8 | 9.0 |
| 100 B-1B bombers | Cancel | 34.3 | 1.4 | 6.0 | 25.8 |
| Ballistic missile defense | Reduce research and development by one-third | 2.0 | 0.1 | 0.3 | 1.5 |
| Continental air defense | Cancel modernization | 6.5 | 0.5 | 1.1 | 4.9 |
| Total | | 54.7 | 3.5 | 9.2 | 41.2 |
| **Baseline budget** | | | | | |
| Trident II missile | Cancel | 7.9 | 0.3 | 1.4 | 5.9 |
| MX missile research and development | Cancel | 10.6 | 0.8 | 1.8 | 8.0 |
| KC-135 tanker re-engining | Cancel | 6.8 | 0.2 | 1.2 | 5.1 |
| Cumulative total | | 80.0 | 4.8 | 13.6 | 60.2 |
| **Not in defense budgets** | | | | | |
| Civil defense (Federal Emergency Management Agency) | Reduce by one-half | 1.0 | 0.1 | 0.1 | 0.8 |
| Nuclear weapons (Department of Energy) | Cancel MX warheads | 1.0 | 0.1 | 0.1 | 0.8 |
| Total, all budgets | | 82.0 | 5.0 | 13.8 | 61.8 |

Sources: *Department of Defense Annual Report to the Congress, Fiscal Year 1983*, pp. III-58–III-66; Congressional Budget Office, *Baseline Budget Projections for Fiscal Years 1983–1987*, report to the Senate and House Budget Committees, part 2 (GPO, 1982), p. 87; and author's estimates.
a. Includes outlays resulting from appropriations in fiscal years 1981–83.

nuclear forces. The airborne TACAMO system for communicating with ballistic missile submarines would be modernized with new aircraft, and a number of ground-mobile command posts would be provided.

ALTERNATIVE PROGRAMS. Table 3-5 shows a number of major strategic programs that could be considered for cancellation or reduction. An intermediate strategic budget would omit the B-1B bomber and continental air defense programs contained in the Reagan budget. It would also forgo MX procurement and support a reduced program of research and development on ballistic missile defense. Five-year savings of $54.7 billion in obligational authority and $41.2 billion in outlays would result. The baseline strategic budget would omit all of these programs and cancel the Trident II missile, MX research and development, and the re-engining of the KC-135 tanker. Five-year savings of $80 billion in obligational authority and $60.2 billion in outlays would follow. In addition, nondefense savings of $2 billion in obligational authority and $1.6 billion in outlays could be achieved by canceling the Reagan civil defense program and the warheads for the MX missile.

Several points about the Reagan strategic programs are worth noting. All of them have some merit and at least one of them—dealing with command-control-communications—would rank high on almost everyone's list of priorities. All of them will take some time to complete; they will not begin to pay off for another few years. When they are deployed they will, for the most part, give somewhat higher confidence to existing U.S. second-strike target coverage rather than increase it. Because the size of the MX program is reduced, at least for the next few years, and the B-1 deployment is added, the five-year cost of the strategic forces may well be no more than was inherent in the program proposed by the Carter administration.

One alternative to the Reagan programs is to concentrate on the essentials of second-strike retaliation. This could mean (1) proceeding with a gradual but high-cost modernization of the penetrating bomber and submarine legs of the strategic nuclear triad; (2) continuing a vigorous program of research and development on ICBM basing and ballistic missile defense; (3) upgrading the strategic command-control system; but (4) canceling or deferring offensive and defensive programs that are more marginal to the U.S. second-strike, retaliatory strategy.

Where does the B-1 bomber fit within this context? It will almost certainly represent an improvement over the B-52H in being new and in having the ability to escape from an airfield on short warning and penetrate the more sophisticated defenses the USSR could have by the late 1980s. As a penetrating bomber, it can also be worth having as a hedge against slippages in the performance of first-generation air-launched cruise missiles. But to make a down payment of at least $34 billion for this hedge when the Stealth bomber is scheduled to follow it so closely in availability can be regarded as excessively conservative, especially since no firm evidence has been presented to suggest either that the B-52H flying at low altitude with modern avionics will have any greater difficulty than the B-1 in overcoming Soviet air defenses for the rest of the decade or that air-launched cruise missiles with even smaller radar cross sections will somehow encounter more obstacles than the B-1 in penetrating these defenses.

How to deal with the MX ICBM is more challenging. The hard-target kill capability it represents can be justified for two purposes: to cover "time-urgent" targets in the USSR such as silos, nuclear storage sites, and command posts; and to bring home to Soviet leaders their folly in allowing the threat to the U.S. ICBM force to develop. For both purposes, in fact, more than 200 MX missiles might be needed, depending on how they were based and how many could be expected to survive a surprise attack. That much said, the probability is low that a basing mode for the MX can be found that will simultaneously meet the conditions of political acceptability, high survivability after a first strike, and rapid reaction with great reliability and accuracy. True, it may be desirable to preserve a triad of offensive forces. But at some point even a triad can become too expensive to warrant its continuation. Whether that point has already been reached deserves analysis in light of the available alternatives.

To the extent that hard targets are worth covering on a second strike (an issue not sufficiently probed), the Trident II submarine-launched ballistic missile will be able to provide the coverage almost as effectively as the MX and with an even shorter flight time. Trident missiles can, after all, be stationed closer to their targets than the MX. And since Trident II is already under development, it could be deployed only a few years after the MX and immediately backfitted into existing Trident submarines. This would permit holding the MX in engineering development, canceling what amounts to a nominal deployment of forty missiles in existing silos (where they will remain vulnerable even if the silos are hardened still more), and waiting to see whether an acceptable basing mode or a more adaptable ICBM can be found. Slowing the development of a system for ballistic missile defense would be compatible with this approach.

Civil defense expansion will add little to deterrence since the main thrust of U.S. strategy is to ensure the destruction of targets in the USSR rather than to prevent the destruction of targets in the United States. In the event of a nuclear exchange, a program for protecting people that depends heavily on trying to evacuate them from cities is of doubtful feasibility and will not reduce damage by much unless the Soviet marshals decide to be highly selective and limited in their own targeting. Thus, with the probability of any strategic nuclear attack remaining low for the foreseeable future, civil defense of this type can hardly be a matter of high priority, however laudable its objectives. Postponement of a major program is not difficult to justify.

Much the same argument can be made about the modernization of U.S. continental air defenses. The present modest capability basically serves as a peacetime warning and surveillance system. Its limited function and effectiveness are not accidental. They are based on three assumptions that date back to the Nixon administration: deterrence will not be affected by the presence or absence of a major antibomber defense; most of the damage from a Soviet attack would be caused by ballistic missiles, not bombers; and there would be little if any follow-on attack from Soviet bombers in any event. Despite the recent rollout of a new Soviet long-range bomber, all three assumptions will probably remain valid for some years to come. Accordingly, modernization of U.S. continental air defenses can also be considered relatively low on the list of defense priorities and subject to postponement or cancellation.

Even with changes in these five programs, the United States will retain an impressive second-strike deterrent throughout the 1980s. Although the existing ICBM force will be at least nominally vulnerable, the on-station SLBMs and the alert bombers alone should be able, from their day-to-day posture with existing payloads, to deliver about 3,000 warheads in a second strike. As Trident submarines and air-launched cruise missiles are added to the inventory, the number of delivered warheads should increase to more than 4,000. In the more likely event of a generated alert—the posture that would be adopted in a major international crisis—the number of deliverable warheads would rise to more than 4,500 with the existing force and to 6,400 with the force planned for the late 1980s.

Although a number of strategic nuclear budgets are of course

Table 3-6. Reagan, Intermediate, and Baseline Strategic Nuclear Budgets, Fiscal Years 1983–87[a]

Billions of dollars

| Item | 1983 | 1984 | 1985 | 1986 | 1987 | 1983–87 |
|---|---|---|---|---|---|---|
| *Total obligational authority* | | | | | | |
| Reagan budget | 37.2 | 45.3 | 50.5 | 55.4 | 55.6 | 244.0 |
| Intermediate budget | 29.9 | 33.6 | 37.5 | 41.8 | 46.5 | 189.3 |
| Saving from Reagan budget | 7.3 | 11.7 | 13.0 | 13.6 | 9.1 | 54.7 |
| Baseline budget | 26.0 | 28.9 | 31.0 | 36.2 | 41.9 | 164.0 |
| Saving from Reagan budget | 11.2 | 16.4 | 19.5 | 19.2 | 13.7 | 80.0 |
| *Outlays* | | | | | | |
| Reagan budget | 31.2 | 39.0 | 43.4 | 48.8 | 49.5 | 211.9 |
| Intermediate budget | 27.7 | 30.1 | 34.2 | 39.0 | 39.7 | 170.7 |
| Saving from Reagan budget | 3.5 | 8.9 | 9.2 | 9.8 | 9.8 | 41.2 |
| Baseline budget | 26.4 | 25.9 | 29.8 | 34.5 | 35.1 | 151.7 |
| Saving from Reagan budget | 4.8 | 13.1 | 13.6 | 14.3 | 14.4 | 60.2 |

Sources: *Department of Defense Annual Report to the Congress, Fiscal Year 1983*, p. B-7; and author's estimates in table 3-5.

a. Budgets reflect appropriations from programs for the strategic forces; they include resources for military personnel, operation and maintenance, procurement, research, development, test, and evaluation, and family housing.

conceivable, only three are considered here. The mixture of high- and low-priority programs recommended by the Reagan administration is one option. A second choice is to go forward with the nominally vulnerable ICBM force; continue the modernization of the bomber force with air-launched cruise missiles, upgraded B-52Hs, and eventually Stealth; continue the Trident program, including the programmed acceleration of the Trident II missile; and hold both MX and ballistic missile defense systems in research and development. Finally, an extrapolation of the baseline strategic budget is made. Its program of modernization is still more modest and includes only the Trident I, air-launched cruise missiles, and Stealth.

The Reagan budget for the strategic nuclear forces is shown in table 3-6, as are the possible reductions in it that would lead to the intermediate and baseline strategic budgets. Estimates of the second-strike delivery capabilities associated with the Reagan and intermediate budgets are shown in table 3-7, given varying assumptions about the ability of the B-52Hs to penetrate Soviet defenses.

### Regional Nuclear Capabilities

The Soviet deployment of medium-range Backfire bombers and SS-20 missiles, with most but not all of them targeted against

**Table 3-7. Second-Strike Delivery Capabilities of Reagan and Intermediate Strategic Nuclear Forces, Fiscal Year 1988**

| Weapon system | Total reentry vehicles | | Day-to-day alert reentry vehicles | | Case 1:[a] delivered reentry vehicles | | Case 2:[a] delivered reentry vehicles | |
|---|---|---|---|---|---|---|---|---|
| | Reagan | Intermediate | Reagan | Intermediate | Reagan | Intermediate | Reagan | Intermediate |
| Minuteman II | 350 | 450 | 315 | 405 | 13 | 16 | 13 | 16 |
| Minuteman III | 1,650 | 1,650 | 1,485 | 1,485 | 59 | 59 | 59 | 59 |
| MX | 1,000 | ... | 900 | ... | 36 | ... | 36 | ... |
| Poseidon | 4,960 | 4,960 | 2,728 | 2,728 | 2,128 | 2,128 | 2,128 | 2,128 |
| Trident | 1,920 | 1,920 | 1,152 | 1,152 | 922 | 922 | 922 | 922 |
| B-52G | 3,000 | 3,000 | 900 | 900 | 720 | 720 | 720 | 720 |
| B-52H | ... | 800 | ... | 240 | ... | 192 | ... | ... |
| FB-111 | 480 | 480 | 144 | 144 | 115 | 115 | ... | ... |
| B-1B | 1,200 | ... | 400 | ... | 320 | ... | 320 | ... |
| Total reentry vehicles | 14,560 | 13,260 | 8,024 | 7,054 | 4,313 | 4,152 | 4,198 | 3,845 |
| Intermediate force as percent of Reagan force | ... | 91.6 | ... | 87.9 | ... | 96.3 | ... | 91.6 |

Source: Author's estimates.

a. In both cases, all systems are on day-to-day peacetime alert. In case 1, all systems have an 0.8 probability of penetrating to targets; in case 2, the B-52H and FB-111 bombers are unable to penetrate.

Western Europe, the renewed belief in overwhelming Warsaw Pact conventional superiority all around Eurasia, and the publicity surrounding enhanced radiation weapons (widely known as neutron bombs) have caused the so-called tactical nuclear forces to become the objects of revived attention and proposals for increased funding. There is, in fact, no such thing as a tactical nuclear weapon, nor are there any tactical nuclear forces. There are only tactical targets, some of which can be attacked just as readily by ICBMs and SLBMs as by shorter-range systems. Indeed, some "strategic" systems carry lower-yield weapons than their "tactical" counterparts. What goes under the name of tactical or theater nuclear forces is a miscellaneous collection of nuclear devices adapted to various delivery vehicles, most of which have nonnuclear warfare as their primary function. To the extent that these vehicles are integrated into any forces, they are the traditional units of the Army, Navy, and Air Force.

Much of what passes for tactical nuclear forces is an artifact of the early nuclear era and its enthusiasm. In those more optimistic days it was assumed that nuclear weapons applied to tactical targets would remain an American monopoly for some years to come, that they could simply be grafted onto the traditional forces as an enhanced form of firepower, and that their use would strongly favor the defense in a campaign against the massed ground forces of the Warsaw Pact.

Whatever the original merit of these assumptions, all are now out of date. The Soviet Union long ago broke the monopoly. It currently deploys a large number of medium- and short-range delivery vehicles specialized for nuclear (and probably chemical) weapons and has presumably stockpiled the bombs and warheads to go with them. The members of both NATO and the Warsaw Pact talk about tactical nuclear campaigns and calculate their "special munitions" requirements as though these campaigns could go on for a matter of days or even weeks. But neither side has figured out how to conduct such a campaign in any organized and systematic way.

This is hardly surprising. Nuclear weapons, even when reduced in firepower to fractions of a kiloton or designed to be small thermonuclear devices, are simply too powerful to permit the traditional series of engagements known as battles and campaigns.

Their use on a battlefield, even on a limited scale, is likely to eventuate not only in terror and total demoralization among all the participants, but also in a rapid escalation of the local conflict. Despite hypotheses about the controlled use of these weapons and ladders of escalation that both sides climb until one clearly stands higher than the other, neither side is in a position to be sure what nuclear yields have vaporized which targets or where those yields have come from. What commanders on both sides will know, however, is that, once nuclear weapons have been used, any and all systems—low-yield, high-yield, nuclear, thermonuclear, short-range, long-range—can be brought rapidly into action. The pressure to use them or lose them, still a problem at the strategic level despite sustained efforts to produce survivable second-strike forces, would be enormous at the regional level, where most of the delivery systems are vulnerable. Faced with this potential instability, neither the Soviet Union nor the United States can have much stomach for lighting the nuclear fires. Both know that to do so is to start a conflagration of unknown but possibly catastrophic proportions.

Despite assertions to the contrary, the Soviet deployment of SS-20 missiles and Backfire bombers has not altered this situation in any meaningful way. It follows that, from a military standpoint, the proposed introduction into Western Europe of intermediate-range Pershing II ballistic missiles and ground-launched cruise missiles will not make matters better or, for that matter, worse. The more likely prospect is that yet another layer will simply be added to what is fast becoming the main archaeological dig of the nuclear age.

It is tempting to believe that this miscellaneous collection of systems, which began their career as the salvation of an alliance supposedly incapable of coping with Warsaw Pact forces by conventional means, can end that career by simply disappearing. Unfortunately, however, history cannot be undone, and both sides now have these systems. Consequently, each must continue to deploy them as the initial deterrent to their use by the other.

Whatever Soviet military leaders may think and say, NATO should be clear about what these systems can and cannot do in their capacity as a deterrent. That they can be used to conduct a nuclear campaign in which armies advance and retreat while tactical air forces and missiles perform their traditional missions is almost certainly a threadbare pretense. That they can prevent the Soviet leaders from destroying Western Europe, if for some unimaginable reason they should choose to do so, is equally a pretense. That it would be to the advantage of the United States and its allies to initiate the use of these weapons has been a myth for more than twenty years. At best, regionally based nuclear weapons can be expected to survive an attack in sufficient numbers to retaliate against a variety of fixed targets such as bases, supply depots, and lines of communication. In doing so, they can probably prevent the Soviet Union from achieving any worthwhile objective in Europe as the result of a first use of nuclear weapons.

Currently deployed weapons, tactical aircraft, Pershing and Lance missiles, and dual-purpose artillery are already sufficient for this modest but destructive task. However, as with most military capabilities, they could usefully absorb more than the roughly $2 billion it takes to operate and support them. They are more vulnerable to conventional or nuclear attack than is desirable; their command and control could use greater survivability; many of the warheads are of archaic design and could be replaced with more efficient devices. Traditionally, the U.S. strategic nuclear forces have targeted the Soviet peripheral attack capabilities: the medium-range bombers, the medium- and intermediate-range ballistic missiles, and the variable-range SS-11 ballistic missiles, most of which have been replaced. But there is no particular reason why these targets could not be covered by equally survivable delivery systems of shorter range, if that should prove politically desirable.

Most of the problems with theater nuclear capabilities have existed for many years without causing undue uneasiness in Europe or the United States. However, when European allies' periodic concern about the credibility of the American strategic nuclear deterrent recurred, the Carter administration proposed and NATO accepted the deployment of 108 Pershing II ballistic missiles and 464 ground-launched cruise missiles under U.S. control, and the United States pledged to engage the Soviet Union in negotiations for a mutual reduction of intermediate-range nuclear systems.

The Reagan administration has embraced the U.S. commitment

**Table 3-8. Potential Cancellations in Major Theater Nuclear Programs, Fiscal Years 1983–87**
Billions of dollars

| Program | Action | Reduction in total obligational authority, 1983–87 | Reduction in outlays 1983[a] | 1985 | 1983–87 |
|---|---|---|---|---|---|
| Intermediate budget | | | | | |
| Nuclear Tomahawk | Cancel | 1.8 | 0.2 | 0.3 | 1.4 |
| 155-millimeter artillery-fired atomic projectile | Cancel | 0.1 | . . . | . . . | 0.1 |
| 8-inch artillery-fired atomic projectile | Cancel | 0.1 | . . . | . . . | 0.1 |
| Total | | 2.0 | 0.2 | 0.3 | 1.6 |
| Baseline budget | | | | | |
| Pershing II missile | Cancel | 2.6 | 0.3 | 0.3 | 2.0 |
| Ground-launched cruise missile | Cancel | 2.0 | 0.2 | 0.3 | 1.5 |
| Cumulative total | | 6.6 | 0.7 | 0.9 | 5.1 |
| Not in defense budgets | | | | | |
| Nuclear weapons (Department of Energy) | Cancel all artillery and missile weapons | 2.4 | 0.3 | 0.3 | 1.8 |
| Total, all budgets | | 9.0 | 1.0 | 1.2 | 6.9 |

Source: *Department of Defense Annual Report to the Congress, Fiscal Year 1983*, pp. III-72–III-73; Congressional Budget Office, *Baseline Budget Projections for Fiscal Years 1983–1987*, p. 87; and author's estimates.
a. Includes outlays resulting from appropriations in fiscal years 1981–83.

to this arrangement. The president also proposes to proceed with the acquisition of at least 600 Tomahawk sea-launched nuclear cruise missiles for deployment on nuclear attack submarines (including eight converted Polaris submarines), the modernization of the U.S. inventory of 155-millimeter and 8-inch nuclear artillery shells, and the production and stockpiling in the United States of enhanced radiation weapons for the Lance missile.

The theater nuclear programs in the Reagan budget that could well be considered for cancellation are shown in table 3-8. Most of the cost of the nuclear weapons would be borne by the Department of Energy.

From a military standpoint, land bases in Western Europe are perhaps the least desirable platforms for a second-strike response to an attack from Soviet intermediate-range systems. Although sea-launched cruise missiles will create difficult counting and verification issues for future negotiators of strategic arms reductions, they—along with fleet ballistic missiles—represent a much more survivable capability. That indeed was recognized many years ago with the commitment of Polaris and then Poseidon warheads to the coverage of targets threatening Western Europe, and by the Reagan administration's continuation of the sea-launched cruise missile program. However, the commitments made by two administrations to the Pershing II and ground-launched cruise missile programs and the beginning of arms control negotiations in Geneva focusing on intermediate-range systems give this program a high political priority, however dubious its military utility may be.

Although the sea-launched nuclear cruise missile program provides a much more survivable basing mode, it is useful primarily, if at all, as a backup to capabilities already deployed in Western Europe and elsewhere and as a hedge against a decision by NATO to reject the deployment of Pershing IIs and ground-launched cruise missiles. As such, its urgency is not high.

The replacement of the existing inventory of 155-millimeter and 8-inch nuclear artillery shells with more efficient and tamper-proof devices is undoubtedly desirable, but it cannot be considered of high priority for deterrence. Enhanced radiation weapons are even less urgent. If used unilaterally, they can be as effective as nuclear weapons of higher yield against some targets yet cause less collateral damage. If their use is followed by enemy retaliation with standard weapons, as seems plausible, obviously these advantages will be erased. Thus, contrary to some fears, enhanced radiation weapons are unlikely to be more tempting to desperate policymakers than any other nuclear weapons. They are also unlikely to add significantly to the credibility of regional nuclear deterrence.

If these brief analyses are correct, only three real choices are available for theater nuclear capabilities. In the first, all programs proposed in the Reagan budget would be funded regardless of their urgency. In the second, or intermediate, budget, acquisition of sea-launched nuclear cruise missiles would be deferred, and funding for all short-range nuclear programs would be canceled. The baseline budget for the theater nuclear capabilities would also cancel the Pershing II and ground-launched cruise missiles. The

**Table 3-9. Reagan, Intermediate, and Baseline Theater Nuclear Budgets, Fiscal Years 1983–87[a]**

Billions of dollars

| Item | 1983 | 1984 | 1985 | 1986 | 1987 | 1983–87 |
|---|---|---|---|---|---|---|
| *Total obligational authority* | | | | | | |
| Reagan budget | 3.3 | 3.6 | 3.9 | 4.2 | 4.2 | 19.2 |
| Intermediate budget | 3.2 | 3.4 | 3.4 | 3.7 | 3.5 | 17.2 |
| Saving from Reagan budget | 0.1 | 0.2 | 0.5 | 0.5 | 0.7 | 2.0 |
| Baseline budget | 2.0 | 2.4 | 2.6 | 2.9 | 2.7 | 12.6 |
| Saving from Reagan budget | 1.3 | 1.2 | 1.3 | 1.3 | 1.5 | 6.6 |
| *Outlays* | | | | | | |
| Reagan budget | 2.8 | 3.1 | 3.4 | 3.7 | 3.7 | 16.7 |
| Intermediate budget | 2.5 | 2.8 | 3.1 | 3.4 | 3.3 | 15.1 |
| Saving from Reagan budget | 0.3 | 0.3 | 0.3 | 0.3 | 0.4 | 1.6 |
| Baseline budget | 1.9 | 2.1 | 2.4 | 2.6 | 2.6 | 11.6 |
| Saving from Reagan budget | 0.9 | 1.0 | 1.0 | 1.1 | 1.1 | 5.1 |

Source: Author's estimates in table 3-8.

a. Budgets reflect appropriations from programs for the general purpose forces; they include resources for military personnel, operation and maintenance, procurement, research, development, test, and evaluation, and family housing.

estimated Reagan budget for theater nuclear systems and the possible reductions in it that would lead to the intermediate and baseline budgets are shown in table 3-9.

*The Nonnuclear Forces*

The detonation of the first Soviet atomic device in 1949 triggered successive attempts to develop U.S. and allied nonnuclear capabilities large enough to deter in their own right the conventional forces of prospective opponents, led by the USSR. Each of these attempts has been followed by a renewed emphasis on nuclear weapons and strategy. The Carter administration, in its attempt, stressed the defense of Western Europe as the centerpiece of nonnuclear planning. But it also began to invest in the forces already programmed for a minor contingency (and renamed them the rapid deployment force) once the revolution in Iran and the Soviet invasion of Afghanistan had made the area of the Persian Gulf appear vulnerable to attack and occupation. Just as the Reagan administration is accelerating these two large programs, the futility of making the attempt is being asserted once more and pleas can be heard for a return by the United States to primary reliance on strategic and theater-based nuclear capabilities.

THE PROBLEM. On its surface, the problem of containing Soviet and satellite conventional power looks daunting indeed. The USSR alone is reported to deploy approximately 180 divisions and 4,800 fighter-attack aircraft, supposedly having added 600,000 men, nearly 40 divisions, and 1,300 tactical aircraft to its conventional forces in the last seventeen years. During this same period, its airlift capability has expanded, and its naval forces, though not larger, have undergone considerable modernization.

This vast array of power, and especially the masses of tanks (allegedly up to 50,000 of them) said to be available to canny, innovative, and flexible though aging Soviet marshals, is staggering enough. When coupled with the forces of the other members of the Warsaw Pact and such nations as North Korea, Vietnam, and Cuba, it is enough to send shivers of inferiority along the spines of U.S. and allied officials, military and civilian alike.

To paraphrase an old slogan, numbers in the raw are seldom mild. But without doubting the fact of a Soviet military buildup, we need to place these numbers in perspective. The total number of Soviet divisions is impressive, but it is worth remembering that 180 of them were created out of a Red Army said to number little more than 1.8 million men. On the average, each division would amount to 10,000 men, including support troops, or about a third the size of most U.S. division forces. Actually, of course, there are no such average Soviet divisions. Approximately 46 of them, or just over 25 percent, are kept at or near full combat strength (but without their full complement of support troops); the remainder are in lower states of readiness and would require a considerable mobilization effort to reach their authorized size and composition. Furthermore, the divisions and tactical aircraft added to the Soviet order of battle since 1965 have for the most part been deployed against the People's Republic of China. What is generally counted as the immediate Soviet threat to Western Europe—the 26 or 27 divisions in East Germany, Czechoslovakia, and Poland—has changed numerically since 1965 in the following respects: (1) the original total of 22 divisions has been increased by roughly 70,000 men and 5 divisions as a result of the Soviet occupation of Czechoslovakia in 1968; and (2) more than 100,000 combat and support troops have been added to the Group of Soviet Forces in East Germany as additional tanks, artillery, and infantry fighting vehicles have been incorporated in the 20 (or possibly 19) divisions located there. In addition, both ground and tactical air forces deployed in Eastern Europe have received a new generation of equipment. These various changes have probably increased the combat power of the units with the newer equipment by as much as 65 percent.

Such selective improvements, which NATO has not fully matched, should not obscure the severe limits on the ability of the Warsaw Pact to project its power. The less ready Soviet and satellite divisions can be filled out rapidly with reservists. But some weeks would probably be required to bring them to full combat effectiveness and provide them with the necessary command and control structure. Even then, questions would remain about the reliability of Polish and other satellite units. How long the ground and tactical air forces could operate in combat and how many major theaters of operation the Soviet logistic system could support simultaneously are uncertain. The Russian transportation system is, after all, fragile and prone to breakdowns even in peacetime.

The fact remains that the Soviet Union is still primarily a land power with a limited military reach. Its long-range airlift capability has grown, but from a negligible base. Of its four fleets, two are virtually landlocked and can be confined to the Baltic and eastern Mediterranean seas. The other two, based at Murmansk and Vladivostok, can probably dominate much of the Barents Sea and the Sea of Japan. Once they move beyond the cover of land-based tactical air power, however, they become highly vulnerable to allied air and sea power. Soviet attack submarines and long-range aircraft, including the Backfires assigned to naval aviation, nonetheless can threaten sea lines of communication in the Atlantic, Pacific, Indian Ocean, and Mediterranean, although geography permits the United States and its allies to establish a number of sea and air barriers to this kind of attack.

THE U.S. RESPONSE. These limitations on Soviet conventional power, together with the long shadow cast by nuclear weapons, have greatly influenced the size and character of the U.S. military response. Since containment in the literal sense seems out of the question, but also since the Soviet Union seems incapable of attacking everywhere at once, the thrust of U.S. strategy has been to emphasize the direct and simultaneous defense of several key regions (with Europe, Korea, and now the Persian Gulf as the main regions used for planning forces). And as conventional conflicts on the scale of World War II seem unlikely, precisely because of the ever-present threat of nuclear weapons, force planning has focused on relatively local and localized ground and air operations directed initially at achieving such limited objectives as the defense or restoration of prewar boundaries in the areas attacked. Furthermore, since it would probably take the Soviet and satellite armed forces several months or more to prepare for an attack, planners have judged it feasible to minimize U.S. overseas deployments and locate major reinforcements in the continental United States. From that central location they could then be rushed to one or more threatened theaters, in some cases to pre-positioned equipment, by a combination of airlift and sealift. The primary role of naval forces in this strategy is seen as the defense of the sea lines of communication over which reinforcements, matériel, and supplies would pass.

Several aspects of this general strategy should be stressed. First, while the number of regions against which the Soviet Union and its satellites might launch large-scale attacks has been estimated to be small, rapid mobility and great versatility built into U.S. forces have been seen as the primary means by which ground and tactical air units, supplemented to some degree by carrier-supported amphibious forces, could be shifted around to meet the threat. Thus the forces themselves might be "sized" to deal with one major and one minor contingency (the 1½-war concept, which replaced the earlier 2½-war concept). But training and equipment for multipurpose operations, pre-positioning of matériel and supplies in the most sensitive regions, and long-range airlift would supposedly permit a timely response to these contingencies wherever they might arise.

It has also been assumed that in most of the regions that could be threatened, U.S. forces would supplement those of staunch allies. Not only would these allies make the task of conventional containment feasible, but they would also permit the U.S. contribution to be held to a manageable size. In Central Europe, for example, a total of 45 divisions and around 4,000 fighter-attack aircraft has usually been considered sufficient for an initial forward defense against the expected threat from the Warsaw Pact forces, estimated at up to 90 divisions.

Of the 45 divisions and roughly 56 fighter wings within the resources of NATO, the U.S. contribution—measured in combat power—would amount to less than 50 percent, or 15 large divisions and 23 wings of fighter-attack aircraft. Similarly, the Republic of Korea would provide most of the forces for its own defense, and allied navies would contribute substantially to the protection of the sea lines of communication.

What might be considered the U.S. baseline conventional force emerging from this strategic concept and the more detailed calculations made about specific contingencies and their needs is shown in table 3-10, along with the estimated costs of the force during the next five years. Basically, its size and composition was determined in the mid-1970s. To the extent that the Soviet threat is seen as having increased in power, readiness, and strategic mobility, these increases have been met by efforts to raise the effectiveness of individual units and improve their ability to deploy rapidly overseas rather than by an expansion of the force structure. This, in turn, has accounted for a part of the real increase in the

Table 3-10. Baseline Conventional Forces and Budgets, Fiscal Years 1983–87[a]

Billions of dollars

| Item | 1983 | 1984 | 1985 | 1986 | 1987 | 1983–87 |
|------|------|------|------|------|------|---------|
| 19 active-duty Army and Marine Corps divisions | 44.6 | 50.3 | 56.3 | 62.6 | 70.2 | 284.0 |
| 13 reserve Army and Marine Corps division-equivalents | 8.2 | 9.2 | 10.3 | 11.5 | 13.0 | 52.2 |
| 41 active-duty Air Force, Marine Corps, and Navy tactical air wings[b] | 27.8 | 31.4 | 35.2 | 39.2 | 43.8 | 177.4 |
| 15 reserve Air Force, Marine Corps, and Navy tactical air wings | 5.7 | 6.4 | 7.2 | 8.0 | 9.0 | 36.3 |
| 535 active-duty and reserve surface ships and submarines | 39.9 | 45.1 | 50.4 | 56.2 | 63.0 | 254.6 |
| 500 active-duty and reserve strategic and tactical airlift aircraft | 6.8 | 7.7 | 8.6 | 9.5 | 10.7 | 43.3 |
| 45 days of modern munitions | 8.8 | 9.9 | 11.1 | 12.4 | 13.9 | 56.1 |
| Total | 141.8 | 160.0 | 179.1 | 199.4 | 223.6 | 903.9 |

Source: Author's estimates.

a. Budgets reflect appropriations from programs for the general purpose, airlift and sealift, and National Guard and Reserve forces; they include resources for military personnel, operation and maintenance, procurement, research, development, test, and evaluation, and family housing.

b. Navy patrol aircraft are included in this category.

cost of new weapons and munitions. It also explains why so much effort has gone into the creation of a rapid deployment force out of existing rather than additional assets, the pre-positioning of growing amounts of matériel in Western Europe, and the expansion of airlift capabilities, sealift (to a modest degree), and equipment stocked on ships in the Indian Ocean.

THE REAGAN PROGRAM. The Reagan administration is not fully comfortable with either the traditional strategic concept or the baseline force. It continues in most respects to plan and program on the basis of the concept, but it also seeks to depart from it in several ways. The hypothesis that conventional wars will be relatively limited in scope and duration has been rejected, with major implications for the supply of war reserve stocks and replacement personnel. Equally important, reliance solely on direct defense in threatened areas has been dismissed, at least rhetorically, in favor of determining enemy vulnerabilities and being prepared to attack them at an early stage in a local conflict. This change of policy, if implemented, could bring about a major expansion of the baseline force structure. In effect, the implied threat of vertical escalation would be replaced or complemented by the explicit threat of horizontal escalation. As one example, Cuba, Libya, other supposed Soviet assets, and even Soviet naval bases would presumably become fair game if the USSR attacked Iran and Saudi Arabia.

So far, these views have had a major impact on only one part of the force structure: the size and composition of the U.S. Navy. How large a particular navy is said to be depends on what categories of ships are counted, as can be seen from table 3-11. For some years now, the U.S. Navy—using the larger definition as the baseline from which to measure any change—has advocated the acquisition of a 600-ship fleet. Since any such plan must take account of aging ships and their replacement or conversion as well as of the construction of new ships, the Navy formerly advocated reaching its goal of 600 ships over a twenty-year period. In fact, when Sea Plan 2000 was first made public, in 1978, the Navy estimated that the shipbuilding and conversion costs required to complete the plan would run to about $9.5 billion a year in 1978 dollars. The Reagan administration has now seized on this goal and moved forward its ostensible date of completion from

Table 3-11. General Purpose Naval Ships, by Category and Type,
at End of Fiscal Year 1982[a]

| Type of ship | Active fleet | Naval reserve | Total | Fleet auxiliary force | Total |
|---|---|---|---|---|---|
| Aircraft carriers | 13 | . . . | 13 | . . . | 13 |
| Surface combatants | | | | | |
| Cruisers | 27 | . . . | 27 | . . . | 27 |
| Destroyers | 84 | 5 | 89 | . . . | 89 |
| Frigates | 84 | 4 | 88 | . . . | 88 |
| Submarines | | | | | |
| Nuclear attack[b] | 91 | . . . | 91 | . . . | 91 |
| Diesel | 3 | . . . | 3 | . . . | 3 |
| Patrol combatants | 6 | . . . | 6 | . . . | 6 |
| Amphibious warfare ships | 60 | 6 | 66 | . . . | 66 |
| Mine warfare ships | 3 | 22 | 25 | . . . | 25 |
| Mobile logistic ships | 56 | 2 | 58 | 14 | 72 |
| Fleet support ships | 15 | 6 | 21 | 19 | 40 |
| Other ships[c] | 6 | . . . | 6 | . . . | 6 |
| Total | 448 | 45 | 493 | 33 | 526 |

Source: *Department of Defense Annual Report, Fiscal Year 1982*, p. 154.
a. Does not include ships in the strategic and mobility forces.
b. Includes former Polaris nuclear ballistic missile submarines converted to nuclear attack submarines.
c. Miscellaneous auxiliaries and combatants.

the year 2000 to the early 1990s. As a consequence, its five-year shipbuilding program contains a total of 133 new ships and 16 conversions of older ships. The main emphasis in the 600-ship plan is placed on the acquisition of 15 attack carrier battle groups; 4 so-called surface action groups based on World War II battleships; the ocean-going amphibious lift ships for 1½ Marine Corps divisions; 100 first-line nuclear attack submarines; and the surface combatants necessary to escort seven military convoys a month. Since it will be impossible to complete the 3 new large-deck nuclear-powered attack carriers necessary for the 15 battle groups before the end of the decade, the 4 battleships to be brought out of mothballs and modernized will also serve as interim substitutes for the missing carriers. Presumably at least 90,000 people will have to be added to the Navy to man and support these ships. The five-year cost of the program is estimated to be $96 billion in current dollars.

This long-term expansion in the Navy has been justified for many reasons in the past, including the value of a peacetime presence: the alleged diplomatic payoff from having ships, particularly large ships, cruising in various oceans and seas and available for visits to the waters of friendly or hostile powers. Since for every major ship on station the Navy in peacetime requires that at least two others be in training or overhaul, maintaining a relatively modest presence overseas can generate a large fleet, of which perhaps 80 percent could be on station in wartime. However, the current rationalization for the 600-ship fleet is probably based more on the need to provide a first line of defense in the vicinity of the Persian Gulf and on the traditional naval objective of obtaining command of the seas by destroying the enemy fleet. Such an offensive is seen as requiring attacks on Soviet naval ports with carrier battle groups.

Whether the ground forces will undergo any expansion in structure still remains to be determined. For the next five years, the administration is proposing to continue the rapid modernization of the nineteen active-duty Army and Marine Corps divisions, increase their stocks of war reserve matériel beyond the needs of short wars, and acquire additional wide-bodied airlift to improve their intercontinental mobility. The Marine Corps will modernize its three large air wings with F/A-18 fighter and attack aircraft and with the very expensive AV-8B vertical-takeoff-and-landing aircraft. The Air Force will initially fill out its twenty-six active-duty wings of fighter-attack aircraft with F-15s and F-16s. It is also tentatively planned to add two more fighter wings to the active-duty Air Force and another two to the twelve wings in the reserves. This will give the Air Force a total fighter force of forty-four wings. Because of the emphasis on attacks preceded by very short warning—an emphasis begun during the last year of the Ford administration—sets of pre-positioned equipment for two more divisions will be stored in Germany to add to the four already there. The proposed acquisition of fifty C-5N airlift aircraft and forty-four KC-10 tanker aircraft will permit the United States to move an additional 72,000 tons to Europe or 36,000 tons to the Persian Gulf in thirty days. Current airlift capability and the effects of this increase in tonnage are shown in table 3-12.

In all, the administration is proposing to invest approximately $1.1 trillion in the conventional forces over the next five years. Of this total, about $900 billion will go for maintenance and modernization of the baseline force. Another $180 billion will be allocated

**Table 3-12. Current Airlift Objective, Capability, and Programmed Increase**
Short tons unless otherwise specified

| 30-day cargo capacity | Europe | Persian Gulf |
|---|---|---|
| Objective (outsize and oversize tonnage only) | 570,000 | 235,000 |
| Capability of current airlift (70 C-5A and 234 C-141 aircraft) | 203,490 | 101,950 |
| Capability of programmed airlift (70 C-5A, 50 C-5N, and 234 C-141 aircraft) | 275,540 | 138,000 |
| Percent increase | 35 | 35 |
| Difference between objective and programmed airlift | 294,460 | 97,000 |

Source: Author's estimates.

to expansions in the baseline force structure, principally for a larger Navy (including more amphibious lift for the Marine Corps), more tactical air wings, additional airlift, and greatly increased war reserve stocks. Table 3-13 summarizes these allocations.

ALTERNATIVE PROGRAMS. This strong emphasis on improving U.S. conventional forces should be welcome in an era of manifest nuclear stalemate and growing Soviet nonnuclear power. The particular nature and magnitude of the emphasis are bound nonetheless to raise three questions. Is the proposed increase in baseline capability worth its cost? Are there other and less costly ways of acquiring needed additions to capability? And considering the negative externalities of rapid increases in defense spending, can the growth be controlled without damaging the conventional posture?

It may help, before answering these questions, to consider the military problems facing the United States and its allies. Perhaps the most worrisome contingency is the loss of the oil supplies from the region of the Persian Gulf. That such a loss would have the highest probability of occurring as a consequence of strife within the region itself is generally conceded. That large-scale American military power would have only a limited role to play in deterring or controlling such an event is also widely acknowledged. But since the stakes in the region are so high for the United States and even higher for its allies, strong arguments can be made for having the capability to come to the defense of friendly states there. And since the USSR can project its military power into the region, there are good reasons for considering it the primary threat for force planning purposes. How much U.S. counterforce this threat requires depends critically on several factors. If Soviet ground forces attempted to make a sudden dash to the head of the Persian Gulf over some of the most difficult terrain in the world, the United States would probably need no more than four divisions and six tactical air wings to halt the dash well short of its goal. However, if the Soviet forces were "invited" into northern Iran and could establish themselves there without outside intervention, as many as nine divisions and fourteen fighter-attack wings might be required to halt what could subsequently prove to be a much heavier attack. But whatever the range of possibilities, a Marine Corps brigade afloat and two sea-based tactical air wings on station in the Indian Ocean would probably be necessary at a minimum to hedge against a surprise attack and, in the event of war, to establish a lodgment in the area and prepare for the reception of larger U.S. forces. Barring extreme and perhaps unrealistic cases of rapid Soviet preparation and movement, fast sealift with a capacity of 300,000 tons should be sufficient to provide whatever additional buildup the threat of such an attack might require. More very expensive airlift, as proposed by the Reagan administration, would certainly be nice to have, particularly as a further hedge against surprise attacks. But it is not at all clear that, under realistic conditions, airlift could deliver the total tonnages required any more rapidly than fast sealift. It takes time to organize a major airlift and, except for Europe and the Far

Table 3-13. **Augmentation of Baseline Conventional Forces in the Reagan Five-Year Defense Plan**

Billions of dollars

| Nature of the augmentation | Five-year cost |
|---|---|
| Baseline budget | 903.9 |
| Increased equipment sophistication and rate of modernization | 64.2 |
| 446 AH-64 attack helicopters (Army) | 6.4 |
| Modernized chemical warfare stockpile (Army and Air Force) | 8.0 |
| 36 ships for general purpose forces (Navy) | 39.9 |
| 4 wings of fighter-attack aircraft (Air Force) | 10.0 |
| 50 C-5N airlift aircraft (Air Force) | 5.7 |
| From 45 to 90 days of supply in modern munitions | 45.0 |
| Total | 1,083.1 |

Sources: *Department of Defense Annual Report to the Congress, Fiscal Year 1983*, pp. III-9, III-36, III-43; *Major Themes and Additional Budget Details, Fiscal Year 1983* (Executive Office of the President and Office of Management and Budget, 1982), pp. 185–89; and author's estimates.

East, there is considerable uncertainty about the availability of overseas bases to receive the aircraft. In the circumstances, if the time available for a response is too short for fast sealift to deliver the necessary cargo to the Persian Gulf, it is probably too short for airlift to make a significant difference. Where political decisions are likely to be delayed, there is no real substitute for forces on station in or near a threatened region to make a rapid response feasible.

If more than four divisions and the equivalent of six Air Force fighter wings are needed (assuming that all other active-duty forces might be committed simultaneously to Europe and Korea), it would make greater sense to draw them from a modernized and better-trained National Guard and Reserve, for which $14.3 billion is already being paid, than to add further expensive active-duty divisions and air wings to the force structure.

Ironically, because of the agitation of the past eight years over the alleged Soviet capability for nonnuclear surprise attacks, the United States may now be better prepared to deal with these rather improbable events than it is to counter slow Soviet conventional buildups that could accompany large international crises and result in greater Soviet combat power. For the former type of contingency, the baseline ground and tactical air forces are probably sufficient, and substitutes for additional rapid deployment capabilities, such as fortifications and more allied forces, almost certainly can be found. For the latter type of contingency, baseline ground and tactical air forces may be too small (depending on the magnitude of allied efforts and the reliability of non-Soviet Warsaw Pact forces) and large amounts of pre-positioning and airlift unnecessary.

Nowhere is this paradox more evident than in Central Europe. If the Warsaw Pact countries launched a large surprise attack there, more than 40 percent of its units would be ill prepared for combat. However, if the buildup stretched out over a period of ninety days or more, the expected threat of up to 90 divisions could be as much as 50 percent more powerful, and perhaps as many as 20 more full-strength divisions could be allocated to the attack from the Russian general reserve. Such an attack would have a high probability of bringing about a collapse of the programmed allied defenses. To compete with this greater-than-expected buildup, the equivalent of 11⅓ more U.S. divisions and 17 tactical air wings might well be necessary. Some of this increased capability could come from active and reserve units that already exist in Great Britain, France, and Germany. The United States could also contribute another 8 divisions and 8 tactical air wings from its National Guard and Reserve, even if there were heavy and simultaneous demands for units from the Persian Gulf commander.

In the worst worldwide case, more or less simultaneous threats of war might develop in Norway, Central and Southern Europe, the area of the Persian Gulf, and Korea. Table 3-14 shows what might be the demand for major U.S. ground and tactical air forces on the following assumptions: the higher-than-expected threat materializes; no U.S. forces are needed for Southern Europe; and U.S. ground and tactical air forces are still required in Korea. In such a crisis there would be a shortfall in U.S. forces even after the inclusion of all available units from the National Guard and the Reserve.

The North Korean army, with 700,000 men, is now considered to be about 67 percent larger than was estimated a decade ago. Nonetheless, there is good reason to believe that South Korea alone, protected as it is by substantial fortifications along the demilitarized zone separating North from South Korea, could

Table 3-14. Worst-Case Requirement for U.S. Conventional Forces

| Theater | Divisions | Land-based tactical air wings | Air-craft carriers | Amphib-ious ships | Convoy escorts | Attack sub-marines |
|---|---|---|---|---|---|---|
| Atlantic Ocean | . . . | 1 | 2 | . . . | 50 | 40 |
| Norway | 1 | . . . | 2 | . . . | . . . | . . . |
| Central Europe | 23 | 31 | . . . | . . . | . . . | . . . |
| Mediterranean Sea | . . . | . . . | 2 | . . . | . . . | . . . |
| Persian Gulf | 9 | 14 | 2 | 65 | 50 | . . . |
| Korea | 3 | 5 | . . . | . . . | . . . | . . . |
| Pacific Ocean | . . . | . . . | 2 | . . . | 30 | 40 |
| Total requirement | 36 | 51 | 10 | 65 | 130 | 80 |
| Available, 1983 | 33 | 46ª | 12 | 66 | 100 | 83 |

Source: Author's estimates.
a. The 4 Marine Corps wings (active and reserve) are counted as the equivalent of 8 Air Force wings; hence a total of 46 rather than 42 wings.

repulse an attack from the North without the loss of Seoul. On that assumption, and with the U.S. forces oriented to the Korean contingency reallocated to the Persian Gulf, the deficiency would disappear. Furthermore, if the three U.S. divisions now based in Hawaii and the Western Pacific were given the Persian Gulf as their primary mission, they could, except in worst-case conditions, provide the South Koreans with ample backup.

If these assumptions are valid, the current five-year defense plan is probably overinvesting in the long-term acquisition of airlift, active-duty fighter wings, and war reserve stocks while underinvesting in sealift and the National Guard and Reserve. Surely, if the Soviet Union can prepare its lowest-readiness divisions for combat in fourteen days (a most dubious assumption), it should be possible for the United States, with an additional investment, to make its reserves ready in ninety.

It should also be possible to control the growth in the cost of the U.S. tactical air forces. Heavy commitment to the missions of deep air superiority and interdiction by the Air Force with the F-15 and F-16 aircraft, and by the Navy with the F/A-18, may well be beyond efficient recall. However, Air Force National Guard squadrons can be reequipped with aircraft more suitable to close air support and combat air patrol: the A-10 and the F-5G. And it may not be too late to cancel the acquisition of the Army's new attack helicopter (the AH-64) and the jump jet of the Marine Corps (the AV-8B). If desired, existing helicopters and aircraft can readily substitute for these two expensive weapon platforms until the missions and ownership of the U.S. tactical air forces are given a clearer resolution than now exists.

Finally, past underfunding of war reserve stocks is no excuse for future overfunding. A buildup of these stocks, particularly of modern munitions, is warranted. But whether at this juncture a five-year investment of $90 billion in such stocks is advisable in light of Soviet supply and logistic limitations is more open to question.

Then there is the proposed expansion of the Navy. Large-deck carriers are almost certainly more efficient than small-deck carriers, and the cost of defending one large deck is less than that of protecting two much smaller decks. But if peacetime presence as the basis for force planning is ignored (as it should be, considering the size of the investment represented by a carrier battle group), three additional large decks and their tactical air wings will not raise the combat effectiveness of the fleet by much. Control of the essential lines of communication can be exercised with twelve battle groups, of which nine could be expected to be on station in wartime. Far more than fifteen such battle groups would be needed to conduct offensive operations with sea-based tactical aircraft against Soviet home ports; and even then, their chances of success, especially against the greatest threat to the sea lanes—the Soviet nuclear attack submarines—would be in doubt. Additional amphibious lift for the Marine Corps may be desirable but not urgent. Renovated battleships fall even lower on the list of fleet priorities. The proposed functions of the four surface action groups, of which the battleships would be the heart, remain obscure.

The Navy is already engaged in a program to extend the service life of its older large-deck carriers. It must also prepare to replace in the late 1980s and early 1990s several classes of destroyers that are reaching the end of their normal service lives, its older nuclear attack submarines, and a number of mundane but essential auxiliary ships. Furthermore, even with a contribution from allies, the Navy may be short of the frigates and destroyers necessary to provide the close-in protection of both fast sealift and the merchant convoys that must sail to and from Western Europe, the Persian Gulf, and the Far East. To remedy these weaknesses alone will require that, on the average, fifteen new ships be built each year and that the five-year cost of shipbuilding run to $40 billion in current dollars. This is a far cry from the minimum of $96 billion (also in current dollars) that the administration will probably have to obligate for shipbuilding during the same period.

In addition to these large issues there is a question of defense management that deserves consideration. Quite simply, the question is whether in light of the continuing competition with the Soviet Union this country wishes to organize its defense programs for what used to be called the long haul. This is not being done now. Periods of relative prosperity and reduced circumstances have admittedly characterized defense budgets in the past. Such ups and downs do not mean, however, that short of an emergency the country is best served by a forced feeding of the armed forces to make up for previous periods of underfeeding. Surely preferable

**Table 3-15. Potential Reductions or Cancellations in or Additions to Conventional and Other Programs, Fiscal Years 1983–87**

Billions of dollars

| Program | Action | Total obligational authority, 1983–87 | Outlays 1983[a] | Outlays 1985 | Outlays 1983–87 |
|---|---|---|---|---|---|
| **Intermediate budget** | | | | | |
| **Land forces** | | | | | |
| Chemical weapons | Cancel | −8.0 | −0.1 | −1.4 | −5.8 |
| AH-64 helicopters | Cancel | −6.4 | −0.3 | −1.1 | −4.6 |
| M-1 tanks | Reduce procurement by one-third | −4.5 | −0.4 | −0.7 | −3.3 |
| Other (including M-2, M-3 vehicles) | Reduce procurement | −6.4 | −0.9 | −0.9 | −4.6 |
| Reserve land forces | Add equipment for 13 reserve divisions | +12.7 | +1.6 | +2.0 | +9.6 |
| **Tactical air forces** | | | | | |
| AV-8B aircraft | Cancel | −6.4 | −0.6 | −1.0 | −4.6 |
| Other (including F-15, F-16 aircraft) | Reduce procurement | −3.9 | −0.3 | −0.6 | −2.8 |
| Reserve tactical air forces | Add equipment for 12 reserve tactical air wings | +12.7 | +1.6 | +2.0 | +9.6 |
| **Naval forces** | | | | | |
| Aircraft carriers | Cancel 2 carriers | −6.8 | −0.2 | −1.0 | −4.4 |
| Attack submarines | Cancel 7 submarines | −9.8 | ... | −1.5 | −6.3 |
| Air defense cruisers | Cancel 8 Aegis ships | −12.5 | ... | −2.0 | −8.0 |
| Other (including battleships, amphibious ships) | Cancel 19 ships | −10.8 | −0.2 | −1.7 | −6.9 |
| **Mobility forces** | | | | | |
| C-5N airlift aircraft | Cancel 50 aircraft | −5.7 | −0.2 | −1.0 | −4.2 |
| Fast sealift | Add 40 roll-on, roll-off ships | +4.0 | +0.1 | +0.7 | +3.0 |

| Defense-wide programs | | | | | |
|---|---|---|---|---|---|
| Military pay | Reduce pay raise to cost-of-living increase | -7.2 | -1.3 | -1.3 | -6.5 |
| War reserve munitions | Reduce objective to 45 days of stocks | -25.2 | -0.5 | -3.9 | -16.1 |
| Real property maintenance activities | Reduce increase to 1982 level | -22.3 | -3.2 | -2.8 | -14.4 |
| Research and development | Reduce to 1981 level of effort | -25.3 | -2.4 | -3.4 | -16.2 |
| Subtotal | | -131.8 | -7.3 | -19.6 | -86.5 |
| Baseline budget | | | | | |
| Reserve land forces | Cancel equipment for 13 reserve divisions | -12.7 | -1.6 | -2.0 | -9.6 |
| Tactical air forces | Cancel F/A-18 aircraft | -14.5 | -2.2 | -2.0 | -10.4 |
| Reserve tactical air forces | Cancel equipment for 12 reserve tactical air wings | -12.7 | -1.6 | -2.0 | -9.6 |
| Mobility forces | Cancel fast sealift | -4.0 | -0.1 | -0.7 | -3.0 |
| Research and development | Reduce defense commitment to space shuttle | -3.5 | -0.5 | -0.5 | -2.6 |
| Total | | -179.2 | -13.3 | -26.8 | -121.7 |

Sources: *Department of Defense Annual Report to the Congress, Fiscal Year 1983*, pp. III-8–III-55; Congressional Budget Office, *Baseline Budget Projections for Fiscal Years 1983–1987*, p. 87; and author's estimates.
a. Includes outlays resulting from appropriations in fiscal years 1981–83.

is a steady course, which avoids sudden spurts of activity followed by the block obsolescence of equipment and large backlogs of maintenance and overhaul, which ensures regular training and the gradual accumulation of war reserve stocks, which neither lives off the inheritance of the past nor tries desperately to make up for past failures (real or imagined), and which takes a leaf from the opponent's book and stops playing hare to the Russian tortoise. For it is after all the tortoiselike budgets, moving upward at a steady rate of 3 or 4 percent a year, that are so frequently proclaimed the mark of the winning side.

Now is a particularly appropriate time to set such a course. The competition exists, but it is quite manageable in scale. The United States has its deficiencies, but it is not exactly a 98-pound weakling. The country is plagued by fiscal and monetary problems, but it remains sympathetic to a strengthened defense posture. It is hardly a better season, as the French might put it, for attacking, always attacking, but without too much zeal.

There are a number of areas in which it might be asked whether current attacks are not showing too much zeal. The Army already has 1,000 modernized AH-1 attack helicopters; does it need 446 more AH-64 attack helicopters at $16 million a copy? Should it plunge ahead (because the money, like Mount Everest, is there) to acquire M-1 tanks and so-called fighting vehicles at a rapid pace when so many questions still exist about their effectiveness? How fast does it need to build up its inventory of trucks? Is there any urgency about acquiring new chemical weapons when the issue of how most efficiently to deliver them still needs to be resolved? Would the Air Force be any worse off in an era of rapid techno-logical change by slowing its commitment to F-15s and F-16s and minimizing block obsolescence in the future? Do the services really want to wipe out all backlogs of maintenance and overhaul, or would they prefer their civilian work force to be kept stable, busy, and proficient? If they thought that funding would be less subject to sudden starts and stops, would they program double the real property maintenance of the recent past, or would they take a more gradual approach? Is it appropriate, after a very large increase in fiscal 1982, to raise military pay across the board by 8 percent when civilian pay is due to go up by 5 percent and when unemployment rates are high in competitive private sector jobs?

Table 3-16.  **Reagan, Intermediate, and Baseline Conventional Forces Budgets, Fiscal Years 1983–87**[a]
Billions of dollars

| Budget | 1983 | 1984 | 1985 | 1986 | 1987 | 1983–87 |
|---|---|---|---|---|---|---|
| *Total obligational authority* | | | | | | |
| Reagan budget | 174.8 | 189.1 | 211.8 | 238.6 | 268.8 | 1,083.1 |
| Intermediate budget | 150.2 | 168.6 | 188.6 | 210.1 | 233.8 | 951.3 |
| Saving from Reagan budget | 24.6 | 20.5 | 23.2 | 28.5 | 35.0 | 131.8 |
| Baseline budget | 141.8 | 160.0 | 179.1 | 199.4 | 223.6 | 903.9 |
| Saving from Reagan budget | 33.0 | 29.1 | 32.7 | 39.2 | 45.2 | 179.2 |
| *Outlays* | | | | | | |
| Reagan budget | 146.3 | 163.6 | 182.3 | 210.3 | 238.8 | 941.3 |
| Intermediate budget | 139.0 | 145.0 | 162.7 | 189.8 | 218.3 | 854.8 |
| Saving from Reagan budget | 7.3 | 18.6 | 19.6 | 20.5 | 20.5 | 86.5 |
| Baseline budget | 133.0 | 138.1 | 155.5 | 182.3 | 210.7 | 819.6 |
| Saving from Reagan budget | 13.3 | 25.5 | 26.8 | 28.0 | 28.1 | 121.7 |

Sources: *Department of Defense Annual Report to the Congress, Fiscal Year 1983*, p. B-7; and author's estimates in table 3-15.
a. Budgets reflect appropriations from programs for the general purpose, airlift and sealift, and National Guard and Reserve forces; they include resources for military personnel, operation and maintenance, procurement, research, development, test, and evaluation, and family housing.

Does it make sense to keep funding research, development, test, and evaluation at 10 percent of the total budget regardless of the budget's size or the merits of the proposed research? Clearly a number of measures can be taken to reduce the rate at which defense spending increases and at the same time place the armed forces in a strong position to achieve steady, realistic, necessary, and acceptable growth in the future. One such list of possible measures is shown in table 3-15.

The Reagan five-year defense plan for the conventional forces is shown in table 3-16, as are reductions from it to an intermediate plan and the baseline program. To go much below the baseline force in size would certainly reduce the premium on the insurance. It would also limit the coverage.

## Summary

Americans increasingly realize that they live in a highly competitive world. Various forms of Marxism may continue to spring up, particularly in the less developed countries. But the Soviet Union has lost the ideological contest. Its place has been taken by a grim military rivalry to which attention in the United States has only recently returned. At almost the same time, it has been recognized that America has lost its competitive edge in many sectors of the international economy. Thus it faces more or less simultaneous demands for investment in both the nation's defense and the nation's economic structure.

The United States has the resources to effect major improvements in both. That is not the problem. The problem, given expected commitments to social expenditures, the needs of the economy, and reduced federal revenues, is how to regulate the timing, pace, and direction of growth in defense investments. The problem can be defined in these terms for several reasons. First, much of the Soviet increase in defense outlays has gone toward the relatively sterile nuclear competition and a buildup of conventional capabilities in the Far East. Second, the United States and its allies currently possess a strong foundation of nuclear and nonnuclear capabilities, and while the allies could do more, their contribution to the common defense is already substantial. Third, as President Reagan has put it, the task is to restore a margin of safety in these capabilities rather than to pursue the will-o'-the-wisp of superiority. Fourth, it is generally accepted by military and civilian officials alike that accomplishing the task requires long-term efforts rather than a declaration of national emergency and crash programs to close this or that window of vulnerability. Accordingly, the timing, pace, and even direction of these efforts can be controlled, to some degree in deference to the need to make the economy more competitive and preserve essential social programs.

Control over the growth in defense obligations and outlays can be exercised in many different ways. Table 3-17 gives a summary of three approaches to the problem of control.

The Reagan option is the most expansive of the three. It envisages an average of 8.1 percent real growth each year in outlays over the period of the five-year defense plan, although the growth surges in fiscal 1983 and 1985. Cumulative outlays for the five years amount to more than $1.4 trillion in current dollars. Total obligational authority for the same period, in current dollars, amounts to more than $1.6 trillion, which means that defense outlays will continue to grow rapidly even after fiscal 1987.

The Reagan option, like the other two, provides for a gradual

**Table 3-17.** Reagan, Intermediate, and Baseline Defense Budgets, Fiscal Years 1983–87
Billions of dollars

| Item | 1983 | 1984 | 1985 | 1986 | 1987 | 1983–87 |
|---|---|---|---|---|---|---|
| *Total obligational authority* | | | | | | |
| Reagan budget | 258.0 | 285.5 | 331.7 | 367.6 | 400.8 | 1,643.6 |
| Intermediate budget | 226.0 | 253.1 | 295.0 | 325.0 | 356.0 | 1,455.1 |
| Baseline budget | 212.5 | 238.8 | 278.2 | 307.9 | 340.4 | 1,377.8 |
| Reduction | | | | | | |
|   Reagan to intermediate | 32.0 | 32.4 | 36.7 | 42.6 | 44.8 | . . . |
|   Cumulative: Reagan to intermediate | . . . | 64.4 | 101.1 | 143.7 | 188.5 | 188.5 |
|   Reagan to baseline | 45.5 | 46.7 | 53.5 | 59.7 | 60.4 | . . . |
|   Cumulative: Reagan to baseline | . . . | 92.2 | 145.7 | 205.4 | 265.8 | 265.8 |
| *Outlays* | | | | | | |
| Reagan budget | 215.9 | 247.0 | 285.5 | 324.0 | 356.0 | 1,428.4 |
| Intermediate budget | 204.8 | 219.2 | 256.4 | 293.4 | 325.3 | 1,299.1 |
| Baseline budget | 196.9 | 207.4 | 244.1 | 280.6 | 312.4 | 1,241.4 |
| Reduction | | | | | | |
|   Reagan to intermediate | 11.1 | 27.8 | 29.1 | 30.6 | 30.7 | . . . |
|   Cumulative: Reagan to intermediate | . . . | 38.9 | 68.0 | 98.6 | 129.3 | 129.3 |
|   Reagan to baseline | 19.0 | 39.6 | 41.4 | 43.4 | 43.6 | . . . |
|   Cumulative: Reagan to baseline | . . . | 58.6 | 100.0 | 143.4 | 187.0 | 187.0 |

Sources: *Department of Defense Annual Report to the Congress, Fiscal Year 1983*, p. B-3; and author's estimates in tables 3-6, 3-9, 3-16.

buildup of U.S. power to counter the increase in Soviet capabilities. It does so by (1) full funding of the baseline forces; (2) a relatively cautious modernization of nuclear capabilities, the payoffs of which will begin to show in the late 1980s with a somewhat higher assurance of delivering about the same number of warheads as the baseline forces; and (3) an expansion of naval offensive capabilities and intercontinental airlift and a possible growth in land-based tactical air power, none of which will materialize before the late 1980s. Whether they will then do much to remedy the main weaknesses in the U.S. conventional defense posture is open to debate.

The intermediate option allows real growth in outlays of 4.8 percent in fiscal 1983; thereafter, the annual rate of growth is 6.5 percent. Total outlays for the five-year defense plan, in current dollars, are $1.3 trillion, $129 billion less than in the Reagan option. Savings in outlays of $68 billion are made during the first three years, beginning with $11.1 billion in 1983 and rising to $29.1 billion in 1985.

Despite these savings, the intermediate option also provides for an increase in capabilities above those of the baseline force. But it differs from the Reagan option in that it attempts to hedge against what could be greater-than-expected Soviet conventional threats in several theaters. It does so by (1) full funding of the baseline forces; (2) a more deliberate modernization of the nuclear forces, largely on the ground that a long-term and relatively stable stalemate exists in the strategic arena, that further modernization of the bomber force (beyond the addition of air-launched cruise missiles) can await the arrival of the Stealth aircraft, and that ICBM modernization can be delayed until there is a resolution of the issues surrounding the future basing mode and mission of land-based missiles; (3) expansion of the available ground and tactical air forces through increased investment in the National Guard and Reserve; (4) improved sea control with emphasis on the modernization and expansion of naval escort capabilities; and (5) greater intercontinental mobility through increased sealift rather than airlift.

The baseline option postulates an increase in real outlays of slightly less than 1 percent from fiscal 1982 to 1983. Thereafter, real growth averages about 6.5 percent through the five-year period. Cumulative outlays, in current dollars, are estimated at more than $1.2 trillion, $187 billion less than required by the Reagan option. Of the total, $100 billion is saved during the first three years of the planning period, beginning with $19 billion in 1983 and increasing to $41.4 billion in 1985.

The assumptions of the baseline option are that (1) existing and foreseeable threats require an upgrading of existing forces rather than an expansion of them; (2) current nuclear and nonnuclear forces will be brought to full combat power through increased training, maintenance, and supplies; (3) war reserve stocks for the conventional forces will be built up to permit forty-five days of intense combat; and (4) real cost growth in the next generation of weapons for the force will be held to 6 percent a year, or a factor of four over the life of the systems to be replaced.

Both lower and higher defense options and budgets are of course imaginable, although there is little basis at present for either. Permanent peace may not be at hand, but neither is a repetition of the Rhineland or Munich. In the circumstances, a declaration that the military competition has ended or that a national emergency is imminent would be unrealistic. Military power still has a role to play in international politics; it remains the system's final voting mechanism. But in a world of ambiguous intentions and motives, there can be no fixed military requirements that must be met within a specified period of time regardless of cost and other opportunities forgone. Instead, as usual, the country faces uncertainties, risks, and competing priorities. America must to some degree rearm. It can acquire a margin of military safety and still reach other goals. But it must also maintain an economy and a national consensus strong enough to sustain that margin. A budget somewhat below that proposed by the Reagan administration will permit both.

Legend has it that John Jacob Astor was in the ship's bar when the *Titanic* hit the iceberg. Supposedly he turned to the bartender and said: "I asked for ice, but this is ridiculous." Real or imagined, these prescient words are not irrelevant to the current debate on the 1983 defense budget.

CHAPTER FOUR

# Nondefense Programs

HENRY J. AARON *and associates*

*Better the occasional faults of a government that lives in a spirit of charity than the consistent omissions of a government frozen in the ice of its own indifference.*
—Franklin Delano Roosevelt

*In this present crisis, government is not the solution to our problem; government is the problem.*
—Ronald Reagan

THE 1983 budget continues the efforts of President Reagan and his administration to minimize the role of the federal government in all areas other than defense. In particular, the federal government is either being withdrawn from the provision of social services and income maintenance or having its activities curtailed.

President Reagan is forthright in stating the reasons for retrenchment. Services and protections offered by the federal government, in his view, are too numerous and too costly. State and local governments, the president holds, should decide whether or not to provide these services, how much to spend on them, and how to organize their delivery, without federal restrictions or financial support. The twin goals of higher spending for defense and lower tax rates, which the administration takes as immutable, lead inexorably to either intolerable budget deficits or drastically curtailed nondefense expenditures. Furthermore, the furor created by his proposals of May 12, 1981, to cut the long-run cost of retirement, survivors, and disability insurance benefits by 22 percent, has led the president to avoid any mention of reductions

Gary Burtless, Anthony Downs, Louise B. Russell, Gilbert S. Omenn, and David W. Breneman assisted in the preparation of this chapter. In addition, Robert D. Reischauer and Darwin G. Johnson made constructive suggestions on drafts of this chapter, and Diane E. Levin and Julie A. Carr provided research assistance.

in social security in his 1983 budget. Instead, he has established a commission to make recommendations for amending the social security system, but not until after the November elections. The 1983 budget proposes to cut nondefense spending on programs other than payment of interest to $43 billion below the current services level, lowering total spending in 1983 to $435 billion from the $478 billion that would be necessary to maintain programs at their current services level. These cuts come on top of the $27.1 billion in reductions enacted last year. Both these proposals would reduce the fraction of gross national product devoted to programs other than defense and interest from 15 percent of GNP in 1981 to 12.7 percent in 1983 and to 11.5 percent in 1985. Moreover, the cuts are unevenly divided; the major entitlement programs decline negligibly as a fraction of GNP over this period, while all other nondefense spending plummets (see table 4-1).

The reductions made in 1981 and those proposed this year constitute the Reagan administration's effort to eliminate or to reduce in size most of the social programs enacted during the last fifty years. Social security, medicare and medicaid, higher education assistance, aid to school districts on behalf of disadvantaged

Table 4-1. Nondefense Outlays in Constant 1981 Dollars, Fiscal Years 1981, 1983, and 1985

Billions of dollars unless otherwise specified

| | | Projected | | Percent of GNP | | |
|---|---|---|---|---|---|---|
| Outlay | 1981 | 1983[a] | 1985[a] | 1981 | 1983 | 1985 |
| Total nondefense | 497.4 | 466.4 | 451.6 | 17.4 | 15.6 | 13.8 |
| Interest | 82.5 | 97.8 | 93.8 | 2.9 | 3.3 | 2.9 |
| Nondefense less interest | 414.9 | 368.6 | 357.8 | 14.5 | 12.3 | 11.0 |
| Payments to individuals[b] | 316.6 | 318.0 | 321.1 | 11.1 | 10.7 | 9.8 |
| Social security and railroad retirement, medical care, and federal employee retirement and insurance | 226.5 | 241.5 | 255.4 | 7.9 | 8.1 | 7.8 |
| Other | 90.1 | 76.5 | 65.7 | 3.2 | 2.6 | 2.0 |
| Other nondefense | 98.3 | 50.6 | 36.7 | 3.4 | 1.7 | 1.1 |

Source: Office of Management and Budget, "Payments for Individuals, 1983 Budget," February 1982 edition.
a. Deflated by the implicit index for all government spending derived from *Budget of the United States Government, Fiscal Year 1983*, p. 9-61.
b. Excludes payments to individuals included in the defense budget.

children, unemployment insurance, housing assistance, grants for urban and rural development, grants for training and job creation, financial aid to the poor, disabled, and elderly, grants for social services, and legal services for the indigent have all been the target of spending cuts proposed by the Reagan administration last year or this year.

In this chapter we examine some of these cuts in federal spending in the areas of income security, housing, health, and education and training. Because President Reagan's proposals express a coherent view of the appropriate role of the federal government in each area, we also review the rationale for creating the programs. The chapter builds on the tension between the view that these programs fulfill necessary responsibilities of the federal government and the contrary view that they are imposing heavy and unnecessary burdens on the economy.

### What Is at Stake

Beginning with the New Deal of Franklin Delano Roosevelt and continuing through successive administrations, both Democratic and Republican, presidents and Congresses have established a series of programs to protect people from economic adversity, to guarantee them minimum quantities of basic goods, and to increase equality of opportunity. To achieve these goals, they created new federal agencies, modified the tax code to promote favored activities, provided grants to state and local governments and private organizations, and issued regulations mandating or prohibiting behavior of various kinds by governments, businesses, and individuals.

In the pursuit of these objectives, the federal government has become an increasingly visible, intrusive, and costly element in the economic and social life of the United States (see table 4-2). Spending has grown; income and payroll taxes have risen (though corporation income tax rates have declined). Federal employment has increased, but less rapidly than the civilian work force. A complex web of economic and regulatory relationships has formed, linking the federal government with subsidiary governments and with private businesses and organizations.

For most of the half-century during which the federal role was

**Table 4-2. Selected Indicators of the Size of the Federal Government**
Percent of GNP unless otherwise specified

| Item | 1950 | 1960 | 1970 | 1981 | 1983 (projected) |
|---|---|---|---|---|---|
| *Taxes* | | | | | |
| Personal income and payroll | 7.6 | 11.1 | 14.1 | 16.4 | 18.4 |
| Corporation income | 4.0 | 4.3 | 3.4 | 2.5 | 2.7 |
| Other | 3.4 | 3.1 | 2.6 | 2.1 | 2.1 |
| *Federal employment* | | | | | |
| Number (millions) | 2.1 | 2.4 | 3.0 | 2.8 | 2.8 |
| As percent of civilian labor force | 3.4 | 3.4 | 3.6 | 2.6 | n.a. |

Sources: Office of Management and Budget, "Federal Government Finances," January 1980 edition, p. 9. Federal employment is from Bureau of the Census, *Statistical Abstract of the United States, 1980* (GPO, 1980), p. 318. The 1983 budget quotes full-time equivalents, which were initiated only in 1981. Civilian labor force is from *Employment and Earnings*, vol. 29 (January 1982), p. 9.
    n.a. Not available.

growing, the economy was expanding, first after the low point of the Great Depression, then during the boom of World War II, and finally during the great postwar expansion that, punctuated by brief recessions, lasted until the early 1970s. Beginning in the late 1960s, however, inflation became progressively more serious, and since 1974 the rate of growth of productivity has been negligible, about 1 percent a year. The administration maintains that reducing the size, cost, and influence of government is a necessary precondition for bringing down inflation and restoring economic growth. Others believe that the economic role of the federal government was an important factor in assuring three decades of growth and price stability unprecedented in modern U.S. history.

The division between those who support an active role for the federal government in dealing with domestic social problems and those who feel that government usually creates more problems than it solves rests on two important trade-offs.

The first trade-off is between equality and efficiency. Most nondefense expenditures, other than those for interest on the national debt, occur under programs that provide benefits either to people who experience certain income-threatening events, such as reaching retirement age, becoming disabled, or losing a job, or to people who are judged needy. These programs help the elderly or the disabled to retire. They relieve workers of some of the economic consequences of unemployment. And they provide the poor with income or with minimum quantities of certain basic commodities. The fraction of the population with money income below the poverty threshold dropped from 22 percent in 1960 to 13 percent in 1980, although there has been little decline since 1968 and the number of poor rose by 3.2 million last year. If in-kind benefits, which have risen faster than money income, are included, as few as 6 percent of the population may be below the official poverty threshold.[1] Also, the taxes levied to pay for these programs are somewhat progressive.[2]

The rationale for such programs is the common observation that many people do not or cannot plan adequately for economic adversity and that the outcomes of the marketplace are sometimes unjust because, in the words of Arthur Okun, they "allow the big winners to feed their pets better than the losers can feed their children."[3] Moreover, there is the plain aversion of many people to indigence, not only for themselves, but also for others. These programs do not seek to equalize incomes so much as to prevent serious declines in income and utter destitution.

Such programs carry a price, however. The most obvious is the taxes imposed to pay for them, which reduce the incomes that taxpayers retain for their own consumption and saving. Taxes distort decisions about how much to work and to save and what to invest in. Furthermore, the programs themselves affect behavior. Retirement benefits may be viewed positively as enabling the elderly to retire, or negatively as discouraging some from working who are capable of doing so. Likewise, welfare payments may be viewed as preventing destitution and providing protection against adversity, or as subsidizing sloth and promoting improvidence. Subsidies for medical care increase the access of the poor, the disabled, and the aged to care they could not otherwise afford, but they reduce the sensitivity of beneficiaries to the cost of care

1. Sheldon Danziger, "The Distribution of Income: An Account of Past Trends and a Projection of the Impacts of the Administration's Economic Program," prepared for the Joint Economic Committee, February 10, 1982.
2. See Joseph A. Pechman and Benjamin A. Okner, *Who Bears The Tax Burden?* (Brookings Institution, 1974), for estimates of the distribution of federal tax burdens.
3. Arthur M. Okun, *Equality and Efficiency: The Big Tradeoff* (Brookings Institution, 1975), p. 1.

and increase the likelihood of waste.[4] Thus there is a pervasive trade-off between the goal of helping people judged to be needy and that of minimizing inefficiencies by maintaining incentives based on the threat of economic adversity.

A second trade-off exists between providing help to as many people who need it as possible and not providing help to those who don't—in other words, between errors of omission and errors of commission. The lower the income ceiling for food stamp benefits, housing assistance, or welfare benefits, the smaller will be the number of people assisted who in some sense do not deserve help, but the greater will be the chance that some deserving people will be denied it. Strict rules for disability benefits minimize the number of people capable of working who will be awarded benefits, but increase the number of people for whom work is painful or impossible who will be denied benefits. Reducing social security benefits to people who retire before they reach sixty-five will cause some people who can continue working with little inconvenience to do so, but will impoverish many who are unable to work or who cannot find work.

In all such cases the fact that defined rules and regulations are necessary to minimize administrative caprice and that the average official is endowed with average wisdom means mistakes will invariably be made. The task of designing social programs is to arrive at a consensus of need and to decide how many people deserving of help should be denied it in order to minimize error, fraud, and abuse.

Many social programs enacted over the past half-century have been criticized as inefficient by people who embrace their objectives and agree that the federal government should be actively involved in income support, health, housing, and education. For example, student loans have been criticized because they provide unneeded subsidies to wealthy families; housing subsidies have been criticized because they are needlessly costly; health subsidies have been criticized because they provide excessive pay-

4. It is worth noting that both private and public "third party" payment systems produce the same effects. Evidence that third party reimbursement increases the demand for health care and that the effect depends on the proportion of total cost of which patients are relieved is reported in Joseph Newhouse and others, "Some Interim Results from a Controlled Trial of Cost Sharing in Health Insurance," *New England Journal of Medicine* (December 17, 1981), pp. 1501–07.

ments to some providers and insufficient payments to others. The 1983 budget accepts these criticisms. But it uses them primarily to justify budget cuts, not to design better ways of achieving previously accepted goals.

The 1983 budget may be read as a brief for leaving many of the nondefense functions now performed by the federal government to state and local governments or to the private sector. Congressional action on the president's 1983 budget is best understood, therefore, as a referendum on the wisdom of retaining a major federal role in the financing and provision of social services and income support. Acceptance of most of the president's budget amounts to agreement that many services previously assured by federal administration, financing, or regulation should be provided by lower-level governments with highly disparate fiscal capacities,[5] by private groups, or not at all. Rejection of most of his proposed cuts may be interpreted as a collective recommitment of the federal role in assuring social services and income support. The issue whether programs should be redesigned to achieve their objectives more efficiently than existing programs do is not seriously addressed in the 1983 budget. Nor does the budget recognize the inability of states or localities to deal with concentrated problems of poverty, because of their fear that if benefits are higher than average, taxpayers will flee to lower-cost jurisdictions and the poor will move in.

Table 4-3 summarizes the proposed reductions in a representative list of programs that provide income support and social services and that promote urban development. In this table and throughout the text *real outlays* refer to outlays in 1981 dollars.[6] Some programs are eliminated or cut to a small fraction of their former size, notably public service employment, other training and employment programs, and legal services for the poor. Others are scaled back by 20 to 40 percent, but the basic structure of

5. The Advisory Commission on Intergovernmental Relations compiles an index of fiscal capacity showing the ease with which different states can raise a given amount of revenue. The average value of that index for the top five states is 159.2; for the bottom five states it is 76.4. ACIR, *Tax Capacity of the Fifty States: Methodology and Estimates*, report M-134 (Government Printing Office, 1982), pp. 20–21.

6. The deflators used were derived from *Budget of the United States Government, Fiscal Year 1983*, p. 9–61. When applicable, the deflator for payments for individuals was used; in all other cases (unless otherwise specified), the deflator for "all other" nondefense expenditures was used.

**Table 4-3. Effect of Congressional Action in 1981 and Reductions Proposed in the 1983 Budget on Real Outlays in Fiscal Year 1983**

Billions of 1981 dollars unless otherwise specified

| Program | Outlay without cuts in fiscal 1982 or 1983[a] | Proposed outlay | Proposed reduction Amount | Percent |
|---|---|---|---|---|
| *Education and training* | | | | |
| Elementary, secondary, and vocational education (budget authority) | 6.7 | 3.9 | 2.8 | 42 |
| Higher education (budget authority)[b] | 10.7 | 6.0 | 4.7 | 44 |
| Public service employment | 2.4 | c | 2.4 | 100 |
| Other training and employment programs | 6.8 | 2.4 | 4.4 | 65 |
| *Health* | | | | |
| Medicaid | 18.2 | 15.6 | 2.6 | 14 |
| Medicare | 47.4 | 44.5 | 2.9 | 6 |
| Other health programs | 4.3 | 4.0 | 0.3 | 7 |
| *Income support, income tested* | | | | |
| Food stamps and other nutrition programs | 17.7 | 12.0 | 5.7 | 32 |
| Aid to families with dependent children | 8.1 | 5.9 | 2.2 | 27 |
| Energy assistance | 1.8 | 1.1 | 0.7 | 39 |
| Housing assistance (units authorized in thousands) | 230.6 | − 36.0[d] | 266.6 | . . . |
| Supplemental security income | 8.0 | 7.8 | 0.2 | 3 |
| *Income support, not income tested* | | | | |
| Retirement, survivors and disability insurance, railroad retirement, and black lung | 159.0 | 153.5 | 5.5 | 3 |
| Federal retirement and disability | 18.9 | 18.4 | 0.5 | 3 |
| Unemployment insurance | 23.9 | 19.8 | 4.1 | 17 |
| *Other* | | | | |
| Social services | 6.5 | 4.5 | 2.0 | 31 |
| Community development block grant and urban development action grants | 4.4 | 3.4 | 1.0 | 23 |
| Legal services | 0.3 | c | 0.3 | 97 |

Sources: *Budget of the United States Government, Fiscal Year 1983*, pp. 5-93, 5-107, 5-130, 5-143; estimates for entitlement programs for 1983 without cuts, from *Budget of the United States Government, Fiscal Year 1983, Special Analysis A: Current Services Estimates;* and OMB, unpublished data.

a. 1983 outlays or budget authority without cuts equal: for entitlement programs, current services estimates as presented in the 1983 budget plus the estimated reductions in 1983 outlays attributable to actions taken by Congress last year, reduced to 1981 dollars by deflators implicit in table 22 of the 1983 budget; for other programs, outlays equal actual 1981 outlays. Proposed outlays equal estimated 1983 outlays from the 1983 budget, deflated to 1981 dollars by the deflators implicit in table 22 of the 1983 budget.

b. Includes social security student benefits, which are also included under retirement, survivors and disability insurance, railroad retirement, and black lung.

c. Less than $50 million.

d. The net reduction in units represents the balance of 121,000 units authorized for assistance in 1983, less 157,000 cancelations of units authorized in previous years.

many of these programs is transformed, and further cuts are promised. In this second category are elementary, secondary, and vocational education, higher education assistance, food stamps and other nutrition programs, aid to families with dependent children, energy assistance, social services block grants, and community development and urban development block grants. Because many of these programs are scheduled to be turned over to states or to be consolidated into block grants, over the spending of which the federal government would exercise few controls, the budget says little about structural reforms to improve their efficiency.

A third category of programs, including medicare, medicaid, supplemental security income, social security cash benefits, and unemployment insurance, are all retained by the federal government but cut in size, either by actions taken in 1981 or by the 1983 budget. The reductions shown in table 4-3 represent the down payments on future reductions that will flow ineluctably from actions already taken, that are sought by the 1983 budget, or that the administration has clearly indicated it intends to seek.

### Income Security

The federal government took up the task of supporting the incomes of needy and dependent people in 1935, when Congress passed the Social Security Act. That law set in place unemployment insurance, retirement and survivors insurance, and aid to families with dependent children (AFDC). Later Congresses initiated housing assistance, disability insurance, food subsidies, and energy assistance. With the notable exception of AFDC, real federal expenditures under each of these programs rose during the 1970s. Now they have all been cut or are the subject of cuts proposed in the 1983 budget. Moreover, the president's proposal that the states assume full responsibility for AFDC and food stamps in exchange for federal assumption of responsibility for medicaid would remove the federal government from involvement with income-tested cash assistance to the nonaged poor.[7]

*Aid to Families with Dependent Children*

AFDC provides cash assistance to low-income families—usually single-parent families—with dependent children present. The

7. See chapter 5 for an examination of this proposed swap.

states administer AFDC (99.5 percent of the people involved in
its administration are state employees) and set benefit levels, but
the federal government shares 50 to 77 percent of the total cost of
the program. Because states have failed to raise AFDC grants in
line with inflation, average benefits for a family of four have fallen
28 percent in real terms since 1972.

In his 1983 budget President Reagan proposes to reduce real
federal outlays on AFDC and related programs from $8.5 billion
in 1981 to $5.9 billion in 1983, a 31 percent reduction. Of this
reduction, $1.3 billion was enacted last year. Proposed changes
in the definition of family needs and available family income
account for most of the 1983 savings. Family units in larger
households will have their basic benefits reduced. Families receiving low-income energy assistance will have this assistance
counted in determining available income, so that their AFDC
grants will be reduced. The president proposes to require state
"workfare" programs, under which recipients of cash assistance
would have to work at specially created jobs in order to receive
assistance. He is also asking Congress to provide new incentives
for states and localities to enforce child support laws, thus reducing
the dependence of children on public support. The savings from
these proposals are estimated to be $1.3 billion in 1983.

The administration also wants to consolidate and cut federal
grants for administering AFDC, food stamps, and medicaid. The
1983 budget proposes not only to reduce grants for administration,
but also to reduce and eventually to eliminate any federal sharing
in the cost of payments erroneously made. But no penalties will
be imposed on states for denial of benefits to people who turn out
to have been eligible. Thus the budget unmistakably conveys the
message that the administration will not tolerate unjust benefit
awards, but is not concerned about unjust denials.

The proposed administrative consolidation of AFDC and food
stamps makes sense, but it would bring few substantive changes,
because these two programs cover overlapping populations and
are already administered by the same state and local agencies.
The conversion of the federal grant for administrative expenses
from a matching grant to a block grant will undoubtedly induce
states to economize on administrative costs, probably to the
disadvantage of beneficiaries.

Starting in 1984, the president proposes to turn over to the states all responsibility for financing and administering AFDC and food stamps. The resulting change in the method of financing these programs would drastically alter the incentives facing state legislatures and governors. At present, states pay on average 46 percent of each additional dollar of AFDC benefits and none of the cost of food stamp benefits. Thus the federal support of the two programs offsets the widely stated fear that providing benefits for the needy at the state or local level will drive up local taxes and drive away business and the affluent. This fear would grow under the administration's plan to give states or localities full financial responsibility for all aid to the poor, and would probably lead to continued and accelerated reductions in that aid.

The changes in AFDC proposed for 1983 (before the program is handed over to the states) continue a pattern established with the president's proposals for 1982. The structure of the program remains unchanged, but proposed technical changes would disqualify some families—especially those with a prime-age potential worker—and reduce the benefits of many more. The reforms enacted last year hit families that have a wage earner especially hard. Until 1981, benefits were reduced by 67 cents for each dollar of earnings in excess of work-related expenses and a $30 a month disregard. As a result of legislation enacted last year, benefits after four months are reduced by a dollar for every dollar of earnings, a 100 percent tax. Also, allowable work-related expenses used in computing net income are sharply reduced. These and other changes add to the restrictiveness of federal welfare regulations, limiting local administrative control of the program and increasing the burden of management.

### Supplemental Security Income

Supplemental security income (SSI) is a federally financed cash assistance program for the low-income elderly, disabled, and blind. Some states supplement federal benefits. If no changes are made in the program, 1983 federal outlays on SSI are expected to be $9.2 billion, up 15 percent from 1982. This rise is due both to the indexing of basic benefits and to the quirk that thirteen rather than twelve monthly SSI payments will be made in 1983.[8]

8. Because the first day of fiscal 1984 falls on a weekend, the SSI payment otherwise due on that day will be made in fiscal 1983.

As in the AFDC program, the president proposes technical changes in the payment formula and eligibility definitions that would reduce 1983 expenditures by $300 million, or about 3 percent. Many of these changes are minor and will lower the annual payments to beneficiaries by only a few dollars. But the president also proposes to tighten the definition of disability and disqualify about 115,000 people now receiving SSI disability benefits. With this exception, however, the SSI program has escaped the large reductions proposed for other assistance programs.

### Food Stamps and Other Nutrition Assistance

Federal spending on food and nutrition assistance rose irregularly, but rapidly, during the 1970s. Real outlays in 1981 were $16.2 billion, or about 88 percent, higher than in 1973. But the rise in per capita real food stamp benefits from 1974 to 1981 was not large enough to offset the decline in real benefits for AFDC families. A family receiving only AFDC and food stamps qualified for about 18 percent less in combined real benefits in 1981 than in 1974. In fact, combined AFDC and food stamp benefits in 1981 for a family of four with no earnings were 4 percent lower in real terms than AFDC benefits alone in 1969, when the food stamp program was not yet nationally available.

In his 1983 budget President Reagan proposes to continue the reduction of food stamp benefits initiated last year. Real spending is projected to decline by 20 percent from its 1981 level. None of the food stamp proposals for 1983 will alter the fundamental nature of the program. All changes are technical and will principally affect families that receive low-income energy assistance or that have a potential wage earner. The president proposes that energy assistance be counted as income in determining food stamp benefits, that earnings disregards be eliminated (effectively raising the tax on earnings), and that the rate at which benefits are reduced as all forms of net family income (including earnings) increase be raised from 30 to 35 percent. The cumulative effect of the latter two changes would be to raise the tax rate on gross earnings in the food stamp program from about 25 to 35 percent and lower the proportion of increased earnings that food stamp recipients will retain. Other reductions would result from eliminating monthly payments of less than $10 and modifying the benefit-rounding convention to the disadvantage of beneficiaries.[9]

Federal outlays for administrative expenses would be reduced by providing a block grant rather than a matching grant for state and local expenses; and federal reimbursements for benefit over-payments would be phased out over the four years ending in 1986. Both these changes would increase incentives for states and localities to adopt rules that minimize payments to ineligible families, even at the expense of denying payments to those that are eligible. The administration also proposes beginning in 1984 to turn over to state governments all financial responsibility for food stamps.

In addition, the 1983 budget proposes to abolish the special milk and summer feeding programs. The school breakfast, child care feeding, and women, infants, and children programs would be converted from entitlement programs to block grants with reduced budgets. The president expects these changes to save $300 million in 1983. Real federal outlays on nutrition programs other than food stamps would be down 30 percent from 1981.

The proposed changes in federal nutrition assistance programs will affect all classes of beneficiaries—children, prime-age work-ers and other adults, and the very old. Such changes as eliminating the special milk program and increasing the food stamp tax on earnings will primarily affect families with modest incomes that are at the upper end of the eligible range, and will probably not have serious nutritional consequences. But such changes as turning the nutrition program for pregnant women, new mothers, infants, and children into a block grant and counting energy assistance in the computation of food stamp benefits are likely to reduce significantly the well-being of the most disadvantaged, especially the very young and the very old. Although there is a sound argument for concentrating nutritional assistance on the most disadvantaged, the president's proposals go beyond this objective and reduce assistance to all types of beneficiaries, even those with no resources of their own. Even the "less disadvan-taged," whose nutritional assistance will be reduced by these proposals, are far from well-to-do; nine-tenths of the proposed

9. Monthly benefits will be rounded to the next lowest dollar, thus reducing payments by a few dollars a year.

nutritional cuts are focused on food stamps, a program restricted to families with incomes below 130 percent of the poverty line.

## Emergency and Energy Assistance

Since 1979 the federal government has provided block grants to states to help low-income families pay for sharply increased fuel bills. This program protects many of the poorest families from some of the loss they suffered when fuel prices rose after the decontrol of energy prices. The promise of such aid diminished political opposition to the decontrol of energy prices and helped secure passage of legislation that improved the efficiency of the allocation of energy. The Reagan administration now proposes to modify and greatly reduce the low-income energy assistance program. The 1983 budget would combine the grant for energy assistance with the grant for emergency assistance, permit states to apply the combined block grant for hardship assistance as they wish, and reduce outlays to $1.3 billion, 30 percent below expenditures in the last two years. A separate requirement would require states to count energy assistance in determining food stamp and AFDC benefits. This requirement would cause AFDC payments to be cut by up to one dollar and food stamps by 35 cents for each dollar of emergency assistance. As a result, the effective reduction in energy assistance for the poor is far larger than the 30 percent cut in the energy assistance budget. As price controls on gas are phased out and natural gas prices rise, real assistance levels will plummet.

The proposal to take energy assistance into account in the computation of food stamps is inconsistent with the original purposes of both programs. Food stamps help low-income families attain minimum nutritional standards; energy assistance reduces financial hardships arising from the recent rises in energy costs. Under the president's proposal, food stamp aid will decline even though there is no real change in the resources families need to purchase a nutritionally adequate diet.

## The Cumulative Effect of Welfare Cuts

The 1983 budget proposals extend President Reagan's cuts in aid to the needy. In 1981 the federal government spent on the needy $33.7 billion through the two cash assistance programs—

AFDC and SSI—and two categories of in-kind assistance programs—food stamps and other nutrition assistance, and low-income energy assistance. If all the president's 1983 proposals were enacted, real spending in 1983 would fall to $26.8 billion, with reductions concentrated in AFDC, nutrition programs, and energy assistance.

Outlays on these programs would decline from just over 1.18 percent of GNP in 1981 to 0.78 percent in 1983. Although the proposed swap of medicaid for food stamps and AFDC, examined in chapter 5, makes projections uncertain, the budget projects a further decline to 0.58 percent of GNP in 1985 if President Reagan's proposals are adopted.[10] Although expected improvements in economic conditions account for part of the reduction, it is the cumulative impact of many small changes in payment formulas, all tending to reduce real benefits to low-income families, that accounts for most of the drop. Because there are so many changes, it is hard to identify the groups that lose most. The increased taxes on income—especially wage income—suggests that low-income families with an earner or potential earner would be hardest hit by the proposed changes.

If beneficiaries get less for working than they did in the past, they would seem to have less incentive to work.[11] But the efficiency argument against raising marginal tax rates is weak. Recent evidence supports the commonsense view that a rise in the rate at which benefits are reduced as earnings rise will discourage work by people who continue to receive benefits.[12] But increasing the rate of benefit reduction lowers the number of people who receive benefits and who are exposed to the program's work disincentives. The net effect is likely to be small.

The fundamental issue is fairness. The largest proposed cuts hit programs for the nonelderly, like AFDC and child nutrition, or programs like food stamps and energy assistance that serve all

10. By comparison, expenditures on these programs equalled 1.10 percent of GNP under the last budget prepared by President Ford.

11. Tom Joe, "Profiles of Families in Poverty: Effects of the FY 1983 Budget Proposals on the Poor," working paper (Washington, D.C., Center for the Study of Social Policy, 1982).

12. Robert A. Moffitt, "An Economic Model of Welfare Stigma," working paper, October 1981, p. 27; and Frank S. Levy, "The Labor Supply of Female Heads, or AFDC Work Incentives Don't Work Too Well," *Journal of Human Resources,* vol. 14 (Winter 1979), pp. 76–97.

age groups. Programs principally for the elderly and disabled, like SSI and medicare, receive much smaller reductions. Families with an earner present suffer the sharpest reductions. The injustice that arises when families with a full-time earner have no more income, and possibly even less, than families dependent exclusively on assistance will be exacerbated. The Reagan changes compress the income distribution among the nation's disadvantaged families by narrowing the income gap between low-income families with wage earnings and those without. Simultaneously, they widen the gap between families with low earnings and those with high earnings, because they deprive the former of income supplements to their wages. Whether the resulting changes in the welfare of different groups are regarded as good or bad will obviously depend on a social judgment.

*Social Security*

In some ways the most remarkable aspect of the 1983 budget is its failure to propose any changes in retirement, survivors, and disability insurance under the social security system. This program accounts for one-third of nondefense expenditures other than interest, provides benefits to 36 million people, and has grown continuously and rapidly. Despite the size of the program and a looming deficit, the 1983 budget is silent on changes in social security.

The reason for such forbearance is clearly political. On May 12, 1981, the administration proposed a long list of cuts in social security benefits that would have reduced expenditures in fiscal 1982 by $2.5 billion and that would have reduced the long-run cost of the system by more than 22 percent. This proposal generated opposition remarkable for its unanimity. The Senate voted 96 to 0 to disassociate itself from one of the major elements of the proposal, the sharp cutback in early retirement benefits effective in less than seven months.[13] The administration rapidly conceded that it would consider other cuts that would save as much as the ones it had put forward, but the proposal continued to provoke intense and angry criticism. On September 24, 1981, the president

13. Harrison Donnelly, "Senate Opposes Social Security Cuts," *Congressional Quarterly* (May 23, 1981), p. 895.

announced in a televised address that he would not press for action on his proposals, but instead would create a commission to study the social security system and its problems and to make recommendations for changes. The commission was instructed to submit its report by December 31, 1982, after the midterm elections.

Dealing with the social security system presents the administration with severe political problems that arise from the structure of the system, the peculiar financial difficulties that it is experiencing, and the powerful political support it enjoys with most voters. Payroll taxes levied on employees and employers flow into three trust funds, from which retirement and survivors benefits, disability benefits, and medicare hospital insurance benefits are paid. The balance of the retirement and survivors insurance trust fund is declining and will soon reach zero if no action is taken, but the two other trust funds have surpluses for the time being. Last year Congress authorized the trustees to shift resources among the three funds through "interfund borrowing." At that time it appeared that this flexibility alone would cover benefit payments until 1985, when a scheduled increase in payroll tax rates would generate increased revenues. The worsening recession has made clear, however, that even if reserves of all three funds are pooled and combined with total payroll tax collections at legislated rates, revenues may not be sufficient to meet all benefits promised under current law beyond 1984.[14] Thus, not later than 1983, Congress will have to take steps either to increase revenues (by raising payroll taxes, permitting the trust funds to borrow from the Treasury, or allocating other taxes to social security) or to cut benefits.

After this problem is dealt with, the cost of cash social security benefits as a percent of taxable wages will not rise for about three decades. In the first decade of the twenty-first century the cost of social security will begin a three-decade-long rise, as children born during World War II and the postwar baby boom retire. The cost of social security as a percent of taxable wages will rise by about 40 percent. Tax increases already legislated will cover some

14. *Summary of the 1982 Annual Reports of the Social Security Boards of Trustees,* p. 10.

of that rise and will be sufficient to cover benefits for the next fifty years, but more revenues will be necessary to meet legislated benefits after about 2030, according to current estimates.[15]

This long-run problem is almost entirely independent of the short-run financing difficulties with which Congress must soon deal. The large deficits in the Reagan budget, despite the draconian cuts in nondefense spending other than social security, have led members of Congress to suggest alternative budget strategies that entail significant immediate cuts in social security.[16]

Congress faces two decisions with respect to social security: whether to take up the issue as part of its deliberations on the 1983 budget or to wait until next year, and whether to address only the immediate financial difficulties or to take on the long-term deficit, as well. In making this decision, members of Congress must take into account the administration's desire, shown by last year's proposals, to make drastic reductions in social security benefits. A decision to make some short-run cuts, such as deferral of part or all of the cost-of-living increase, would solve the short-run financing problems of the system and let Congress duck the long-run question for the time being. A decision to wait until next year to take up the issue, after the commission created by President Reagan makes its recommendations, would heighten pressure on Congress to deal with the long-run financing questions as well.

### Housing and Urban Policy

The Reagan administration has assigned most federal urban-related programs low priority and considers them useful offsets for real increases in such other budget categories as defense. The administration is rapidly withdrawing from previous commitments to spend federal money in urban areas (see table 4-4).

The main issue for federal policy toward urban areas is how the federal government can help big cities cope effectively with the

15. The Social Security Act requires the annual presentation of estimates of costs and revenues of the retirement, survivors, and disability insurance systems over the succeeding seventy-five years. Traditionally the actuaries have presented three estimates. In 1981 they presented five. The statements in the text refer to projection IIB, which is based on intermediate assumptions about economic and demographic events.

16. Senator Ernest F. Hollings (Democrat of South Carolina) and Senator Pete V. Domenici (Republican of New Mexico) have each put forward plans under which the annual cost-of-living adjustment in social security would be skipped for one year.

**Table 4-4.  Outlays for Urban and Regional Programs in Constant 1981 Dollars, Fiscal Years 1981, 1983, and 1985**
Billions of dollars unless otherwise specified

|  |  | Projected | |
| --- | --- | --- | --- |
| Program | 1981 | 1983 | 1985 |
| Community development block grant | 4.0 | 2.9 | 2.7 |
| Urban development action grant | 0.4 | 0.5 | 0.4 |
| Economic Development Administration and | | | |
| Appalachian Regional Commission | 1.0 | 0.5 | 0.1 |
| Other community and regional development | 2.4 | 2.3 | 2.0 |
| Total | 7.8 | 6.2 | 5.2 |
| *Addendum* | | | |
| Housing assistance (net number of units newly | | | |
| authorized for assistance) | 230.6 | −36.0 | n.a. |

Sources: *Budget of the United States Government, Fiscal Year 1983*, p. 5-93; and Department of Housing and Urban Development, *Summary of the HUD Budget for Fiscal Year 1983* (HUD, 1982), p. H-5.
n.a. Not available.

fiscal consequences of heavy concentrations of poor people. Providing such help has long been regarded as a proper federal role because poverty results in part from the operation of the national economy and because big cities contain a disproportionate share of the poor.

Past experience indicates that poverty, unemployment, crime, arson, drug addiction, and related maladies among the unskilled urban poor remain disproportionately high even during periods of high economic growth and low unemployment at the national level. In 1980 the fraction of people in central cities with incomes below the official poverty level was 17.2 percent, higher than the 15.4 percent in nonmetropolitan areas, and more than double the 8.2 percent in all suburbs combined.[17] Moreover, aiding the poor requires some federal involvement. State or local governments cannot effectively alleviate the problems of the poor, because they fear that if they try to tax the nonpoor heavily to aid the poor, many of the nonpoor will move, usually to nearby suburbs where taxes are lower and they command a political majority. Hence only the federal government, with its relatively inescapable tax system, can finance assistance to poorer citizens and the local governments that serve them.

17. Bureau of the Census, *Current Population Reports*, series P-60, no. 127, ''Money Income and Poverty Status of Families and Persons in the United States: 1980'' (Advance Data) (GPO, 1981), p. 4.

Recognizing these facts, every administration in recent decades has supported programs that extend financial aid to certain areas. The Nixon administration, for example, initiated community development block grants. The Carter administration spent billions of dollars in its first two years on various antirecession programs tilted toward big cities, assisting both their residents and their governments. Examples are local public works grants, comprehensive employment and training programs, and countercyclical revenue sharing. This aid declined in the last two Carter years but remained sizable through fiscal 1981. Big-city governments received over 40 percent of their revenues from transfers directly from the federal government or from states (which in turn received aid from the federal government).

Most of these programs have been condemned as failures by the Reagan administration, with varying degrees of accuracy. But even programs that produced little useful real output transferred income to hundreds of thousands of low-skilled, low-income urban citizens who were having difficulty finding employment in the private economy. Insofar as the Reagan budget recognizes the problems caused by concentrated urban poverty, it proposes mainly to rely on private-sector economic growth and locally raised public-sector revenues.

*Community and Regional Development*

The budget explicitly identifies community and regional development as areas where federal spending should be reduced, both to ease budgetary strains and to "get out of the way" of the private sector. The budget authority for both the Economic Development Administration and the Appalachian Regional Commission is virtually eliminated in 1983, a saving of $817 million from 1981. Real outlays taper off more gradually, from $961 million in 1981 to $492 million in 1983 and $132 million in 1985. (Other regional economic development commissions were abolished earlier.) These agencies are good candidates for elimination. The actions of both have always been gestures of federal concern, more symbolic than effective in reviving the depressed areas they were supposed to serve.

Real spending on community development block grants and urban development action grants is scheduled to fall by 23 percent from 1981 to 1983, and by 30 percent from 1981 to 1985. Obligational authority in nominal terms is constant at $3.9 billion a year from 1982 through 1985, after a drop from $4.4 billion in 1981. These grants are an important way of providing public support to city governments and of helping them cope with their disproportionate share of the nation's poor residents. The money can be used for many physical improvements at the discretion of local governments. The budget states that by not giving inflation allowances for discretionary programs, the federal government "will provide a powerful incentive to reduce overhead, waste, and low-priority activities."[18] It seems likely that a 30 percent real cut in four years will reduce "truly productive" activities too.

Although the 1983 budget frowns on urban areas, it smiles on the countryside. Real spending on rural development in 1983 is 27 percent higher than in 1981, though it falls back close to the 1981 level by 1985. As a result, federal spending on rural development rises from 19 percent of combined community development block grant and urban development action grant outlays in 1981 to 31 percent in 1983 and 28 percent in 1985. The budget provides no explanation for this disparity of treatment. Many rural areas have grown rapidly in population and need added community facilities, but the problems faced by urban areas continue to be serious.

Altogether, outlays on community and regional development are scheduled to fall in real terms from $9.4 billion in 1981 to $6.3 billion in 1983 and $5.3 billion in 1985—declines of 33 percent and 44 percent, respectively, from 1981. About $1 billion of this drop results from assuming that no further disasters like the Mount Saint Helens eruption will occur, but the rest consists of genuine cutbacks.

### Housing Subsidies

Because expenditures for housing assistance start several years after initial commitments, housing subsidies will continue to increase from 1981 through 1985 despite sharp cuts in the number of units to be added. Outlays on housing assistance in real terms rise from $6.9 billion in 1981 to $7.8 billion in 1983 and 1985 (up 13 percent over 1981). In contrast, nominal budget authority for

18. *Budget of the United States Government, Fiscal Year 1983*, p. M18.

housing assistance plummets from $26.1 billion in 1981 to − $3.9 billion in 1983 and $2.1 billion in 1985.[19]

This drop reflects a major policy decision to end almost all subsidies for newly constructed units and to slash commitments to other housing assistance as well. The Department of Housing and Urban Development (HUD) plans to cancel about half the 700,000 new subsidized units in process or under construction in 1982. After 1983 HUD will authorize construction of only 10,000 new subsidized units a year (exclusively for the handicapped and the elderly), more than 90 percent fewer than the 111,600 new or substantially rehabilitated units authorized in 1981 and than comparable totals in preceding years. Nevertheless, HUD expects the number of subsidized units to rise from about 3.4 million at the end of 1981 to about 3.8 million at the end of 1985. Half this increase of 100,000 units a year will come from completion of units already in progress, the other half from assistance under a revised housing voucher program. Under this program eligible households would be given a certificate whose value would depend on local housing costs and family income. Households could use the voucher to pay for all or part of the cost of any rental housing unit they might select.

The voucher program resembles the section 8 existing rental housing program, under which eligible households receive subsidies based on family income, but only if they reside in specified existing housing units.[20] The voucher program contains three administrative changes designed to improve cost-effectiveness. Payments under the voucher program will depend solely on incomes of assisted households and average area-wide housing costs, not on individual rents. Each household will be free to negotiate its own housing arrangements with no rent ceiling, as long as it occupies a standard unit. And assistance will be provided in five-year, no-increase contracts with households, rather than fifteen-to-forty-year contracts with landlords. Present section 8 existing rental housing contracts will gradually be converted to

19. For housing programs, budget authority is the sum of new budget authority in the current year less rescissions of previous budget authority. The 1983 budget would rescind $3.9 billion more of budget authority from years before 1983 than it would provide in 1983.

20. Section 8 consists of two parts. Under one part, subsidy contracts are tied to the construction of new housing units. Under the other, subsidies are provided to tenants of existing housing units.

this same arrangement. Experience with the Experimental Housing Allowance Program, a multiyear study of housing vouchers, indicates that these improvements will induce recipients to strike improved bargains with their landlords.

About 111,600 households will be authorized to receive aid through such vouchers in 1983. About 60,600 of these households will be shifted from present rent subsidy programs; 30,000 will be housed in units to be rehabilitated under a new program that is to provide grants of up to $5,000 a unit; and 10,000 will be placed in units now owned by HUD.

Assistance to occupants of existing public housing units will also be cut. The fraction of income required for rent will rise from 25 to 30 percent, and the cash value of food stamps will be included in the income used as a base for computing rents. Families in public housing that receive food stamps will experience a rent increase in 1983 averaging 26 percent, though their rents will still be significantly below those available in the private sector.

HUD defends these cuts in federal housing aid on three grounds. First, the administration holds that its economic program will boost the incomes of the poor and reduce their need for housing subsidies. Second, budget cuts, it is argued, must be made somewhere, and housing subsidies are a reasonable target, because the vast majority of Americans—including most poor households—are well housed. Third, creation of new subsidized housing can be ended because the existing inventory, plus new unsubsidized private construction, is sufficient to provide basic shelter for everyone. As HUD points out, "the major housing challenges we now face are how to help the very poor afford decent housing, how to maintain and preserve the existing housing stock, and how to assure equal opportunity and access to housing markets for all households."[21] Thus the key housing problem of the poor is no longer physically inadequate units, but high housing cost. In 1979 the fraction of renters paying 50 percent or more of their incomes for rent was 49 percent among those with incomes under $7,000, and 73 percent among those with incomes under $3,000.[22]

21. Department of Housing and Urban Development, *Summary of the HUD Budget for Fiscal Year 1983* (HUD, 1982), p. H-2.
22. Bureau of the Census, *Current Housing Reports,* series H-150-79, *Annual Housing Survey, 1979,* pt. C: "Financial Characteristics of the Housing Inventory" (GPO, 1981), p. 7.

Does it make sense to curtail financial assistance when high housing expense, rather than physically inadequate housing, is the main housing problem faced by the poor? It is certainly sensible to shift from subsidizing costly new units for the poor to helping them pay rents on existing units. But it does not seem reasonable to cut back on the second kind of assistance too—unless other income assistance to the poor is simultaneously being expanded. But in fact it is being cut.

Furthermore, the administration's increased reliance on the existing housing inventory and unsubsidized new construction to aid the poor coincides with two factors likely to create at least a mild rental housing shortage. First, high interest rates in 1981 and 1982 have depressed new housing construction. Second, housing demand will increase as more people born during the baby boom reach their late twenties and early thirties. Also, because the real cost of homeownership is much higher in the 1980s than in the 1970s, housing demand is likely to shift from owner-occupied housing to rental units. As a result, rents will probably rise faster than consumer prices generally for the first time in twenty years.

For many years the designers of urban policy have been unable to resolve the conflict between providing aid for people, such as income support or social services, and providing aid to places, such as grants for commercial redevelopment or new housing. The Reagan administration has resolved that conflict by seeking major reductions in both.

*Urban Transportation*

Real federal outlays on ground transportation will fall from $17.1 billion in 1981 to $11.4 billion in 1983 (down 33 percent) and to $9.7 billion in 1985 (down 43 percent from 1981). Specific declines from 1981 to 1983 stated in 1981 dollars are $2.6 billion in railroad subsidies (down 71 percent), $1.8 billion in highway subsidies (down 20 percent), and $1.1 billion in urban mass transit subsidies (down 28 percent). The most important of these reductions for cities is in urban mass transit aid, because federal operating-cost subsidies will be eliminated. In 1981 the federal government paid about 15 percent of the operating costs of all urban public transit systems. The administration proposes to continue some capital subsidies, though not for new fixed-rail systems, which are more costly to build and operate than alternative modes of transportation. But it also plans to phase out operating-cost grants over a three-year period. It argues that federal subsidies have let local governments avoid raising fares to cover costs and have perpetuated inefficient forms of service. Not only are these claims valid, but federal subsidies also contribute to another major inefficiency: high wage settlements by labor unions with power over wage levels and organization of local transit service. Transit drivers are paid as much as $12 an hour, as against $5 an hour for taxi drivers and nothing for the millions of auto commuters who drive themselves. In 1978 over half of all federal spending on urban highways and mass transit went into mass transit, which accounted for only 3 percent of all urban passenger miles traveled.[23]

Withdrawal of federal subsidies for operating costs would create critical problems for many public transit systems. Systems that provide overexpensive service to low-density areas at fares below cost will change to less extensive routes and more diversified services, not confined to those operated by union-wage drivers. Such services could include jitneys, taxis for the elderly and handicapped paid for by vouchers, van pools partly financed by employers, and higher-priced peak-hour buses.[24]

Because mass transit is locally produced and consumed, placing responsibility for both funding and operating it on states and localities appears sensible. Abolition of federal subsidies would force localities to confront the true costs of their present transit services, which are now masked by those subsidies. The transition would be painful in many cases, especially for the New York area, which has 32 percent of all mass transit patronage. But it should improve the efficiency of the transportation system.

Complete abandonment of responsibility for mass transit operations by the federal government raises two important equity issues. One concerns the disparity of resources among different regions. It seems reasonable for each region to pay for its own public services, like mass transit, but such energy-rich states as Oklahoma have abundant taxable resources, while others like

23. This estimate applies to spending in 1975. It was made by Alan Altshuler in *The Urban Transportation System: Politics and Policy Innovation* (MIT Press, 1979), p. 35.
24. For an excellent analysis of the future of urban mass transit, see Milton Pikarsky and Christine M. Johnson, "After the Dust Settles: Transit in Transition," working paper (Chicago, 1981). Pikarsky is at the Illinois Institute of Technology Research Institute, and Johnson is with the Checker Taxicab Company.

Maine do not. Is it just that the former with lower tax rates can buy much better public services, in general, and mass transit services, in particular, than the latter can?

The second issue arises because mass transit is used disproportionately by people with little income, the aged, and those with disabling handicaps. In the United States public transit is mainly an "inferior good"; that is, as soon as you can afford a car, you stop using the bus. Thus many transit patrons—especially those who travel outside of rush hours—cannot afford private cars, or cannot use them because of handicaps. Forcing transit systems to raise prices would increase the economic burden on these involuntary patrons, many of whom are poor. However, the most deprived could often be provided superior service by alternative systems that do not cover such extensive routes or use such expensive drivers. Examples are taxi service for the handicapped or non-union-driven van service for the elderly. In the case of public mass transit, therefore, the stimulus to greater efficiency caused by withdrawal of federal operating-cost subsidies probably outweighs the negative effects.

**Health**

Federal health policy has long pursued three objectives that now are in open conflict with one another. The federal government has tried to improve access to medical services of the poor, the aged, and selected groups such as Indians. It has underwritten the largest program of biomedical research in the world, principally through the National Institutes of Health. Finally, it has sought to hold down the costs both of its own programs and of those financed by private expenditures or by state or local governments.

The 1983 budget sustains federal interest in research and emphasizes cost containment, but signals a broad retreat in efforts to improve the access to medical care of groups that cannot afford it.

*The Health Budget*

Expenditures on health care are among the most rapidly growing in the federal budget because of rising outlays under medicare (see table 4-5). Medicare has covered the aged since it began in

Table 4-5. Outlays for Federal Health Programs in Constant 1981 Dollars, Fiscal Years 1981, 1983, and 1985

Billions of dollars

| Program | 1981 | Projected | |
| --- | --- | --- | --- |
| | | 1983 | 1985 |
| Medicare | 39.1 | 44.5 | 50.2 |
| Medicaid | | | |
| Federal | 16.9 | 14.9 | 16.3 |
| State | 13.2 | 14.4 | n.a. |
| National Institutes of Health | 3.4 | 3.1 | 2.8 |
| Other[a] | 6.6 | 5.8 | 5.2 |

Sources: *Budget of the United States Government, Fiscal Year 1983*, p. 5-130; and Health Care Financing Administration, unpublished data.

n.a. Not available.

a. Excludes Department of Defense and Veterans Administration programs, Federal Employees Health Benefits, health-related student loans, and assistance to health maintenance organizations.

1966 and the disabled and those with end-stage kidney disease since 1973. Medicaid, the next largest federal health program, pays for acute and long-term care for recipients of AFDC, for the aged and disabled poor, and, in thirty states, for the "medically indigent," or people with low incomes who are not receiving welfare. To obtain federal matching grants under medicaid, states must offer seven mandatory medical services and cover all persons who are receiving supplemental security income or aid to families with dependent children. But states may cover additional people and offer additional services. The rest of the health budget will have been reduced 11 percent in real terms between 1981 and 1983 if all changes proposed by the president are adopted. These outlays consist of $4 billion on health research, mostly by the National Institutes of Health, $1.5 billion on four new block grants created last year that absorbed many grant programs, and the remainder on a variety of programs that for the most part were significantly cut last year and are slated to be cut again this year.[25]

Under medicare and medicaid the federal government, with some help from the states, has shouldered primary responsibility for financing medical care for groups that have great need for care but often little capacity to pay for it. Both programs have tried to

25. The budget does not include in the health function the large expenditures for health care undertaken by the Defense Department for members of the armed services and their families and by the Veterans Administration or health insurance premiums for federal employees.

bring their beneficiaries into the mainstream of American medical care, paying for almost the same care, in the same institutions, that is available to more affluent Americans.

The results have been impressive. All indicators show that the elderly use hospital and nursing home services far more than they did before medicare. The poor that are covered by medicaid now use about as much medical care as the more affluent. The increased use of medical services may have contributed to the large gains in life expectancy among the elderly since 1965 and to the sharp drop in infant mortality, especially among blacks.[26]

National medical expenditures have also risen dramatically in constant 1980 dollars, from $124 billion, or 6.0 percent of GNP, in 1965, to $247 billion, or 9.4 percent of GNP, in 1980. The main forces behind this growth have been the increased range and power of medical services and the rising income of American consumers, accompanied by spreading third-party coverage, since World War II. The aging of the population has contributed only slightly to past increases in health care expenditures, but it will be more important in the future.

### Background on Efforts to Contain Costs

By the early 1970s it was clear that the growth of medical expenditures, both governmental and national, was not a temporary problem, but one with deep and persistent causes. The first efforts to slow the growth of federal expenditures did not alter the basic nature of medicare and medicaid. In 1972 Congress authorized professional standards review organizations, groups of physicians charged with reviewing hospital stays for medicare and medicaid patients and empowered to disallow payment for medically unnecessary services. The same legislation gave medicare administrators the right to limit hospital payments. Individual states began to require hospitals to obtain state approval before undertaking major investments, seeking thereby to eliminate "unnecessary" or duplicative facilities. In 1974 Congress required all states to enact legislation requiring health care providers to obtain a certificate of need for new investments and stated that payments under the Public Health Service Act could be denied if states failed to comply.

26. See Louise B. Russell, "Medical Care," in Joseph A. Pechman, ed., *Setting National Priorities: Agenda for the 1980s* (Brookings Institution, 1980), pp. 178–80.

The Nixon administration imposed wage and price controls on the health industry (from August 1971 to early 1974) as part of the economic stabilization program and left these controls in place for some months after those on the rest of the economy had been lifted. The controls interrupted the rapid growth of health expenditures, which averaged 8.4 percentage points more than the increase in the consumer price index for the five years preceding the freeze. As soon as controls were removed, expenditures shot up and rose an average of 11.1 percentage points a year more than the consumer price index through 1977.

Continued growth in expenditures led Presidents Ford and Carter to propose more fundamental changes. President Ford proposed limits on the rates of increase of reimbursement for hospitals and physicians under medicare. He also proposed billing patients for 10 percent of the costs of hospitalization. In return, coverage of very large bills would have been improved. Congress never considered these proposals seriously, and President Carter withdrew them.

Instead of trying to control the growth of medicare and medicaid alone, President Carter asked Congress to limit the growth of hospital expenditures in general. Such a limit would have reached not only the 75 percent of medicare and almost 40 percent of medicaid expenditures represented by hospital bills, but also private expenditures. Confronted with intense lobbying from the hospital and business sectors, Congress did not enact the Carter proposals, ostensibly because it wanted to see whether the so-called voluntary effort by hospitals to hold down costs would prove effective and obviate the need for federal regulation. The voluntary effort survived as long as the possibility of federal legislation seemed real, and held growth of hospital expenditures to only 3.4 percentage points more than the rise in the consumer price index from 1978 through 1979. Cost containment legislation was defeated definitively in 1979. By 1981 hospital expenditures were rising 8.4 percentage points more than other prices.

As the years of swelling medical expenditures have become decades, it has become clear that fundamental changes are necessary if expenditures are to be controlled. Effective cost control must alter the incentives of patients and providers, either through cost sharing or through some kind of budget limit. Cost sharing forces patients to consider whether the care they seek is worth what it costs them.[27] Budget caps place a limit on the revenues of hospitals or other providers. Implementing a budget limit would require a considerable amount of regulatory interference, however. How should hospital limits vary with the facilities, case mix, and fixed costs of each hospital? Before increasing reliance on cost sharing, it would be necessary to decide whether payments should depend on the income or other characteristics of patients or providers. If beneficiaries were required to choose among alternative health insurance plans, it would be necessary to decide what protections to give patients, particularly the elderly, who may be too uninformed or bewildered to make sound judgments. These and other questions will have to be addressed in the competition plan that President Reagan has promised to present.

Some people hold out hopes that two other approaches to medical care—consumer education and scientific advances—may reduce costs, but these are at least as likely to raise costs as to lower them. Consumer education may deter people from seeking care for trivial or self-healing illnesses, but there is considerable risk that improved consumer education will increase demand for medical care, and, in any event, consumer education itself is costly. In the long run scientific advances may reduce the cost of health care. But though discovery of the fundamental causes of major life-threatening or disabling diseases may prevent premature deaths, it may also increase the frequency of slow and costly decline and the opportunities for costly medical intervention to improve the quality of life during these declining years.

## 1983 Budget Proposals

The health proposals in the 1983 budget reflect no unifying theme or philosophy other than the desire to hold down costs. They constitute a mélange of short-term measures to slow the growth of health outlays while the administration completes the design of its competitive strategy to slow the long-run rise in the cost of medical services. Because federal programs focus on

27. Results from a major health insurance study initiated by the Office of Economic Opportunity, continued by the Department of Health, Education, and Welfare (now the Department of Health and Human Services), and managed by the Rand Corporation show that the demand for health care is 14 percent greater when there is no cost sharing than when patients must bear 25 percent of the cost (up to $1,000 or a certain fraction of income, if less). See Joseph P. Newhouse and others, "Some Interim Results," p. 1501.

vulnerable populations, notably the aged, disabled, and poor, the reductions will cut the access of these groups to medical care, thus reversing a trend dominant since medicaid and medicare were enacted in 1965.

Proposed cuts in medicare total $2.5 billion in 1983. The most important would disallow reimbursement for 2 percent of every medicare hospital bill. Hospitals would be paid 98 percent of their incurred costs and would be prohibited from charging the patient the remainder. This proposal would reduce federal spending by an estimated $653 million in 1983. A large part of these costs would reappear as increases in private insurance, as hospitals tried to shift costs to other payers. An additional $306 million would be saved by requiring employers to provide the same insurance for workers aged sixty-five through sixty-nine as they offer to younger workers and by requiring such insurance to pay for care before medicare is billed. At present, private health insurers are usually charged for the medical costs of elderly workers only after medicare has paid for all covered services. Because medical care is more costly for elderly persons than for younger workers, and because most employers pay premiums that cover the actual cost of care for their employees, this provision may deter employment of older workers. The administration has eliminated professional standards review organizations on the ground that they do not save money, yet it claims $362 million in savings from the proposed expansion of utilization review by contractors who process medicare claims. A variety of smaller changes—shifting the update of physician fees from July to October (the next fiscal year), raising the deductible charged for coverage of physician bills to take account of inflation, reducing reimbursement for hospital-based radiologists and pathologists, delaying medicare coverage until the first full month of eligibility, and others—make up for the rest of the proposed $2.5 billion cut.

The administration also seeks to impose medicare payroll taxes on federal employees, most of whom acquire eligibility from nonfederal employment during their working lives. This proposal is a new, but justified, tax for these federal employees, yielding $619 million in 1983.

The list of proposed changes in medicaid is almost as long as the list for medicare, but the effects on access are likely to be more serious, because medicaid benefits in many states are already far more restrictive than medicare benefits.[28] For example, medicaid in New Hampshire covers only twelve days of hospitalization a year; Tennessee and Kentucky cover fourteen days.[29] A 1975 survey of the Health Care Financing Administration found that medicaid fees were roughly three-quarters of those under medicare. Another survey found that medicaid reimbursements were 40 percent below normal fees.[30] Only half the people living in families with incomes below the official poverty line ($8,450 for a family of four in 1980) are eligible for medicaid.

The most important cuts in medicaid would reduce the federal matching rate for optional services and optional beneficiaries by three percentage points. All states offer some optional services; the most important, intermediate care, accounts for 27 percent of total medicaid expenditures.[31] In addition, the administration proposes to stop matching payments for the medicare part B premiums of those medicaid beneficiaries who are also eligible for medicare. In combination, these cuts would save $803 million in 1983 if adopted.

In addition, the administration would require medicaid patients to pay small sums for physician and hospital services; this cost sharing is projected to save $329 million. Reductions in eligibility for AFDC and SSI welfare payments, increased authority for states to collect nursing home costs from patients' relatives and estates, a cap on administrative costs, and other changes, are expected to bring net savings to almost $1.6 billion, a $2 billion saving for the federal government and a $0.4 billion increase in costs for the states. These proposals follow the administration's attempt last year to place a cap of 5 percent on the allowable annual increase in medicaid expenditures. Bipartisan congres-

28. One very important exception to this statement is the coverage of long-term care or nursing home services, which is far more generous under medicaid than under medicare. In fact, 41 percent of medical expenditures under medicaid in 1981 went for long-term care.

29. National Governors' Association, *Catalogue of State Medicaid Program Changes* (Washington, D.C.: NGA, 1981), pp. I-7–I-10.

30. Data provided by the Congressional Budget Office.

31. Intermediate care includes some costly nursing home care for the elderly. But it also permits physicians to discharge patients who are unable to care for themselves from hospitals to less costly nursing home beds.

sional rejection of that proposal last year suggests that the proposed cuts in medicaid will face considerable opposition.[32]

The most striking proposed change in medicaid, announced by President Reagan in the State of the Union Message, calls for federal assumption of full financial responsibility for medicaid in return for full assumption by the states of the costs of food stamps and AFDC. Unfortunately, no detailed plan existed at the time of the speech. It was not clear whether the enormous geographic variations in medicaid would be allowed to persist. The best guess is that some attempt will be made to set national standards, but it is unclear at what level these standards would be set and what protections would be afforded present beneficiaries. It is also unclear whether administration, now almost wholly in the hands of the states, would be federalized and, if so, what protections would be afforded state administrative employees. The Department of Health and Human Services began the task of answering these questions only after the president's speech in which the plan was unveiled.

### Block Grants in Health Services

During the 1960s and 1970s successive administrations sought, and Congress enacted, many narrowly targeted grant programs to achieve specific health objectives. Almost as the programs were being created, these same administrations and Congresses recognized that their number bred confusion. As early as 1966 President Johnson sought to consolidate nine formula grants under the Partnership in Health Act. Last year President Reagan requested that twenty-six programs be lumped together in two block grants, one for preventive health and one for health services. The president sought simultaneously to reduce authorizations of these programs from $1.9 billion to $1.4 billion, a 25 percent cut in both preventive health and health services.

Congress gave the president some of what he sought. It created four block grants: in preventive health and health services; in

32. Instead of a cap, Congress merely cut its projections of the growth of medicaid expenditures in the budget resolution. Of greater significance, Congress authorized the negotiation by states of lower charges through restrictions on providers, capitation, and prospectively determined payments, instead of relying on cutbacks in eligibility and benefits. It is too early to know what savings will be achieved.

maternal and child health; in alcohol, drug abuse, and mental health (little changed from previous structure); and in primary care (which simply renamed the existing community health center program). Real expenditure on these programs was reduced by 28 percent. Of greater significance was the complete exclusion from the block grants of ten programs that the president had wanted to include, among which venereal disease control, family planning, and migrant health centers were the most visible and most controversial. But the real outlays for these programs were cut 19 percent. Given the financial difficulties that many states are experiencing, few are likely to find resources to make up for reduced federal spending.

For 1983 the administration again proposes to include in block grants the programs whose separate status Congress protected last year. In particular, the 1983 budget again seeks to fold migrant health and family planning into the primary care block grant. The maternal and child health block grant would absorb the nutrition program for women, infants, and children, now administered by the Department of Agriculture, and $284 million would be cut from the $934 million allocated to the program in 1982.

### The Plan to Promote Competition

The administration's long-awaited proposals to promote competition in the medical system are expected later this year. The administration must decide whether to try to promote competition in private insurance, in medicaid and medicare, or in both. Application of the competitive strategy to private insurance raises very different issues from those relating to publicly financed programs.

If the administration decides to tackle private insurance, the legislation is expected to resemble the competition bills submitted in the past by, among others, former congressman David A. Stockman and former senator Richard S. Schweiker. These proposals sought to control the cost of health care by increasing the sensitivity of patients and providers to the costs of the services they seek and provide, primarily by requiring employers to offer several plans to their employees (ideally, one a health maintenance organization [HMO]—an organization of physicians that undertakes to provide or arrange for virtually all the medical care required by the plan's subscribers in return for a fixed annual payment—and another with substantial cost sharing) and by setting a limit on health insurance premiums that employers may deduct as legitimate business expenses or that employees may exclude from taxable income.[33] These measures are designed to encourage workers to weigh the value of additional health benefits against other consumer goods. An employee who chooses a plan that costs less than the employer's contribution (which would be required to be uniform for each plan) would receive a rebate.

The chief obstacles to applying the competitive strategy to the private sector are political. Few groups involved in the delivery of health care stand to gain from an increase in competition; most, therefore, will fight it. Furthermore, slowing growth in the cost of private insurance has little direct effect on the federal budget.

Applying the competitive strategy to public programs would directly affect the budget and should have considerable political appeal, but it is not clear how to implement the strategy. In principle, the competitive strategy is simple enough: the government would offer beneficiaries vouchers for the purchase of private insurance, rather than automatically reimburse providers for a predetermined list of services. In practice, however, vouchers are an unknown quantity, and a host of questions must be resolved before they can be issued. A decision must be made on the value of the vouchers and on how the value should vary according to the characteristics of the beneficiary. No one knows how much coverage private insurers can offer for a payment equal to the current cost of medicare per enrollee, particularly because private insurers must incur selling costs that medicare is spared, and would be less able or less willing than medicare to bargain for or to impose low rates of hospital reimbursement.[34] If successful, the competitive strategy might offset these disadvantages in the long run; but in the short run costs might well increase, and even

33. Employers now may deduct without limit the cost of health insurance purchased for employees. Individuals are not required to include in adjusted gross income the value of such employer-financed health plans. In addition, individuals may deduct 50 percent of the health insurance premiums they pay, up to $150, and include additional premiums in health expenditures, which may be deducted to the extent that they exceed 3 percent of adjusted gross income.
34. Some estimates put the initial cost of vouchers offering the same benefits as medicare at 130 percent of current per capita medicare expenditures.

long-run success is speculative. Nor does anyone know how to handle nursing home care, which is seldom covered by private insurers but which accounts for 41 percent of the cost of medicaid.

Faced with such vexing problems, the task forces working on the administration's proposals may treat vouchers as experimental and permit enrollees the option of retaining basic medicare coverage. If this course is followed, a competition plan will have little effect on federal outlays; it may even increase them if high-cost patients remain with medicare while low-cost patients accept the voucher and purchase private insurance. Another course of action, reportedly under consideration, would require hospitals to accept payments fixed in advance under medicare (and conceivably under medicaid when it is federalized). Prospective reimbursement, however, is nothing other than a particular form of budget limit, much like those previously proposed by Presidents Ford and Carter.

In summary, the 1983 budget joins a long list of budget documents that have expressed concern over runaway medical costs and have taken only modest steps to curb them. The administration promises a new competitive strategy for dealing with this fundamental problem and attributes large savings to it in 1983 and later years, but the plan has not been worked out. The 1983 budget makes clear, however, that the twin problems of rising medical costs and federal deficits have terminated efforts to equalize access to medical services. Rather, efforts to curb federal health care expenditures are reviving the question whether the poor, the aged, and the disabled are to be assured health care on the same terms as others.

### Education

The central question posed by the Reagan administration about education is whether there should continue to be an active federal role at all. Education programs rank high among the federal activities that the administration hopes to return to state and local control. This proposed shift would be accompanied by sharp reductions of federal financial support. Real budget authority for elementary, secondary, higher, and vocational education in 1983 will be 43 percent lower than in 1981 if Congress heeds President

**Table 4-6. Total Federal Budget Authority for Education in Constant 1981 Dollars, Selected Fiscal Years, 1981–85**
Billions of dollars

| | | Projected | | |
|---|---|---|---|---|
| Item | 1981 | 1982 | 1983 | 1985 |
| Elementary, secondary, and vocational education | 6.7 | 4.9 | 3.9 | 3.0 |
| Higher education[a] | 10.7 | 9.1 | 6.0 | 4.4 |
| Total | 17.4 | 14.0 | 9.9 | 7.3 |

Sources: *Budget of the United States Government, Fiscal Year 1983*, pp. 5-106–5-107; and table 4-8. Figures are rounded.
a. Includes Department of Education programs, Social Security benefits, GI Bill benefits, and health training.

Reagan's budget requests (see table 4-6). The budget projects a further 26 percent cut between 1983 and 1985. Reductions of this magnitude cannot be construed as simple reforms to eliminate waste, fraud, and abuse. They challenge the assumptions and fundamental purposes that have guided federal policy in education for the last two decades. This year the debate should focus on whether those assumptions and purposes remain valid and important.

Although the history of federal involvement with education begins with the Northwest Ordinance Act of 1787, the rapid growth of federal support for education occurred during the last twenty-five years. The post-sputnik emphasis on improved scientific and technical training gave way during the 1960s and early 1970s to a concern for equality of educational opportunity. For the last decade the main objective of most federal elementary, secondary, and higher education programs has been to increase educational opportunities for those who have lacked them. The largest elementary and secondary programs serving this goal are title I of the Elementary and Secondary Education Act of 1965,[35] which provides extra money for school districts serving low-income, low-achieving youngsters, and the Education for All Handicapped Children Act of 1975, which requires a "free, appropriate education" for all children, regardless of handicap. In 1981 title I provided over $3 billion in compensatory education services for more than 5 million children in 14,000 school districts, and over $1 billion was appropriated to help states and localities

35. Now chapter 1 of the Education Consolidation and Improvement Act of 1981.

meet the costs of educating handicapped children. Other categorical programs, such as Indian education, bilingual education,
follow-through, and the Emergency School Aid Act, assisted
other needy children.

In higher education, the basic educational opportunity grant
program (renamed Pell grants after Senator Claiborne Pell of
Rhode Island) was enacted in 1972 to assist students from low-
income families pay for college. Pell grants, together with other
grant, loan, and work-study programs, contributed over $6 billion
to the support of low- and middle-income students in 1981. Social
security provided nearly $2 billion to eligible families on behalf of
students over eighteen, and the GI Bill contributed more than $1.5
billion in educational benefits to veterans. Enactment of the
education amendments of 1980 reaffirmed the federal partnership
with state, local, and private agencies in supporting equal educational opportunity for all citizens. It is this commitment that the
Reagan administration has cast in doubt.

*Elementary and Secondary Education*

Table 4-7 presents the budget authority requested for the
principal elementary and secondary programs in 1983 and projections for 1985.

The Education Consolidation and Improvement Act of 1981
rewrote the Elementary and Secondary Education Act of 1965 by
combining twenty-nine categorical programs into a state education block grant (chapter 2, ECIA). It retained compensatory
education as a separate program (chapter 1, ECIA), but relaxed
the requirements governing state and local allocation of funds.
When added to the actions taken last year, the proposed 1983 cuts
would reduce real budget authority for compensatory education
by more than 45 percent from 1981 and block grants by 38 percent.
This year the administration proposes two further consolidations,
one for programs serving the handicapped and the other for
vocational and adult education, with increased state and local
discretion in the use of funds.

The administration justifies the proposed cuts in budget authority by noting the "overall need for fiscal restraint" and by
stating that the cuts "represent lower priorities for Federal funding

Table 4-7. **Federal Budget Authority for Elementary, Secondary, and Vocational Education in Constant 1981 Dollars, Selected Fiscal Years, 1981–85**
Billions of dollars

| Item | 1981 | Projected 1982 | 1983 | 1985 |
|------|------|------|------|------|
| Compensatory education | 3.1 | 2.3 | 1.7 | 1.2 |
| State education block grant | 0.6 | 0.4 | 0.4 | 0.2 |
| Indian education | 0.4 | 0.3 | 0.3 | 0.2 |
| Impact aid | 0.7 | 0.4 | 0.3 | 0.2 |
| Education for the handicapped | 1.0[a] | 0.7[a] | 0.7[b] | 0.7[b] |
| Vocational and adult education | 0.8[a] | 0.6[a] | 0.4[b] | 0.4[b] |
| Other | 0.2 | 0.1 | 0.1 | 0.1 |
| Total | 6.7[c] | 4.9 | 3.9 | 3.0 |

Source: *Budget of the United States Government, Fiscal Year 1983*, p. 5-106. Figures are rounded.
a. Existing law.
b. Proposed legislation.
c. The Carter administration had estimated budget authority in fiscal 1981 at $7.3 billion. The main differences are in vocational and adult education ($139 million), education for the handicapped ($50 million), and other ($307 million).

than other activities."[36] The administration also claims that increased flexibility in the use of funds at the state and local level will make it possible for the neediest children to be served despite the sizable cut in resources. This assertion may have some validity, but increased efficiency will not offset a 43 percent cut in real resources over two years. Instead, fewer instructional services will be provided to a smaller number of students.

The administration candidly acknowledges that it does not place much value on the expenditure of federal revenues for the purposes served by these programs, preferring instead to turn back these responsibilities to the states. Some states may take up the responsibilities that the Reagan administration proposes to abandon. But the same incentives that discourage states from providing income assistance to the poor will deter states and, especially, municipalities and school districts from fully replacing federal assistance. The decision to accept or to reject the administration's proposals must address the question of the degree to which a just society will permit large differences in educational opportunities for its citizens.

36. Office of Management and Budget, *Major Themes and Additional Budget Details, Fiscal Year 1983*, p. 152.

Equity, however, cannot be the sole criterion for judging the proposed budget cuts. If programs such as title I did not produce gains in educational achievement, then the funds should be cut, and their loss would have little effect on educational opportunity. But a recent comprehensive evaluation of title I found statistically significant gains in achievement by title I students relative to control groups.[37] Educational gains were made in mathematics in all six primary grades and in reading in grades one through three.

The more difficult question is whether the increased achievement of 15 to 20 percent per student in the primary grades is worth the roughly $460 spent per child from title I funds.[38] Until more is known about the subsequent education and employment of students helped by title I, it is not possible to compare benefits with costs. What is clear is that the proposed real cut in title I budget authority of 45 percent between 1981 and 1983 will reduce the number of children receiving compensatory education by approximately 1 million and reduce assistance to those who remain in the program.[39]

Most federal support for handicapped students comes from the state grants authorized by the Education for All Handicapped Children Act, but in 1982 about $360 million also came from compensatory education for state-operated programs (chapter 1, ECIA), from preschool incentive grants, and from other discretionary programs. The administration proposes to consolidate these programs and to provide block grants to the states, which will allow increased flexibility in the use of the funds.[40] The $846 million requested for the consolidated program is roughly half what would be required in 1983 to maintain the federal share at 12

37. Launor F. Carter, *The Sustaining Effects Study: An Interim Report,* prepared for the Department of Education, Office of Program Evaluation (Santa Monica: System Development Corporation, 1980).
38. Janice Anderson, "Executive Summary, Study of the Sustaining Effects of Compensatory Education," memorandum, Department of Education, Office of Planning, Budget, and Evaluation, November 1981, p. 17.
39. The administration estimates that 4.3 million children can be served in fiscal 1983 if states can lower costs per student to $400.
40. The Carter administration early considered a comparable consolidation, but dropped it when political opposition became evident. Constituent groups argued that more federal support for handicapped children would be forthcoming from several programs than from one.

percent of the national average expenditure per pupil, the level achieved in 1981.

The administration also proposes to consolidate vocational and adult education and to cut real spending between 1981 and 1983 by 50 percent. Previous administrations, as well as the Congressional Budget Office, have viewed vocational education as a likely candidate for budget cuts because it is assumed that most states would make up the 10 percent of total costs represented by the federal contribution. Roughly half the federal support is unrestricted, while the other half is bound by various set-asides for disadvantaged students and for activities of particular federal interest. Protected groups are likely to bear a disproportionate share of the cuts if the proposed block grant eliminates the set-asides.

The Reagan administration is proposing to continue the policies for education it established last year—consolidation, large budget cuts, and reduced federal influence on state and local decision-making. A logical extension of these policies would be the eventual elimination of any federal involvement in elementary and secondary education, for as budgets shrink and the focus on target populations weakens, the rationale for federal participation is lost. In 1981 Congress went along with the president with little debate as legislative changes were made under the pressure of the budget reconciliation procedure. This year Congress will have a second chance to consider whether the older purposes are still valid and whether new national needs in education are emerging that may require federal support.

As stated earlier, for at least the last decade, the dominant rationale for federal support of elementary, secondary, and higher education has been to equalize educational opportunity. Federal programs were created because schools and colleges, financed and governed by local, state, and private agencies, were not meeting this objective. Federal financial support enriched the education of low-income, low-achieving children in primary and secondary schools and provided aid for low-income students who could not otherwise have paid for college. These programs have not met all the early expectations held for them, and many need reform. Now, because of the president's budget, Congress must address the question whether to slash these programs as no longer affordable luxuries and return essentially all responsibility for education to state, local, and private sources. Fewer federal dollars and increased state and local discretion are almost certain to reduce spending for education in many states and to diminish opportunity for low-income or disadvantaged groups.

*Higher Education*

The 1983 budget continues the policy begun last year of reducing both the number of college and university students receiving federal assistance and the aid that the remaining beneficiaries will receive (see table 4-8).[41] Most financial aid to students comes through need-based grants or subsidized loans or through such entitlements as the GI bill and social security student benefits. Between 1981 and 1983 the administration proposes to cut these programs by 44 percent in real terms. Additional reductions are scheduled for later years. If the president's program is adopted, the number of awards, other than guaranteed student loans and health training grants, will drop from an estimated 6.1 million to 3.3 million between 1981 and 1983, a decline of nearly 46 percent. An unduplicated count of student recipients does not exist. Nor is it known how many students would be forced by the cuts to withdraw or to cancel plans to attend college, how many would be forced to enroll part-time rather than full-time, and how many would shift from higher-priced to lower-priced colleges. Some of the students whose aid is cut off under these programs might receive aid under the vestiges of other programs. The fate of individual colleges and universities would be strongly affected as well, for the cuts coincide with the decline in the eighteen- through twenty-one-year-old population, and would thereby accentuate the anticipated drop in enrollments.[42]

The main changes proposed by the 1983 budget for higher education are (1) a sharp cut in Pell grants that would reduce the number of students receiving this form of need-based aid by nearly 1 million, and a decline of 16 percent in the real value of the maximum grant between 1981 and 1983; (2) the elimination of

41. Excluded are support for research conducted in universities and tax expenditures that benefit higher education.
42. Because most of the grant programs are forward funded, the effect of cuts in budget authority proposed for 1983 would not be felt until the 1983–84 academic year.

**Table 4-8. Federal Budget Authority for Higher Education in Constant 1981 Dollars, and Number of Students Aided, Selected Fiscal Years, 1981–85**
Awards in billions of dollars; students aided in thousands

| Item | 1981 | 1982ᵃ | 1983 | 1985 |
|---|---|---|---|---|
| *Budget authority* | | | | |
| Pell grants | 2.3 | 2.1 | 1.2 | 0.8 |
| Supplementary educational opportunity grants | 0.4 | 0.3 | 0.0 | 0.0 |
| National defense student loans | 0.2 | 0.2 | 0.0 | 0.0 |
| College work-study program | 0.6 | 0.5 | 0.4 | 0.3 |
| State student incentive grants | 0.1 | 0.1 | 0.0 | 0.0 |
| Guaranteed student loansᵇ | 2.5 | 2.6ᶜ | 2.2 | 2.0 |
| Health training | 0.7 | 0.4 | 0.3 | 0.3 |
| General institutional assistance and other | 0.6 | 0.5 | 0.4 | 0.4 |
| Social security | 1.9 | 1.3 | 0.7 | 0.1 |
| GI Bill benefitsᵈ | 1.5 | 1.1 | 0.9 | 0.5 |
| Total | 10.7 | 9.1 | 6.0 | 4.4 |
| *Students aided* | | | | |
| Pell grants | 2,770 | 2,400 | 1,800 | n.a. |
| Supplementary educational opportunity grants | 615 | 463 | 0 | 0 |
| National defense student loansᵉ | 266 | 256 | 0 | 0 |
| College work-study | 916 | 880 | 666 | n.a. |
| State student incentive grants | 300 | 296 | 0 | 0 |
| Guaranteed student loansᵇ | 3,500 | 2,900 | 2,800 | n.a. |
| Parent loans | 0 | 943 | 1,400 | n.a. |
| Social securityᶠ | 590 | 610 | 316 | 50 |
| GI Bill benefitsᵍ | 681 | 585 | 492 | 331 |

Sources: *Budget of the United States Government, Fiscal Year 1983*, p. 5-107; OMB, *Major Themes and Additional Budget Details, Fiscal Year 1983*, pp. 74–75; and data provided by the Social Security Administration, Veterans Administration, and the American Council on Education. Figures are rounded.
n.a. Not available.
a. Based on funding levels in the fiscal 1982 continuing resolution.
b. For 1982 and after, figures are based on proposed legislation.
c. An additional $300 million may be required to cover the costs of this program.
d. For veterans in higher education only. Figures are awards offset by receipts.
e. Students aided from new capital contributions only; students aided from repayments of previous loans are not included.
f. Figures are for September and are generally lower than figures for months later in the academic year.
g. For veterans in higher education only.

supplemental educational opportunity grants, national direct student loans, and the state student incentive grant programs, all of particular importance to private colleges and universities; (3) reduced subsidies for the guaranteed student loan program and the exclusion of graduate and professional students from borrowing under it; (4) the beginning of the four-year phaseout of social security student benefits enacted last year on the ground that needy recipients, 72 percent of whom are from families poor enough to qualify for need-based grants, could turn instead to grants and loans; and (5) cuts in health professions training programs of nearly 75 percent in real terms from the 1981 figure. No new health professions student loans would be made, nursing student loans and exceptional need scholarships would be eliminated, the national health service corps would receive no new starts, nursing programs would be cut from $50 million to $12.5 million, and no subsidies for physician education would be provided.

The proposed cut in Pell grants would more than reverse the expansion of aid to middle-income students enacted in 1978. The Middle Income Student Assistance Act extended aid to students from families with incomes up to $25,000; the current proposal could limit grants to families with incomes of $15,000 or less, depending on the formula adopted. When the program was created in 1972, the maximum grant was $1,400; after adjustment for inflation, the value of the $1,600 maximum award proposed for 1983 is half that initial award. With the average cost of a year in college currently at $5,500, even the maximum Pell grant available to the neediest students covers less than 30 percent of direct costs.

Costs of the guaranteed student loan program have soared in recent years as the number of borrowers has increased and climbing interest rates have driven up the interest subsidy. Proposals this year to curtail costs include increasing from 5 to 10 percent the fee paid to banks for originating loans, applying a needs test to every borrower, charging a market rate of interest after the second year of repayment, and eliminating graduate and professional student borrowing. Graduate students would be allowed to borrow under a new auxiliary loan program that carries a higher interest rate (14 percent as opposed to 9 percent) and no in-school interest subsidy (the loan enters repayment sixty days after borrowing). Because of the repayment provisions, many banks may be unwilling to lend to graduate students under this program, which operates now in less than half the states.[43]

The need to limit costs in the guaranteed student loan program is clear, but the flat exclusion of graduate students from the

43. Efforts are being made to secure participation of lenders in all states.

program would simply cut off in mid-course an estimated 600,000 graduate and professional students at the very time that there is a perceived shortage of scientists and engineers. Measures to reduce the interest subsidy, while preserving eligibility for graduate students, would reduce use of the program, lower costs, and would preserve options for students who need to borrow to attend a university.

How would the various sectors of higher education fare under the Reagan budget if enacted in its current form? Private colleges would be hit particularly hard, since their students have come increasingly to depend on federal student aid to help cover tuition. The National Institute of Independent Colleges and Universities has estimated that the 1.1 million students receiving aid at private colleges and universities in 1980–81 would lose about $1.3 billion in federal aid, leaving 500,000 students unable to cover the cost of an independent college in 1983–84.[44] Graduate and professional schools would also suffer large drops in enrollments if borrowing under the guaranteed student loan program is prohibited. Public universities would be affected by cuts in both grants and loans, while community colleges would be affected most by the cuts in Pell grants. Bankruptcies and closures of small, nonselective, private liberal arts colleges would increase. Community colleges alone might gain, as students who lack resources shift to relatively inexpensive institutions. Access to elite institutions, both at the undergraduate and professional levels, by students who are not wealthy will be curtailed. If most of the reductions proposed in the 1983 budget are adopted, the proportion of the generation of students nearing college age that will be able to acquire a higher education will be smaller than it has been in recent generations.

In defining the federal role in education, Congress may also consider issues relating to the quality of education. How can brighter and more capable people be lured into teaching? How can links be established and strengthened between the school curriculum and the increasingly technical employment market? At the college and university level, concerns are growing about the obsolescence and deterioration of research equipment, library

44. Virginia Hodgkinson, "The Impact of the President's Budget Proposals upon Students Attending Independent Colleges and Universities" (Washington, D.C.: National Institute of Independent Colleges and Universities, March 1982).

collections, and the physical plant, as well as with the vitality of an aging faculty.

In short, federal educational policy today must address two central questions. Is the goal of equality of educational opportunity still a national concern? And should the national government help states and localities to achieve and maintain high-quality education from primary through professional school? Whether Congress agrees with the administration's negative answers to both questions remains to be seen.

*Employment and Training Programs*

The federal government supports a variety of locally administered manpower training programs under the Comprehensive Employment and Training Act (CETA).[45] In 1981 President Reagan proposed to eliminate public service employment, and Congress agreed. Because of this change and a large drop in training, real expenditures on employment and training programs will fall from $7.9 billion in 1981 to $2.4 billion in 1983.

CETA is due for reauthorization this year, and the president has proposed further cuts in his 1983 budget. He also seeks to eliminate the work incentive program that provides training and jobs for people otherwise dependent on welfare; in its place states would be empowered to require welfare recipients to take special jobs under community work and training programs. He also proposes to reduce sharply the size of the state-federal employment service.

COMPREHENSIVE EMPLOYMENT AND TRAINING. The details of the administration's CETA proposal are contained in a reauthorization plan recently submitted to Congress. Most of CETA's titles will be consolidated into a single block grant to states to pay for the training of welfare recipients and economically disadvantaged out-of-school youths. The proposed plan would permit states to spend a small fraction of the federal grant on other disadvantaged groups. Presumably states would distribute the funds to local

45. CETA provides public service jobs for economically disadvantaged adults in two programs, one designed to handle cyclical unemployment, the other for structural unemployment. Titles II-A, II-B, and II-C give workers training and work experience. Programs for migrant farm workers and native Americans are grouped under Title III. Title IV gives on-the-job work experience for unemployed youth; the Job Corps is administered under this title. Title VIII created the young adult conservation corps.

authorities similar to existing CETA prime sponsors, who would provide training services or contract with others to provide them. States and localities would be prohibited from spending federal funds on public service employment, training stipends, or "work experience" programs. Thus enrollees in local programs would be restricted primarily to on-the-job training with private employers or to formal classroom training in training institutions. A major feature of the proposal is to give substantial control in design and control of the training programs to private business. Real outlays on CETA programs would decline from $8 billion in 1981 to $1.9 billion in 1983.

These changes depart radically from past practice. In 1980 work experience and public service employment constituted two-thirds of the service years provided under CETA. Training stipends, usually set at the minimum wage, have accounted for about half the cost of classroom training to CETA enrollees. Many present CETA participants who are neither young nor welfare recipients would be prevented from participating in training under the president's 1983 proposals.

Contrary to popular belief, manpower programs have been effective in improving enrollees' earnings, though frequently by modest amounts. An exhaustive recent study concludes that four of CETA's five basic employment and training programs—including public service employment—succeeded in raising the post-program earnings of enrollees by 6 to 18 percent.[46] Only CETA's work experience programs failed to raise enrollee earnings. Questions remain about whether the gains in earnings justify the costs. But it does appear that these programs have made progress toward their main objective. In addition, public service employment earnings and training stipends in some measure replace welfare payments on which beneficiaries otherwise would be forced to depend; and public service employees and work experience trainees often provide valued local services for financially hard-pressed counties and municipalities.

WORK INCENTIVE PROGRAM. This program provides manpower counseling and training for AFDC recipients. Participation is

46. Westat, Inc., *Impact on 1977 Earnings of New FY1976 CETA Enrollees in Selected Program Activities,* Employment and Training Administration, Office of Policy, Evaluation, and Research (ETA, 1980).

mandatory for most able-bodied adult AFDC recipients without very young children, and is voluntary for others. The president proposes to eliminate this $381 million program in 1983. The budget states that the work incentive program will be unnecessary in 1983 once states have set up mandated community work experience or "workfare" programs. Presumably the training that would otherwise have been provided by the federal program would then be provided in these community public service projects, where AFDC recipients would be required to work off their welfare grants. Past experience suggests that little if any training would be given on state or local work projects.[47] Although such social services as child care will be curtailed with the elimination of the work incentive program, the effects on AFDC recipients may be mitigated by the concentration on them of such CETA training benefits as remain.

EMPLOYMENT SERVICE. The employment service provides labor market information, especially for low-wage workers who are not well served by private alternatives. Since the 1930s the employment service has told workers and potential workers about available jobs and has sought to make the labor market operate more efficiently by reducing frictional unemployment. Because higher-wage workers tend to find employment through other means, the employment service disproportionately serves low-wage workers and their employers.

The administration proposes to reduce real federal outlays for this service from $804 million in 1981 to $511 million in 1982, and to $426 million in 1983 and subsequent years, a cut of nearly half. The employment service recently has had low placement rates, but there is some evidence that it has nonetheless shortened the duration of unemployment for people it served.[48] What makes this proposed budget reduction puzzling is that job referral assistance is one of the cheapest methods of helping disadvantaged workers

47. See Ketron, Inc., *Food Stamp Workfare Demonstration Project: Interim Report on the Short-Term Impact of the Program* (Wayne, Pa.: Ketron, 1981), pp. 28–31; Wellington Webb and Carla Bodaghi, "Utah Work Experience and Training Assessment," Department of Health, Education, and Welfare, Region 8 (Denver, Colorado: HEW, 1978); and Barry Friedman and others, *An Evaluation of the Massachusetts Work Experience Program* (Center for Employment and Income Studies, Brandeis University, 1980).

48. Terry Johnson and others, *A Pilot Evaluation of the Impact of the U.S. Employment Service* (Menlo Park, California: SRI International, 1979).

to raise their earnings. Since the administration proposes to reduce or to abandon such assistance as training and public service employment, an increase in efforts to make the private labor market work more effectively would seem prudent. The employment service is the most important existing state-federal instrument for accomplishing this goal.

EFFECTS OF THE CHANGES. Because benefits from the work incentive and CETA programs accrue largely to the unemployed and economically disadvantaged, the population that suffers most from the cutbacks is easy to identify. It is the same population hurt most by recent and proposed changes in means-tested transfer programs, namely low-income families with a potential earner.

Taken in combination with the proposed changes in transfer programs, the scheduled reductions in manpower programs appear to represent a systematic withdrawal of both income assistance and manpower services from the working poor in the midst of the most serious economic decline since the 1930s.

**Conclusion**

Emboldened by his success in securing approval for most of the program he proposed in 1981, President Reagan is returning for even larger cuts in domestic programs than he obtained last year. These reductions do more than extend last year's program. Most of the cuts enacted in 1981 reduced the size of the programs they affected but did not change their basic structure. Last year the president persuaded Congress that many programs could be trimmed without undermining their capacity to achieve their basic goals. Furthermore, he assured Congress and the American people that certain programs, basic to economic security, would be preserved as a "social safety net."

Proposals advanced after his budget amendments last year together with the 1983 budget make clear that President Reagan intends to eliminate major social programs and shrink even those that constitute the safety net. In some cases federal spending is to be curtailed enough to require a change in traditional objectives. In others the federal government will withdraw completely and leave to states the decision about whether any services at all are to be provided. The 1983 budget for domestic programs must be viewed not merely as one element in an overall economic plan, but as the boldest and most controversial attempt in fifty years to roll back the place of the federal government as a guarantor of equal opportunity and provider of social services.

CHAPTER FIVE

# The New Federalism

EDWARD M. GRAMLICH *and* DEBORAH S. LAREN

THE ECONOMIC and social changes implicit in President Reagan's budget proposals represent some fundamental alterations in the policies that have been developing since the Great Depression. But nowhere is the change more apparent than in the area of federalism. The United States has fashioned one of the most intricate federal structures in the world, with the federal government underwriting a host of state and local services through an extensive set of grant programs. Reagan's goal is to end many of these arrangements and turn a wide range of spending and taxing decisions back to state and local governments.

In his budget proposals for fiscal 1982, the president called for a consolidation of existing categorical grant programs into more or less unrestricted block grants, coupled with large reductions in funding levels. The proposals for 1983 call for still more consolidations. And for 1984 Reagan proposes what would be the biggest rearrangement of programs in U.S. history: (a) the federal government will "swap" programs with state governments, assuming sole responsibility for the large and rapidly growing medicaid program and giving the states sole responsibility for the aid to families with dependent children (AFDC) program and food stamps; and (b) the federal government will "turn back" respon-

The authors are indebted to Henry J. Aaron, Thomas J. Anton, Harvey E. Brazer, Paul N. Courant, Harvey Galper, Robert W. Hartman, Larry L. Orr, Robert D. Reischauer, and Daniel L. Rubinfeld for their comments on early versions of this paper.

151

sibility for forty-four other grant programs to state governments. For the first four years these programs are to be financed by a special trust fund consisting of excise and some other tax revenues; beginning in 1988 the trust fund will wither away, and states will be responsible for financing and operating any of these programs that they choose to retain. All this takes place against the background of sharp cutbacks in federal grant levels: by 1983 the ratio of grants to GNP will be the lowest it has been since the 1960s.

The president's proposals provide an opportunity to examine carefully the present-day grant system. It has grown rapidly over time, and many problems have developed with it. In this chapter we first review some of these problems. We then discuss all aspects of the president's proposal—the grants that are to be consolidated in fiscal 1983; the swaps envisioned for medicaid, AFDC, and food stamps; and the further arrangement whereby the forty-four other programs would be turned back to states to be financed by the transitional trust fund. Finally, we explore several modifications that could be made in the president's plan and suggest some basic alternatives to it.

**The Role of Grants in the Federal System**

The broad system of governmental responsibilities that has evolved in the United States features extensive sharing of functions. The federal government is solely responsible for such functions as national defense, foreign aid, and space, and for the operation of trust funds for programs like social security. But it leaves the responsibility for the actual operation of almost all other programs to state or local governments. State governments usually operate programs in the areas of mental health, higher education, AFDC, and medicaid, while local governments take responsibility for operating such services as elementary and secondary education, police, fire, and sanitation.

But financial responsibility is not divided in the same way as functional responsibility. The federal government now makes numerous grants to state and local governments, as shown in table 5-1 for the pre-Reagan fiscal year 1981. These grants are the means by which the federal government influences the operation and shares in the cost of many public services actually run by state or

**Table 5-1. Outlays for Federal Grants, by Function and Type, Fiscal Year 1981**
Billions of dollars

| Item | Total | Categorical, payments to individuals | Other categorical | Noncate-gorical[a] |
|---|---|---|---|---|
| | | *Type of grant* | | |
| Energy | 0.6 | . . . | 0.6 | . . . |
| Natural resources and environment | 4.9 | . . . | . . . | . . . |
| Environmental Protection Agency construction grants | 3.9 | . . . | 3.9 | . . . |
| Other | 1.0 | . . . | 1.0 | . . . |
| Agriculture | 0.8 | . . . | 0.8 | . . . |
| Transportation | 13.5 | . . . | . . . | . . . |
| Highway trust fund | 8.6 | . . . | 8.6 | . . . |
| Urban mass transit | 3.8 | . . . | 3.8 | . . . |
| Other | 1.1 | . . . | 1.1 | . . . |
| Community and regional development | 6.1 | . . . | . . . | . . . |
| Community development block grants | 4.0 | . . . | . . . | 4.0 |
| Other | 2.1 | . . . | 2.1 | . . . |
| Education, training, employment, and social services | 21.1 | . . . | . . . | . . . |
| Social services block grants | 2.6 | . . . | . . . | 2.6 |
| Services to selected groups | 2.7 | . . . | 2.7 | . . . |
| Comprehensive employment and training | 5.9 | . . . | . . . | 5.9 |
| Compensatory education | 3.3 | . . . | 3.3 | . . . |
| Other | 6.6 | . . . | 6.6 | . . . |
| Health | 18.9 | . . . | . . . | . . . |
| Medicaid | 16.8 | 16.8 | . . . | . . . |
| Other | 2.1 | 2.1 | . . . | . . . |
| Income security | 21.3 | . . . | . . . | . . . |
| Child nutrition | 3.3 | 3.3 | . . . | . . . |
| AFDC | 8.5 | 8.5 | . . . | . . . |
| Emergency and energy assistance | 1.6 | 1.6 | . . . | . . . |
| Subsidized housing programs | 4.0 | 4.0 | . . . | . . . |
| Other | 3.9 | 3.9 | . . . | . . . |
| Administration of justice | 0.3 | . . . | . . . | 0.3 |
| General government fiscal assistance | 6.8 | . . . | . . . | . . . |
| General revenue sharing | 5.1 | . . . | . . . | 5.1 |
| Other | 1.7 | . . . | . . . | 1.7 |
| Other | 0.5 | . . . | 0.5 | . . . |
| Total | 94.8 | 40.2 | 35.0 | 19.6 |

Source: *The Budget of the United States Government, Fiscal Year 1983, Special Analysis H: Federal Aid to State and Local Governments*, pp. 29–36. Figures are rounded.
a. Items may include some miscellaneous categorical grant outlays.

local governments. As seen in the table, grants are mainly in the areas of health, income security, education and training, and transportation. The largest individual grant programs are medicaid, AFDC, and the highway trust fund.

Since the grant system is so extensive, it is hard to characterize it simply. Broadly speaking, there are two types of grants: categorical and noncategorical. Categorical grants, intended to support specific state and local activities, are the oldest and most diverse, and almost all the early grants (existing before 1970) were of this type. Noncategorical grants grew in the 1970s, but categorical grants still amounted to nearly 80 percent of the grant budget when the Reagan administration took over.

There are several rationales for categorical grants. One is income maintenance. Many of the important income maintenance programs in the United States—AFDC and medicaid most prominently—are financed by federal grants. Grants that ultimately finance payments to individuals totaled $40 billion in fiscal 1981, two-fifths of all grants and over half of all categorical grants. Most of these grants will revert either to the federal government or state governments if the president's proposed program rearrangements are made.

The rationales for other categorical grants vary from program to program. The textbook rationale for grants is based on the presumed existence of benefit spillovers, or gains to other states and communities when the recipient community spends on a public service. Accordingly, the federal government shares in recipient community expenses by providing a matching grant, to encourage the recipient community to spend on the program in question. Grants for natural resource programs and some transportation grants probably adhere closest to this rationale. But sometimes grants seem more to reflect the federal government's desire to preempt state and local program management, or even to have states and localities act as subcontractors to the federal government in operating what are essentially federal programs. Many of the social services grants appear to fit this mold. Others, like grants for compensatory education, can be justified by a combination of income maintenance and subcontracting motives. For some other categorical grants, often those given for very small programs, it is hard to find a strong rationale for federal budgetary expenditure.

Whatever the case, since the usual categorical grant is designed to raise total (federal plus state or local) spending on a particular project, the federal money is accompanied by restrictions on what kinds of state or local spending qualify for federal sharing. Often these categorical grants are given only after federal approval of a state or local project application.

Whereas categorical grants go to states or localities if and only if they are spent on a particular public service, noncategorical grants go to communities as a matter of legal entitlement. Federal controls on the kinds of expenditures are much less binding than for categorical grants. Usually the main point of noncategorical grants is not to raise public spending on a particular program, but to raise local fiscal resources, either because the federal tax system is felt to be more efficient or because state and local fiscal capacities are unequal and the grants try to reduce the disparities.[1]

The least restrictive of the noncategorical grants are called general purpose grants. The main general purpose grant, general revenue sharing, was introduced by President Nixon in 1972. Nixon also made a series of proposals for what were first called special revenue sharing grants and are now called block grants. These block grants, of which the three largest programs are for community development, comprehensive employment and training, and social services, are a hybrid of categorical and noncategorical grants. States and localities simply receive money for spending in a functional area and are relatively free of federal restrictions on how the money is to be spent. If states on their own are already spending amounts as large as the block grant, they can have this spending satisfy the conditions of the grant, and in effect use the grant for tax reduction.

### The Grant System before and after Reagan's Changes

The federal grant system has grown rapidly since the Second World War. As seen in table 5-2, federal grants to states and localities amounted to only $2.3 billion, less than 1 percent of GNP, in 1950. Large highway grants were added in the late 1950s,

---

1. Obviously this short summary does not cover all the rationales and institutional arrangements surrounding either categorical or noncategorical grants. For a thorough discussion, see George F. Break, *Financing Government in a Federal System* (Brookings Institution, 1980), pp. 73–122.

**Table 5-2. Outlays for Federal Grants, by Type, Selected Fiscal Years, 1950–85**
Billions of current dollars unless otherwise specified

| | Total | | Type of grant | | | Programs to be turned back to states |
|---|---|---|---|---|---|---|
| Year | Amount | Percent of GNP | Cate-gorical | General purpose | Block | |
| 1950 | 2.3 | 0.9 | 2.0 | 0.1 | 0.2 | ... |
| 1955 | 3.2 | 0.8 | 2.7 | 0.2 | 0.3 | ... |
| 1960 | 7.0 | 1.4 | 6.5 | 0.2 | 0.3 | ... |
| 1965 | 10.9 | 1.7 | 10.3 | 0.3 | 0.3 | ... |
| 1970 | 24.0 | 2.5 | 23.2 | 0.4 | 0.4 | ... |
| 1975 | 49.8 | 3.4 | 38.2 | 7.0 | 4.7 | ... |
| 1980 | 91.5 | 3.7 | 72.6 | 8.6 | 10.3 | ... |
| 1981 | 94.8 | 3.3 | 77.9 | 6.8 | 10.0 | ... |
| 1982 | 91.2 | 3.0 | 72.4 | 6.5 | 12.3 | ... |
| 1983 | 81.4 | 2.4 | 60.8 | 6.7 | 13.9 | ... |
| 1984[a] | 73.8 | 1.9 | 24.8 | 2.2 | ... | 46.8 |
| 1985[a] | 73.8 | 1.8 | 24.2 | 2.5 | ... | 47.1 |

Sources: *Special Analysis H*, pp. 17, 21; *Budget of the United States Government, Fiscal Year 1983*, pp. 5-130, 5-143, 9-60; *Special Analyses, Budget of the United States Government, Fiscal Year 1980*, p. 230; breakdowns by type of grant for 1950–70 are based on data in the national income and product accounts.

a. Totals differ from amounts shown in the budget for 1984 and 1985 because the budgetary projections do not incorporate the proposed program rearrangement. We have adjusted the budgetary figures by subtracting medicaid ($18.7 billion), no longer a federal grant under the president's proposal, and then adding food stamps, to be made a federal grant. We also deducted all grants on the Office of Management and Budget's "illustrative list" from their present columns and put them in the column on the right. The dollar amount of programs to be turned back then equals that of the forty-four grants ($30.2 billion in 1984), the projected federal AFDC expenses ($6.0 billion), and the projected food stamp expenses ($10.6 billion). Amounts are administration estimates incorporating effects of the proposed funding reductions.

a number of Great Society categorical grants in the late 1960s, general revenue sharing in the early 1970s, and the new block grants in the late 1970s. By 1981 grants equaled $94.8 billion, or 3.3 percent of GNP—a share of GNP almost four times as large as in 1950.

President Reagan's proposals have already changed this picture considerably, and the changes will be even more dramatic if the new program rearrangements are enacted. From the $94.8 billion figure in 1981, the cutbacks in grants already made and those proposed in the 1983 budget lower grants in nominal terms to $81.4 billion by fiscal 1983, a cut of $13.4 billion in two years. By 1983 grants are scheduled to be down to 2.4 percent of GNP, as low as the ratio has been since the 1960s. In addition, Reagan has continued the process started by Nixon of consolidating categorical grants into block grants. Congressional action on his recommendations last year resulted in the consolidation of fifty-seven categorical programs into nine new block grants; this year he proposes converting another forty-one categorical grants into seven new block grants. These changes will shift $10 billion from categorical to block grants between 1981 and 1983, accounting for most of the decline in categorical grants in this period. Block grants will not rise as much as this because Reagan is proposing to cut heavily the block grants resulting from earlier Nixon consolidations and to cut funding for the grants he himself has consolidated. This stands in strong contrast to the strategy followed by Nixon during his grant consolidations: as table 5-2 shows, all types of grants—categorical, general purpose, and block grants—rose sharply in the seventies. In President Reagan's budget proposals, all types of grants decline.

The program rearrangements to take effect in fiscal 1984 make even more significant changes in the historical evolution of the grant system. To begin with, the federal government will assume full responsibility for medicaid and states will assume full responsibility for AFDC and food stamps. These changes lower grants to $73.8 billion, less than 2 percent of GNP. The drop in categorical grants is particularly steep—they are down to just $24.8 billion, or 0.7 percent of GNP, by 1984. General purpose grants are also greatly reduced from their high point in 1980, first because President Reagan has continued a change made initially by President Carter of not appropriating funds for the state share of general revenue sharing, and second because Reagan has proposed to turn general revenue sharing back to state governments. Block grants grow to $13.9 billion in 1983 and then drop to nothing, since they would almost all be turned back. Hence in 1984 the total amount of grants to be transferred to states under the rearrangement is $30.2 billion for the forty-four categorical and general purpose grants that are turned back, $6.0 billion for AFDC, and $10.6 billion for food stamps, making a total of $46.8 billion. The funds to finance these programs would come from the funds that states would no longer need to match medicaid grants and from a special trust fund set up for this purpose. By 1991 the trust fund would be eliminated and states would be on their own, with the federal government having relinquished some of its revenue sources.

## Problems with the Federal Grant System

Since the proposed changes are so dramatic, the existing federal grant system might appear to have serious problems. In fact, it is hard to draw up a consensus list of its problems. What some observers see as problems, others see as advantages. Nevertheless, there are at least a few important agreed-on characteristics of the grant system.

One alleged problem is the sheer size of the grant system. The budget message makes much of the fact that grants grew from $2.3 billion to $94.8 billion between 1950 and 1981. In large part this expansion was caused by the trend growth in prices, population, and real output: as noted earlier, the numbers are not nearly so dramatic when viewed as a share of GNP. An expansion, both in scale and in the types of grants, clearly did occur. But that grants had already declined from their peak levels (as a percent of GNP) even under President Carter suggests that their growth might have been halted even without the Reagan cutbacks.

Another way to look at size is in terms of numbers of grant programs. In one place the budget says there were more than 500 grant programs, in another, only 362, in 1980.[2] Whatever the correct number, the 1982 Reagan proposals consolidated 57 categorical grants into 9 block grants. In addition, the Reagan administration eliminated numerous grant programs, making a net reduction of 141 in the number of grants by 1982. The 1983 proposals would convert 41 categorical grant programs into 7 new block grants, add 4 health programs to 2 existing block grants, and combine the energy and emergency assistance program with the low-income energy assistance block grant. This plus the turnback proposals would bring the net reduction to 222, leaving either more than 278 or 140 grant programs still in existence. This is both a large absolute and percentage reduction in numbers of grant programs and implies a concomitant drop in federal, state, and local management burdens.

A second problem, raised by both fiscal liberals and conservatives, is that grant strategy is not consistent across functions. On

2. The first number comes from Office of Management and Budget, *Major Themes and Additional Budget Details, Fiscal Year 1983*, p. 18; the second from *Budget of the United States Government, Fiscal Year 1983, Special Analysis H: Federal Aid to State and Local Governments*, p. 21.

one side, grants are sometimes given for programs in which the federal interest seems marginal. It is easy to see why a national grant system would be needed to subsidize the development of a national highway system, but harder to see why federal grants should be used to finance local transportation programs that could be left up to local communities. Also, it is hard to justify using national grants for local economic development programs, particularly if these programs merely entice industries away from other areas. One can find many such examples of federal grants dominating what should be state, local, or regional decisions.

But examples can be found on the other side, too. In some cases grants are used when direct federal expenditures seem more appropriate—that is, when states are being asked to share in the expenses of what should be national programs. The prime example of this kind of overuse of the grant system—really the underuse of direct expenditures—is usually taken to be the welfare programs that the president is now proposing to turn over to the states completely. Discussion of this matter will be deferred until the alternatives to Reagan's program are treated.

A third problem with the grant system involves "displacement." Since the system enables government spending programs to be conducted at one remove—the federal government pays and states and localities operate the programs—a slip can occur in the process. Funds will be transferred to states and localities, but they may be able to use these funds to finance state and local spending that would have been made in any case. This will free up the grant funds for a different use—spending on other programs, tax reduction, or even spending on programs that work at cross-purposes with the grant program. Empirical research on existing federal grants indicates a significant amount of displacement, even for categorical grants.[3]

The reason that grant displacement exists and may be so widespread involves two important facts about categorical grants. First, in the average categorical grant not used to finance payments to individuals, the federal matching share is very high, about 80

3. See Edward M. Gramlich, "Intergovernmental Grants: A Review of the Empirical Literature," in Wallace E. Oates, ed., *The Political Economy of Fiscal Federalism* (Lexington Books, 1977), pp. 219–39, for a summary of many studies of federal grants.

percent.[4] If states or localities expect to receive substantially more than 20 percent of the benefits from a program financed by a categorical grant, as they probably do for most grant-financed programs, they may be induced to overspend on the public service in question by the large (80 percent) effective cut in the price of the service. Second, to prevent overspending by states and localities, the federal government must put a cap on grants—that is, limit the amount of grant money individual states and localities can receive. If these limits are small relative to what states and localities would otherwise have spent on the program, the states can claim that their spending satisfies the conditions of the grant and use the new grant money for their own purposes.[5] As one example, a careful study of the federal ABC (noninterstate) highway program indicates that in forty-one states federal grants paid for highways the states would probably have built on their own, and that in the remaining states it was not even clear that the federal grants stimulated road building.[6] Hence the combination of high federal matching shares and caps on grants works to make grant displacement very likely.

Grant displacement is partly responsible for a fourth problem, paperwork. To try to assure that grants do support the intended expenditures, Congress often adds restrictions to grant programs. One kind is an effort-maintenance clause, which attempts to ensure that states spend more on the program in question than they spent before receiving the federal grant. Although such a clause might be effective in the early years of a grant, over time it becomes more and more difficult to define spending in the absence of the grant, and effort-maintenance clauses probably become

4. This share was computed from *Special Analyses, Budget of the United States Government, Fiscal Year 1982*, p. 255. The overall ratio was adjusted to remove the influence of general purpose grants (for which there is no matching) and grants to individuals (where the federal share is close to one-half).

5. A numerical example illustrates the point. Suppose that a state was initially spending $100 on a public service not supported by any federal grant program. The federal government then passed a categorical grant for that service, offering to pay 80 percent of state expenses. If the grant had no cap, the state would presumably be influenced by the lower effective price for the public service and spend more, say $200. At this level the federal grant would be 80 percent of $200, or $160. The federal government might then try to limit its own costs by capping the grant at $80, implying state spending of $100. But this is just what states spent on their own before the grant: the states can claim that their initial spending of $100 fulfills the grant conditions and use the new $80 federal grant for their own purposes.

6. The example is taken from Edward Miller, "The Economics of Matching Grants: The ABC Highway Program," *National Tax Journal*, vol. 27 (June 1974), pp. 221–29.

ineffective. As the typical grant program is being designed, more potential abuses are imagined, more restrictions are added, and more bureaucrats are needed to oversee the restrictions and fill out the forms, so that many of the perceived management inefficiencies of the grant system take life. In addition, grants are often given for small programs without an enduring rationale and sometimes even for programs that work at cross-purposes. As a result, state and local governments have become subjected to an extensive set of federal regulations. Restrictions on federal grants are not the only cause of this red tape, but they are certainly an important cause.[7]

Although nobody will actually come out in favor of paperwork, it should be stressed that elimination of paperwork does not necessarily improve the grant system. As paperwork requirements are eliminated, fewer bureaucrats will be needed to process the forms, but also state and local governments will find it easier to use federal money to displace their own expenditures and hence divert the grant money to their own purposes. A different solution to the joint problem of paperwork and displacement will be described later, when alternatives to the president's program are discussed.

### The President's Program

The president's program consists of several major parts: the further consolidation of categorical grants planned as part of the 1983 budget; the financial arrangements set up for financing the forty-four grants turned back as part of the 1984 budget; and the transfers of AFDC, food stamps, and medicaid from one level of government to another. We now examine each component in more detail.

*Proposed Block Grant Consolidations for 1983*

For fiscal 1982 President Reagan proposed the consolidation of eighty-three categorical grants into six block grants. Though not

7. For an instructive look at federal regulation of states and localities in general, see David R. Beam, "Washington's Regulation of States and Localities: Origins and Issues," *Intergovernmental Perspective,* vol. 7 (Summer 1981), pp. 8–18. The president's message in OMB, *Major Themes,* states that "a typical grant program imposes from 300 to 500 separate requirements and mandates on State and local governments as a condition for receipt of funds" (p. 18).

all these proposals were accepted by Congress, many were. Eventually fifty-seven categorical programs were collapsed into nine block grants, still a large reduction in the number of grant programs. For fiscal 1983 the president is proposing to consolidate another forty-one categorical grants into seven block grants in the areas of vocational and adult education (eight programs), education for the handicapped (thirteen programs), employment and training (four programs), rehabilitation services, child welfare (four programs), rental rehabilitation (two programs), welfare administration, and others. In addition, some consolidations already made last year would be expanded to include more programs. The outlays for all these consolidations made or proposed—the fifty-seven programs in 1982 and the more than forty in 1983—are $5.7 billion for fiscal 1982, rising to $11.9 billion by fiscal 1985. In other words, these block grants are for rather small programs even after the consolidations—the sixteen new block grants average less than $1 billion apiece. The programs, indeed, are so small that it is hard to evaluate the proposal one way or the other.[8]

The consolidations will almost certainly streamline the grant process and improve management efficiency. At the same time, since they involve very small grant programs, states will find it easy to claim that the funds they were spending on similar programs satisfied the spending requirements of the block grant and then to divert grant funds to their own purposes. If important federal goals were being served by the grants, they are likely to be lost in the shuffle.

*The Transitional Trust Fund Arrangement*

Beginning in fiscal 1984, the states will have the option of taking over responsibility for forty-four other grant programs accounting for $30.2 billion in that year. The net drain on state and local budgets will be that amount less the estimated $2 billion saving from the medicaid, food stamp, AFDC exchange. This net cost of $28.2 billion is to be financed by a trust fund consisting of

---

8. For a detailed look at the consolidations already made, which indicates that there is even less to them than meets the eye, see Claude E. Barfield, *Rethinking Federalism: Block Grants and Federal, State, and Local Responsibilities* (Washington, D.C.: American Enterprise Institute for Public Policy Research, 1981), chap. 3.

earmarked alcohol, tobacco, and telephone excise taxes, two cents of the four-cent-per-gallon federal gasoline tax, and a portion of the windfall profits tax on oil.[9]

Leaving aside the big programs—medicaid, AFDC, and food stamps—the first question concerns the grant turnbacks. According to the Office of Management and Budget guidelines, during the first four transition years, 1984–87, "states can use their trust fund money in either of two ways. If they want to continue receiving some or all Federal grants that are designated for turnback, they can use their trust fund money to reimburse the Federal agencies that make those grants, and abide by Federal conditions and rules. Or, to the extent they choose to forgo the Federal grant programs, they can receive their trust fund money directly as super revenue sharing, to be used for these or other purposes."[10] After 1988 the federal government will no longer operate the programs, and the states will be free to continue or discontinue them.

If states take the first option, leaving the present grant programs pretty much intact, the changes are minimal. But if states take the second option, the turned-back grants are immediately converted to general purpose fiscal assistance, less restrictive than even current block grants because the grant money need not be spent for a particular class of programs.

The initial effect of the plan will depend on the extent to which the turned-back programs are now categorically restricted. While detailed descriptions of the proposals are not yet available, OMB has prepared an "illustrative list" of programs to be turned back.[11] The list indicates that the changes implicit in this arrangement may be less significant than most observers are anticipating, since a large share of the grants to be turned back have already been converted to block grant form. Of the $30.2 billion total to be transferred, general revenue sharing, already the most general

9. The amounts of funds involved in the program turnbacks may not balance out in the way the administration envisions. The Congressional Budget Office has calculated that the cost of running the grant programs may be as much as $15 billion above the revenues provided by the designated taxes unless big program cuts are made in the grants. See the testimony of Alice M. Rivlin, director of CBO, before the Senate Committee on Governmental Affairs, March 16, 1982.

10. OMB, *Major Themes*, p. 21.

11. Ibid., pp. 24–25.

purpose of grants, accounts for $4.6 billion. The main block grants from the Nixon administration—community development, comprehensive employment and training, and social services—account for another $3.2 billion (all for community development because the other two grants are scheduled to be eliminated by fiscal 1984). Most of the block grants created by President Reagan, accounting for $12.1 billion in fiscal 1984, are also included in the turnback. This leaves only $10.3 billion from present categorical programs, all of which are rather small.[12] Therefore, the 1984 turnback essentially means converting another $10.3 billion of categorical grants to block grant form, with the constraints even looser than on present block grants because a wider array of categorical programs are involved. The same questions raised above about the 1983 consolidations can be raised about these: in truth, there is not much evidence at this level of detail to know whether such consolidations are desirable or not.

In the long run the effect of the grant turnback will be more significant than that of a straightforward consolidation, since the fiscal ability of state and local governments to sustain the programs will vary. Through 1988 OMB will try to prevent financial hardships by "holding harmless" all states, and by mandating that super revenue sharing be passed through to local governments. The holding harmless clause means that the trust fund will be set so that "the share of each state in the trust fund will be based on its 1979–81 share of specified Federal grants now slated for 'turnback'. . . with an adjustment for any gains or losses for individual states resulting from the Medicaid-welfare swap."[13] The pass-through clause attempts to do the same for localities. But after 1987 the trust fund is to be reduced by one-quarter a year, so that it will be phased out completely by 1991. During and after this transitional period, states must assess taxes on their own.

As the trust fund disappears, states that have higher incomes and tax bases will be able to operate the turned-back programs with lower tax rates than other states. Hence there will no longer

12. Since these grants are not identified by dollar totals on OMB's illustrative list, it is difficult to identify the categorical grants to be included. Most are in the areas of education, social services, transportation, and community development.
13. OMB, *Major Themes*, p. 21.

be a way to assure that public services are consumed approximately on equal terms in rich and poor states, or that funds are passed through to localities, many of which are now beset by high rates of poverty and unemployment.

To take one illustration of these changes in the distribution of funds, an important program being turned back is general revenue sharing. These funds now go only to local governments; and it can be estimated that central cities receive an average of about $27 per capita, whereas their generally richer suburbs receive an average of $15 per capita.[14] If the pass-through arrangement works, there should be no major change in the distribution of funds through 1987. But after that, when the pass-through provisions lapse, the poorer central cities will probably lose more than their richer suburbs. The same will happen with other grants, such as community development block grants, that now go directly to local governments.

## Medicaid

Medicaid is a program of uncapped federal matching grants made to states for the financing of medical care for low-income persons. The federal matching rate for medicaid varies inversely with the ratio of state to federal per capita income, but cannot be lower than 50 percent or higher than 78 percent. Since richer states have much larger medicaid programs, the sharing rate nationwide is close to one-half: OMB has estimated that by fiscal 1984 medicaid will cost both the state and the federal government about $19 billion.

The medicaid program was enacted in 1965 under Title XIX of the Social Security Act. It was initially intended as a catchall program to cover the medical needs of residual groups left out of the medicare program adopted that same year. While states could choose whether or not to institute medicaid (the one state without a program, Arizona, has only recently applied for a medicaid demonstration grant), participating states were required to make eligible for medicaid all recipients of public assistance (including AFDC), and were permitted to make eligible the "medically

---

14. Based on data in Advisory Commission on Intergovernmental Relations, *Central City-Suburban Fiscal Disparity and City Distress, 1977*, report M-119 (Government Printing Office, 1980), p. 84.

needy," those whose incomes fell below some state-determined limit (once medical expenses were deducted) and who would be eligible for public assistance if poor enough. Initially there were no federal constraints on the income limit a state could use in defining the medically needy, so that income limits varied widely from state to state. States had to fund inpatient and outpatient hospital care, physicians' services, laboratory tests and x-rays, and skilled nursing home services, and could fund other medical services. Providers of hospital services were to be reimbursed at "reasonable costs," which came to mean pretty much whatever hospitals demanded. There were, in other words, only minimal constraints on program eligibility and cost per recipient and almost no price incentives for cutting costs. Not surprisingly, federal program outlays grew rapidly, from less than $3 billion in 1970 to $16.8 billion by fiscal 1981.

Many attempts have been made to limit the growth of medicaid outlays. In 1967 Congress limited the income level defining "medically needy" to 133 percent of the level used for the states' AFDC program. In 1969 the Department of Health, Education, and Welfare issued guidelines limiting physician payments to 75 percent of customary charges. In 1972 health maintenance organizations, with prepaid insurance and more incentives for cost cutting, were made eligible for inclusion in medicaid. Also in that year legislation mandated the establishment of professional standards review organizations to monitor costs and the quality of care. In 1981 Congress passed a measure intended to reduce the federal share by 3 percent in 1982, by 4 percent in 1983, and by 4.5 percent in 1985 and to give states more flexibility in management.

The administration is proposing some further changes in medicaid before the program is to be assumed by the federal government. One change would reduce the federal matching rate for optional medicaid services, another would impose modest copayments for medicaid services, others would tighten medicaid eligibility, and another would eliminate the higher federal matching rate on supplementary medicaid services. These changes would decrease federal outlays for medicaid by $2 billion in fiscal 1983. Of course, once the federal government takes control of the program, all recent changes in matching rates become irrelevant: the federal share jumps to 100 percent.

The main advantage of centralizing medicaid at the federal level is that it will help prevent interstate disparities in benefits. State determination of eligibility and reimbursement schedules, even subject to the restrictions now imposed, leads to varying benefit levels across states. Although specific proposals have not yet been put forward by the administration, presumably centralization of the program will eliminate many of these disparities. But that raises another problem: once the federal government begins standardizing benefits and eligibility, it will have to determine a norm for setting program benefits. Given the cuts being proposed for almost all federal domestic programs, the federal benefit norm will probably be below that now offered in many states. This would mean that standardization of medicaid eligibility would reduce or eliminate benefits for many people formerly on welfare and eligible for medicaid. The number of people hurt could be held down by so-called grandfather clauses, which allow previously eligible people to preserve eligibility for a certain time. Nevertheless, the reduction or loss of medicaid benefits could cause serious difficulties for many people.

## Aid to Families with Dependent Children

The AFDC program, which the federal government plans to turn over to states under the proposed program exchange, is much older than medicaid. It was first established by the Social Security Act of 1935. This act extended assistance to women with dependent children but no husbands, still the main target group for AFDC. This group was always viewed as a "residual" category, and up to the late fifties official presidential statements indicated that the AFDC program was expected to wither away or remain small as other social insurance programs matured. But the rise in national divorce and desertion rates meant that the program did not remain small. It, too, grew, with federal outlays increasing from less than $1 billion in 1960 to $8.5 billion in fiscal 1981. Like medicaid, AFDC is now set up as a matching grant program for which the federal government pays from 50 to 78 percent of state expenses, with no cap on the federal grant.[15]

15. In 1965 states were given the option of being reimbursed by an older AFDC benefit formula, which had a cap, or the medicaid formula, which depends on state income but has no cap. By now all states except Arizona, which has not yet got medicaid, and Texas, which pays very low AFDC benefits, have changed over to the medicaid reimbursement formula.

AFDC has changed relatively little in the last two decades. Roughly half the states have taken advantage of an unemployed parent option whereby families with fathers are eligible if the father has a specified amount of unemployment. A work incentive program requiring certain recipients to work or accept training for their benefits was added in 1967. Also starting in 1967 families were allowed to keep one-third of their earnings from work, so that those who worked could have higher incomes than those who did not. The Reagan administration has advanced various proposals to require recipients to work, to search for private jobs, and to count as income family resources that have previously not been counted; their purpose is to lower benefit levels and eliminate overlapping between assistance programs. Probably the administration's most important change has been to weaken the provision allowing families to keep one-third of their earnings from work—for many families this provision has now become worthless, and AFDC tax rates are effectively 100 percent. This change is in direct opposition to proposals being made regarding the positive tax side of the system, and violates supply-side principles by discouraging work.[16]

As an income maintenance system, AFDC has been the object of intense criticism by both conservatives and liberals. Conservatives have attacked the program because they feel that in some states benefit levels are too high, incentives to work too weak, and budget costs and expenditure growth too high, and that the program is conducive to fraud and cheating. Liberals have sought to improve the program's work incentives, and they have also focused on two destructive incentives within the program. First, since families without fathers are eligible for benefits and families with fathers are usually ineligible, the program has incentives for family separation.[17] Second, since states can set their own eligi-

16. The effects of the Reagan proposals on low-income families are described in detail by Tom Joe, "Profiles of Families in Poverty: Effects of the FY 1983 Budget Proposals on the Poor," working paper (Washington, D.C.: Center for the Study of Social Policy, 1982).

17. Exactly how important these incentives are has been the subject of a violent controversy among social scientists. Social experiments with more general income support programs, called negative income taxes, have found that such plans increase family separation, contrary to what would be expected. See Michael T. Hannan, Nancy B. Tuma, and Lyle P. Groeneveld, "The Effects of Negative Income Tax Programs on Marital Stability: A Summary and Discussion of Results from the Seattle-Denver Income Maintenance Experiments," working paper (Menlo Park, California: SRI International, 1978); and John H. Bishop, "Jobs, Cash Transfers, and Marital Instability: A Review and

bility and benefit standards, benefit levels vary greatly across states. As in medicaid, this causes families with the same income but living in different states to be treated unequally and could give an incentive for recipients to move to high AFDC benefit states.[18]

How significant these differences are can be seen in table 5-3, which shows monthly payments for a family of four with zero outside income in 1979. These monthly payments, or basic benefit levels, range from highs of $546 in Hawaii, $524 in Vermont, $510 in Wisconsin, and $487 in California to lows of $120 in Mississippi and $140 in Texas. Nationwide, benefits average $330, with about one-sixth of the states paying benefits above $450 and one-sixth less than $200.

If AFDC were given to states under the program exchange, their grant levels would remain constant. Federal funds that now go to states for financing their AFDC program would, in essence, be available for financing programs in general. But the marginal cost to states of paying AFDC benefits would rise sharply: in effect, states would no longer have to pay AFDC benefits to get the federal funds. To illustrate, the present average federal matching rate of 58 percent implies that it costs states only 42 cents to raise AFDC benefits one dollar. After the program exchange is made, it will cost states one dollar to raise benefits one dollar; thus the effective rise in the price of AFDC benefits will be about 80 percent (depending on how the rise is measured).[19] Econometric studies of existing state benefit-setting behavior indicate that changes of this magnitude would lower average benefit levels by about 19 percent.[20] Hypothetical monthly payments across states

Synthesis of the Evidence," *Journal of Human Resources,* vol. 15 (Summer 1980), pp. 301–33. On closer inspection, however, these findings are not necessarily unfavorable for a negative income tax, because almost all the program-induced breakups were by couples without children, and many were related to the wife's desire for independence once she had greater financial resources.

18. Nobody is sure how important these migration incentives are. One amusing anecdote from the negative income tax experiment in Gary, Indiana, suggests that they are not unimportant: welfare offices in the state of Indiana used to post the (higher) AFDC benefit levels in Michigan and Illinois.

19. The rise in price is 138 percent when measured against the initial price ($0.42) and 58 percent when measured against the final price ($1.00). A more impartial method is to measure the rise in price against the average of initial and final prices ($0.71); then the effective rise in price is about 80 percent.

20. See Larry L. Orr, "Income Transfers as a Public Good: An Application to AFDC," *American Economic Review,* vol. 66 (June 1976), pp. 359–71.

**Table 5-3. AFDC Monthly Payments for a Family of Four with Zero Income, by State, Calendar Year 1979**

Payments in dollars

| State | Monthly payment | Federal matching share at margin, 1981 (percent)[a] | Hypo-thetical monthly payment after swap[b] | Unemployed parent option |
|---|---|---|---|---|
| Alabama | 148 | 71 | 111 | No |
| Alaska | 450 | 50 | 381 | No |
| Arizona | 240 | 0 | 240 | No[c] |
| Arkansas | 188 | 72 | 139 | No |
| California | 487 | 50 | 413 | Yes |
| Colorado | 327 | 52 | 274 | Yes |
| Connecticut | 446 | 50 | 376 | Yes |
| Delaware | 287 | 50 | 243 | Yes |
| District of Columbia | 253 | 50 | 214 | Yes |
| Florida | 230 | 58 | 187 | No[c] |
| Georgia | 170 | 66 | 132 | No |
| Hawaii | 546 | 50 | 462 | Yes |
| Idaho | 366 | 65 | 285 | No |
| Illinois | 315 | 50 | 267 | Yes |
| Indiana | 275 | 57 | 225 | No |
| Iowa | 419 | 55 | 356 | Yes |
| Kansas | 350 | 53 | 292 | Yes |
| Kentucky | 235 | 68 | 179 | No |
| Louisiana | 187 | 67 | 144 | No |
| Maine | 332 | 71 | 248 | No |
| Maryland | 294 | 50 | 249 | Yes |
| Massachusetts | 419 | 54 | 348 | Yes |
| Michigan | 480 | 50 | 406 | Yes |
| Minnesota | 454 | 54 | 377 | Yes |
| Mississippi | 120 | 77 | 86 | No |
| Missouri | 270 | 60 | 217 | Yes |
| Montana | 331 | 65 | 258 | Yes |
| Nebraska | 370 | 58 | 300 | Yes |
| Nevada | 297 | 50 | 251 | No |
| New Hampshire | 382 | 59 | 308 | No |
| New Jersey | 386 | 50 | 327 | Yes |
| New Mexico | 242 | 67 | 186 | No |
| New York | 476 | 51 | 401 | Yes |
| North Carolina | 210 | 68 | 160 | No |
| North Dakota | 389 | 62 | 309 | No |
| Ohio | 327 | 55 | 270 | Yes |
| Oklahoma | 349 | 60 | 280 | No |
| Oregon | 456 | 53 | 380 | No |

**Table 5-3** (continued)

| State | Monthly payment | Federal matching share at margin, 1981 (percent)[a] | Hypothetical monthly payment after swap[b] | Unemployed parent option |
|---|---|---|---|---|
| Pennsylvania | 373 | 57 | 305 | Yes |
| Rhode Island | 389 | 58 | 316 | Yes |
| South Carolina | 142 | 71 | 106 | No |
| South Dakota | 361 | 68 | 275 | No |
| Tennessee | 148 | 69 | 112 | No |
| Texas | 140 | 51 | 118 | No |
| Utah | 389 | 69 | 295 | Yes |
| Vermont | 524 | 69 | 397 | Yes |
| Virginia | 263 | 57 | 215 | No[c] |
| Washington | 483 | 50 | 409 | Yes |
| West Virginia | 249 | 68 | 190 | Yes |
| Wisconsin | 510 | 58 | 414 | Yes |
| Wyoming | 340 | 50 | 288 | No[c] |
| Mean | 330 | 58 | 269 | . . . |

Sources: Monthly payments from Department of Health and Human Services, Social Security Administration, Office of Family Assistance, *Research Tables Based on Characteristics of State Plans for Aid to Families with Dependent Children: Need, Eligibility, Administration,* 1980 ed. (Government Printing Office, 1980), pp. 59–60; federal shares from Department of Health and Human Services, Office of the Secretary, "Federal Financial Participation in State Assistance Expenditures," *Federal Register,* vol. 45 (December 1, 1980), p. 79582.

a. Federal medical assistance percentages. States with approved medicaid plans may claim federal payments for other aid programs as well, at these higher rates. Both Arizona and Texas use the pre-1965 AFDC matching formula in which the federal government pays 83 percent of the first $72 a month (for a family of four) and 50 to 65 percent of the balance up to $128 a month. Arizona was above the cap on maximum amounts per recipient and got no matching payments, but it could not change over to the medicaid formula because it did not have medicaid in 1981.

b. Based on responses to changes in federal matching rates computed by Larry L. Orr, "Income Transfers as a Public Good: An Application to AFDC," *American Economic Review,* vol. 66 (June 1976), pp. 359–71.

c. Unemployed parent program approved, but funds not appropriated.

based on these econometric calculations are shown in the third column of table 5-3: not only do the benefits in all states (except Arizona) go down because of the higher marginal price, but the decline in absolute benefit levels is roughly constant across the country. Mississippi and other states with very low benefit levels might be expected to lower benefits less in dollar terms, but this effect is offset by the fact that the rise in price at the margin for these states is much larger than for wealthier states. Under these hypothetical calculations, average AFDC basic benefits are reduced to $269 a month, with only one state paying more than $450 a month and one-quarter of the states paying less than $200 a month.

These numbers are, of course, hypothetical and subject to error. Any changes in AFDC benefits will probably be made only gradually over time, and state responses to small changes in matching rates may not accurately predict responses to the large changes in matching rates proposed by the president. But even though the calculations are rough, they bring out an important point that should not be lost in discussions of the AFDC change. Even if the program rearrangement is conducted so that the states' effective income is not changed, as the administration intends, the loss of federal matching implies a big rise in the cost of maintaining AFDC benefits or of adjusting them to keep up with inflation. Since matching rates are inversely correlated with state income, the effective price change is largest in the low-income states. This price change will probably lower AFDC benefits across the board and not even narrow disparities much, because the price increase is higher in low-income states. Current dollar differences in benefit levels will then be expected to persist, and average benefits will probably be somewhat lower, estimated here to be about 20 percent. This is one important reason why the president's new federalism plan is likely to work to the disadvantage of low-income people.[21]

*Food Stamps*

The food stamp program originally began under President Kennedy as a small pilot program operating in economically depressed areas. A series of amendments in 1964 and 1970 expanded it into a national program, with benefit levels that are uniform across the country. Food stamps is not and never has been a matching grant program. Also, since people can qualify for food stamps simply by having a low income—they do not have to be unemployed, aged, or disabled or have a broken family—the

21. It should be noted that this change comes on top of those already made in the early Reagan budgets, which have had adverse effects on low-income people. Based on estimates prepared by the Congressional Budget Office, the net impact of the 1981 tax and benefit changes has been to *reduce* after-tax income about 4.5 percent for households with incomes of less than $10,000; and to *increase* after-tax income by 6.7 percent for households with incomes of more than $80,000. See Congressional Budget Office, "Effects of Tax and Benefit Reductions Enacted in 1981 for Households in Different Income Categories," Special Study prepared by the Staffs of the Human Resources and Community Development Division and the Tax Analysis Division (CBO, 1981). Similar changes are under way as a result of the 1982 and 1983 expenditure proposals and scheduled tax cuts.

food stamp program is now the only nontargeted federal income support program. Budget expenditures for food stamps totaled $11.3 billion in fiscal 1981.

Families with very low incomes can get food stamps free, but the price of stamps to a family rises with its income. As the price rises, the difference between the value of the food stamps and their cost, the so-called bonus value of the stamps, falls. This fall in bonus value is the way in which higher earnings are effectively taxed away by the program. Before the program exchange takes place, the Reagan administration proposes to raise this implicit tax rate from 26 to 35 percent, again a change that will reduce the incentives for beneficiaries to work.[22]

Since food stamp benefits are nationwide and available to almost all low-income families, the food stamp program has the effect of narrowing the disparities in benefits existing under AFDC. The basic AFDC monthly benefit level is four times as high in California as in Mississippi, but when the food stamp bonus value of $204 a month (for a family of four with zero income in 1979) is added, total benefit levels become $691 in California and $324 in Mississippi, a ratio of somewhat more than two to one.[23] At the same time, making payments to families with fathers present should reduce the incentives to separate.

The equalizing property of food stamps will also be lost if the program is turned back to states. Instead of paying nothing for food stamp benefits, states will bear the full burden of the cost. As with AFDC, average food stamp benefit levels can be expected to fall, probably by more in the low-income states (since benefits are now very different from what these states would be apt to pay with their more limited incomes). Hence besides lowering all benefits, as with the AFDC change, turning the food stamp

22. Since AFDC benefits are counted as income in determining food stamp bonus values, for families on both AFDC and food stamps the 100 percent AFDC tax rate implies that food stamp bonus values are unaffected. Hence the new change in food stamp tax rates mainly affects families not on AFDC. Also, it should be noted that the statutory tax rate in the food stamp program before the Reagan changes was 30 percent. It was effectively lowered to 26 percent because some working expenses were disregarded in computing benefits. But besides raising the tax rate, the administration disallowed the working expense disregard, which raised the total effective tax rate from 26 to 35 percent.

23. Actually it is more complicated than this to determine the effect of adding food stamps onto AFDC. If states set AFDC benefits in the knowledge of food stamp levels, food stamps may simply displace AFDC benefits and not narrow the state disparities at all.

program over to states will have the effect of *widening* the disparities in benefits around this lower base.

### Alternatives to the President's Program

There are essentially four kinds of alternatives to the president's program: an increase in the amount of funds transferred to state and local governments, a change in the mix of programs being centralized or decentralized, a change in the distribution of funds available to states and localities in the programs to be turned back, and a modification of the block grant consolidation favored by both the Nixon and Reagan administrations.

#### *Maintaining Current Federal Grants*

As table 5-2 shows, federal grants are scheduled to fall by $13.4 billion between fiscal 1981 and fiscal 1983, a year before the great program rearrangement takes effect. This cutback in the nominal level of grants will drop grants as a share of GNP from its pre-Reagan level of 3.3 percent to just 2.4 percent in two years, reversing more than a decade's growth. Indeed, to a large extent the president's program rearrangement proposals have pushed into the background grant cutbacks that in normal years would have been front-page news. Should federal grants be cut by less, or not be cut at all?

The decline in grants, whether measured in nominal or real terms, comes at the same time as two other events that are also likely to complicate state and local budgets. One is the economic recession of 1981–82 (discussed in more detail in chapter 2), the other is the tax limitation movement at the state level. The recession has been especially painful for the older industrial states of the Midwest—the unemployment rate in Michigan reached 16 percent at the start of 1982, and was nearly as high in surrounding states like Ohio and Indiana. Unemployment has been accompanied by high interest rates and by new opportunities for investors to save in tax-free form, which have both greatly increased the cost of borrowing for state and local governments. The high-grade municipal bond rate jumped from 7.09 percent in December 1979 to 12.77 percent in December 1981, even though interest rates normally fall in a recession.

Deep recessions can have an adverse effect on the budgets of state and local governments. Since states and localities rely heavily on income and sales taxes whose rates are hard to change, tax revenues can be expected to fall nearly in proportion to GNP in the short run. But most expenditures are for quasi-contractual obligations that are not likely to decrease much in a recession, and might even increase. The combination of tax revenue losses and fairly stable expenditures will cause an immediate drop in the budget surplus or rise in the deficit of state and local budgets, the biggest change occurring in areas where cyclical unemployment is increasing the most.

Although these cyclical changes would appear to present problems for state and local governments, it is hard to say how serious they might become in the 1982–83 period. Probably the best indication of short-run fiscal stress for state and local governments is the change in their budget surplus or deficit. Econometric studies show that cyclical developments have surprisingly little effect on overall state and local surplus: a dollar's drop in GNP seems to lower the surplus by $0.025 in the short run. This means that even big cyclical changes in GNP would lead to changes in the surplus well within the fluctuations observed historically.[24]

Current data do not show much indication of danger either. Over the ten-year period 1971–80 the state-local general government budget surplus in the national income accounts averaged $1.7 billion. For the first three quarters of 1981 this surplus averaged $5.3 billion at annual rates, indicating that the typical state and locality went into the recession in a strong fiscal position. Press reports show that particular governments are in financial difficulties, but since official budget data for individual state and local governments are available only after a long lag, it is impossible to verify the claim systematically. Those data that are available from the Census Bureau are summarized in table 5-4. Since government budget totals vary widely, the table gives

24. The econometric results are taken from Edward M. Gramlich, "State and Local Budgets the Day after It Rained: Why Is the Surplus So High?" *Brookings Papers on Economic Activity, 1:1978*, pp. 191–216. A recent survey, sponsored by the Joint Economic Committee, does indicate fairly large cutbacks in real expenditures and increases in user fees in response to the recession and grant cutbacks. See *Emergency Interim Survey: Fiscal Condition of 48 Large Cities*, Joint Economic Committee, 97 Cong. 1 sess. (GPO, 1982).

**Table 5-4. Frequency Distribution of General Government Surpluses or Deficits for States and Cities, Fiscal Years 1978 and 1980**

Number of governments unless otherwise specified

| Item | 1978 | 1980 |
|------|------|------|
| *Fifty state governments* | | |
| Ratio of surplus to revenue (percent) | | |
| More than 10 | 7 | 3 |
| 5 to 10 | 19 | 11 |
| 0 to 5 | 15 | 25 |
| 0 to −5 | 9 | 7 |
| −5 to −10 | 0 | 3 |
| Less than −10 | 0 | 1 |
| Median ratio | 5.2 | 2.7 |
| Mean ratio | 4.6 | 3.1 |
| *Fifty large city governments* | | |
| Ratio of surplus to revenue (percent) | | |
| More than 10 | 17 | 8 |
| 5 to 10 | 11 | 14 |
| 0 to 5 | 12 | 15 |
| 0 to −5 | 5 | 3 |
| −5 to −10 | 1 | 4 |
| Less than −10 | 4 | 6 |
| Median ratio | 6.3 | 4.3 |
| Mean ratio | 4.4 | 0.8 |

Sources: Bureau of the Census, *State Government Finances in 1980*, series GF80, no. 3 (GPO, 1981), p. 11; Bureau of the Census, *State Government Finances in 1978*, series GF78, no. 3 (GPO, 1979), p. 11; Bureau of the Census, *City Government Finances in 1979–80*, series GF80, no. 4 (GPO, 1981), pp. 12–67; and Bureau of the Census, *City Government Finances in 1977–78* (GPO, 1980), pp. 12–65.

frequency distributions of the ratios of the general government surpluses (excluding pension funds, utilities, and transportation systems) to general revenues. The table compares 1980, a normal surplus year for states and localities (the overall surplus was only slightly above the decade average), with 1978, a very good year (the overall general government surplus was $9 billion, well above the decade average). As expected, the fiscal health of the fifty states and fifty large cities shows some decline: both the mean and median surplus–revenue ratios fell for both states and cities. As of 1980 eleven states and thirteen cities (in the representative sample of fifty) had deficits. But these figures should be understood in context, because even in 1978 nine states and ten cities had deficits. The number of individual governments apparently experiencing fiscal problems was increasing, but not at an alarming rate. Hence while it is likely that the combination of grant cutbacks, high interest rates, and the recession will create fiscal problems for many states and localities, the seriousness of the problem is not yet clear.

The other complication, which in the long run could cause more serious fiscal problems for states, is the spread of tax limitation amendments at the state level. Since 1976 voters in sixteen states have added statutory or constitutional tax or expenditure limitation measures to their fiscal regulations. These measures vary greatly in the revenue or expenditure item being limited, in the tightness of the limits, and in the ease with which they can be overridden (table 5-5). Opinions differ over why the measures passed—whether they were a vote for governmental cutbacks, a call for greater productivity or efficiency at the state-local level, or a complaint reflecting the national economic difficulties of inflation, unemployment, and real wage decline.[25] But there is no question that now that the tax limitation amendments have passed, states and localities will be constrained in their ability to raise taxes to cover federal grant cutbacks.

A few examples will show how the presence of tax limits could complicate the response to grant cutbacks. In Tennessee, Michigan, Texas, North Dakota, Montana, and Missouri, the limit prevents state revenues or income taxes from growing more than state income. In the first place, income growth in these states will be reduced by the recession. And as federal grants are cut back, the state government will have no opportunity to raise its taxes to pick up the federal program unless it begins the period below the revenue ceiling or explicitly votes an override to the limit. Therefore, whether it is desirable or not, many programs cut out by federal grants will probably not be picked up at the state level. As another example, in California, Idaho, Alabama, and Massachusetts, the tax limitation measure required a large initial cut in local

---

25. At least three extensive survey studies have been made to try to answer the question. See Jack Citrin, "Do People Want Something for Nothing: Public Opinion on Taxes and Government Spending," *National Tax Journal*, vol. 32, Supplement: Proceedings of a Conference on Tax and Expenditure Limitations (June 1979), pp. 113–29 (California); Paul N. Courant, Edward M. Gramlich, and Daniel L. Rubinfeld, "Why Voters Support Tax Limitation Amendments: The Michigan Case," *National Tax Journal*, vol. 33 (March 1980), pp. 1–20; and Helen F. Ladd and Julie B. Wilson, "Proposition 2½: Explaining the Vote," working paper (Harvard University, 1981) (Massachusetts).

**Table 5-5. State and Local Tax and Expenditure Limitation Measures Enacted 1976–80**

| State | Year | Type of law | Jurisdiction | Type of limitation | Item limited | Initial cut | Growth limit | Override provision |
|---|---|---|---|---|---|---|---|---|
| New Jersey | 1976 | Statutory | State, Local | Expenditures | Total | No | Income, 5 percent | Majority referendum |
| Colorado | 1977 | Statutory | State | Expenditures | Total | No | 7 percent | Majority of legislature |
| Rhode Island | 1977 | Statutory | State | Expenditures | Total | No | 8 percent | Nonbinding |
| Tennessee | 1978 | Constitutional | State | Taxes | Total | No | Income | Majority of legislature |
| Arizona | 1978 | Constitutional | State | Expenditures | Total | No | Income | Two-thirds of legislature |
| Hawaii | 1978 | Constitutional | State | Expenditures | Total | No | Income | Two-thirds of legislature |
| Michigan | 1978 | Constitutional | State, Local | Total, Property tax | No | Income, Price level | Two-thirds of legislature, Majority referendum |
| Texas | 1978 | Constitutional | State | Taxes | Total | No | Income | Majority of legislature |
| California | 1978 | Constitutional | State, Local | Taxes | Total, Property tax | Yes | Income, 2 percent | Two-thirds of legislature, Two-thirds of registered voters |
| Idaho | 1978 | Statutory | State | Taxes | Property tax | Yes | 2 percent | Majority of legislature |
| Alabama | 1978 | Constitutional | Local | Taxes | Property tax | Yes | Property value | Majority of legislature and majority referendum |
| North Dakota | 1978 | Statutory | State | Taxes | Income tax | Yes | Income | Majority of legislature |
| Arkansas | 1980 | Constitutional | Local | Taxes | Property tax | No | 10 percent | None |
| Massachusetts | 1980 | Statutory | Local | Taxes | Property tax | Yes | Property value | Two-thirds referendum |
| Missouri | 1980 | Constitutional | State, Local | Taxes | Total, Property tax | No | Income, Price level | Majority referendum |
| Montana | 1980 | Statutory | State | Taxes | Income tax | No | Income | Majority of legislature |

Sources: Advisory Commission on Intergovernmental Relations, *Significant Features of Fiscal Federalism, 1979–80 Edition* (GPO, 1980), pp. 186–87; Jane F. Roberts, "States Respond to Tough Fiscal Challenges," *Intergovernmental Perspective*, vol. 6 (Spring 1980), pp. 17–18; "States Tackle Tough Fiscal Issues," *Intergovernmental Perspective*, vol. 5 (Winter 1979), p. 10; John Shannon and Carol S. Weissert, "After Jarvis: Tough Questions for Fiscal Policymakers," *Intergovernmental Perspective*, vol. 4 (Summer 1978), p. 10; "Tax Revolt Continues as 12 States Vote on Reductions, Controls," National Governors' Association, *Governors' Bulletin*, October 24, 1980; and unpublished data.

property taxes. State governments could either bail local governments out with additional state aid, as was done in California and Massachusetts, or watch local services deteriorate. When the cut in federal grants is combined with the revenue drain of additional state aid to local governments, these states too will be in a fiscal squeeze and will probably be unable to raise enough taxes to cover the full deficiency. As a final example, Colorado and Rhode Island have limited the growth of state expenditures to 7 or 8 percent in nominal terms, which implies stable or declining real expenditure levels as long as prices in general and state and local wages in particular grow at this rate or more. If inflation does not decline quickly, these states will be forced to serve growing population and income levels with declining real expenditures, with an expenditure gap that is likely to increase over time. If grants are cut back too, the forced decline in real public services consumption levels becomes even more pervasive.

That citizens in state and local governments around the country have seen fit to constrain their fiscal choices by these binding limitations certainly does not mean the federal government should be prevented from cutting its own grants to state and local governments. Indeed, the tax revolt movements at the state and federal levels are being interpreted as electoral mandates for spending reductions that reflect the same general mood of voters. But while federal grant cutbacks and state tax limitations may conform politically in this sense, they do not necessarily complement each other from a fiscal standpoint. Tax limitation amendments, imposed at a time when the economic recession and interest costs may already be eroding state financial cushions, could severely restrict fiscal choices in dealing with grant cutbacks. Hence there is likely to be a sharp, and unprecedented, drop in state and local expenditures resulting from the grant cutbacks, and at least a risk of some serious governmental financial difficulties.

The obvious way to prevent these problems from occurring is to modify or defer the cuts in grants proposed by the president. General cuts in grants could be deferred until any recession-induced fiscal problems had passed. Or an attempt could be made to target more grant money to particular states and localities that have lower taxable incomes or are facing particular fiscal difficulties, perhaps by adding to direct support programs like general revenue sharing or community development block grants.

## Sorting Out the Programs

A second alternative to the president's program involves changing the composition of programs to be turned back to state governments. Concerned with what it referred to as congestion of the federal grant system, the Advisory Commission on Intergovernmental Relations recommended in June 1980 that all federal grant programs be examined with the aim of nationalizing those with the greatest national purpose, devolving to other levels of government those with the least national purpose, and retaining as grants those with a shared purpose. This approach has been endorsed by the National Governors' Association and the National Conference of State Legislatures.

In some ways President Reagan's plan is similar to the advisory commission's recommendation. The block grant consolidations do greatly reduce the number of grants and provide much more state and local freedom in managing the programs. But unlike the president's plan, the advisory commission's recommendations singled out income maintenance as a federal responsibility, and AFDC and food stamps (along with medicaid) as programs that should be operated at the federal level. That judgment was in keeping with two earlier welfare reform proposals by Presidents Nixon and Carter, both of which entailed greater national standardization of AFDC levels.

There are two important reasons for making income maintenance a federal responsibility and for setting benefit standards nationally.[26] One is that on the positive tax side the national income tax provides for approximately the same treatment of families with the same income levels living in different states. Another, and more practical reason, is that the population receiving income maintenance is likely to be fairly mobile. States choosing to set generous AFDC benefits might find that their generosity is rewarded only by attracting low-income families

___

26. Professional opinion is by no means unanimous that income maintenance should be solely a federal responsibility. For an argument that it should not be, see Richard W. Tresch, *Public Finance: A Normative Theory* (Plano, Texas: Business Publications, 1981), chap. 30.

from other states, which would raise their own tax costs and lower those of surrounding states with less generous benefits. This could in turn lead to increased state competition in cutting benefits to try to send the AFDC recipients back to other states. The result might be AFDC benefits that are below those desired by taxpayers in any state, but that are kept down by the fear of generating incentives for beneficiaries to immigrate.[27] Another possible outcome might be a series of exclusionary laws such as welfare residency requirements, now outlawed by the Supreme Court.[28]

Earlier we showed that the effect of turning AFDC and food stamps over to states will most likely be to lower the general level of income maintenance and to increase state disparities in benefit levels. When this first-round effect is combined with the longer-run problem of beneficiary migration, or really perceptions that AFDC beneficiaries will migrate, a multiplier is added to the process—the low-benefit states can drag down benefits in the high-benefit states. Whether in the short or the long run, turning AFDC and food stamps back to state governments is likely to harm the poor.

The obvious way to solve the problem is through the advisory commission's approach of federalizing income maintenance programs. The food stamp program is already federalized, supplemental security income (income support for the aged, blind, and disabled) is federalized, and medicaid is proposed to be federal-

27. It is commonly alleged that high AFDC benefit levels and state tax rates drive taxpayers out of the state. A simple numerical calculation shows that this effect, if present at all, should be of little importance. To take one example, a 30 percent increase in AFDC benefit levels would change the disposable income of AFDC recipients by about 30 percent. It would cost about $4 billion (federal plus state cost) at present levels. This represents a decline in the disposable income of taxpayers of less than 0.33 of a percent at present levels, surely a change most taxpayers would never notice.

28. It is at this point not clear whether this ruling, based on a 1969 decision of the Supreme Court, would apply to completely state-financed AFDC programs. The Court decision held that residency requirements were unconstitutional restrictions on free interstate travel and that such laws constituted an "invidious discrimination" in distinguishing between poor persons who were long-term residents and those who were not, thereby violating the equal protection clause of the Constitution. The decision held that such requirements could be justified only by "compelling governmental interests." *Shapiro, Commissioner of Welfare of Connecticut* v. *Thompson*, 394 U.S. 627 (1969). In later challenges, fiscal problems were *not* permitted as a justifying factor. Since the fact that the federal government financed part of AFDC benefits was not mentioned in the Court opinion, and since fiscal problems are not considered as justification for residency requirements, it may prove impossible for states to impose constitutional residency requirements even if they operate AFDC on their own. On the other hand, some states have recently adopted residency requirements that are yet to be challenged in court.

ized; the added burden of federalizing the AFDC program would be about $6 billion in fiscal 1983, should present average benefit levels be maintained. Comparable federal tax contributions could be deducted from the trust fund to finance the turned-back programs to prevent either the federal government or states from gaining or losing from the transfer. And while the costs appear small, the gains—as a way to standardize benefits, eliminate migration incentives, and possibly avoid competitive benefit cuts—could be large.

Presidential spokesmen have taken pains to point out that the program exchange proposal was preliminary and could be altered by negotiation with the states. One way of altering it would be to change the treatment of AFDC and food stamps in line with the advisory commission's recommendations. Another way, not explicitly ruled out by the administration, is to leave the program exchange as is, but to combine it with nationally mandated standards for minimum welfare benefits, allowing states to supplement the benefits (at full cost to them) if they wish. The nationally mandated standard could even be financed by a federal grant. Options of this sort were included in both President Nixon's and President Carter's welfare reform plans. From a theoretical standpoint, the difference between a federal AFDC-food stamp program and a program administered locally but subject to national standards is not great. But from a political-institutional standpoint, it is likely to be: states may object to the federal government restricting their behavior without the promise of federal money. But if centralization of AFDC is ruled out politically, the possibility of a program exchange subject to national standards, with or without a grant, might be worth pursuing.

*Altering the Distribution of Funds*

The president's proposal to turn back forty-four grants to states and localities for their eventual financing and operation raises two separate questions. Is there a valid federal rationale being served by the grant? And will the change ultimately lead to a shift in spending power toward richer areas?

By holding harmless states and localities, as the trust fund arrangement attempts to do until 1987, the second question is made moot, and the only issue to be dealt with is the first. But once the trust fund begins to wither away in 1988, there will be no way to protect the funding of poorer states and localities. Richer states will be able to consume public services with lower income and property tax rates than poorer states. In that sense the tax price for these services will become lower in richer states. This in turn could lead to public spending differences in rich and poor states, and would be another instance of the differential tax treatment of persons with the same income living in different states.

Since the turnback essentially confounds the question whether the federal grant should be eliminated with the question whether the tax price structure should move in favor of richer states, proposals for reforming the system could try to disentangle the two issues. For the period in which the trust fund exists, the president's proposal essentially does that. One option, then, is to adopt the president's turnback proposal but not have the trust fund wither away. This option would allow states to decide, as the president wants them to do, whether to assume these programs on their own, but it would not alter the tax treatment of individuals with similar incomes in different states. A potential problem with the option is that the 1979–81 share of grant monies becomes enshrined for all time in the distribution rules of the trust fund. The problem could be met by devising, as was done for general revenue sharing and community development block grants, some distributionally and politically acceptable formulas for apportioning funds and updating these formulas when new income and population statistics become available.

A less drastic revision in the president's plan would be to exclude all grants going to local governments from the turnback arrangement. Ensuring that states are held harmless in the trust fund arrangement is difficult enough; ensuring that localities are protected raises many more complications and introduces a set of new provisions into the trust fund distributional arrangements. Moreover, since localities are much more vulnerable to taxpayer mobility to escape from poor areas with high tax rates, any distributional shifts caused by the dismantling of the grant system could cause much greater geographic inequities. A solution to both problems might be simply to leave grants to localities out of the turnback arrangement and include only grants now going to state governments. Some redistribution of funds toward higher-income states would still occur, but the potential distributional effects would not be nearly as adverse as under the present plan.

*Changing the Structure of Grants*

A final change has not received much publicity, since it has not been suggested by any important political group. At the same time, this change does offer a potential solution to the difficult trade-off mentioned earlier in reforming those categorical grants not financing payments to individuals: tight constraints on funding lead to bureaucratic and management inefficiencies; loose constraints increase the risk that the funds will not be used for federally intended purposes.

The problem arises in the first place because federal matching rates are set so high that state governments have a powerful incentive to spend on the grant-supported program and take advantage of the federal money. This leads to a growth in federal outlays and may ultimately force the federal government to cap the grant. That, in turn, makes displacement likely, and is at least one cause of the growth of paperwork and regulation. A vicious circle of management inefficiency is the result.

An obvious solution to the problem is to lower federal matching shares to a level that properly reflects the balance of interests within and without the state. If Ohioans appear to gain about 60 percent of the benefits of a particular program, the federal matching share should be set at 40 percent. Were it so set, states would be less likely to overuse federal grants and overconsume public services; caps might still be necessary, but they would not bring about as much displacement as they do now; and less federal regulation would be required to prevent displacement. Since the states would have more of their own money at stake in the program, they might also be more diligent in weeding out program abuses. This change would be, in effect, an alternative way of decentralizing decisions in order to limit government spending and improve management.

Of course, the idea of lowering federal matching shares would not be easy to implement. In general, it is no easier to estimate the share of the benefits from a program received internally than it is to know whether grant consolidation makes sense. On the other hand, for those grants not financing payments to individuals, federal matching shares are so much above any reasonable estimate of benefits received outside the community that some reductions in matching rates will almost certainly improve the efficiency of the federal grant system, from both an economic and management standpoint.

Another potential problem with this change is that in the new regime there is no reason why matching shares should be the same for all grant programs, or even for all states within a program. Matching shares already differ for individual grant programs, but usually not very much within a grant. Some efficiency could be gained if matching shares were varied more from program to program; much efficiency could be gained if they were also varied within programs. In general, large states will gain a higher share of the benefits of a particular public program and should receive less generous federal matching provisions. Whether the introduction of variations of these kinds strains the ability of Congress to abstain from logrolling remains to be seen: Congress already is forced to deal with the more inflammatory issue of how funds are to be distributed geographically.

**Summary**

The 1983 budget proposes what is probably the biggest change in the United States federal structure in history—a number of grants will be consolidated, forty-four more will be turned back to the states, medicaid will be federalized, and AFDC and food stamps will also go to the states. These measures will take place against a background of very large cutbacks in federal grant levels—in its first two years the Reagan administration proposes to reduce federal grants from 3.3 percent of GNP to 2.4 percent, reversing a decade of growth.

The proposed consolidations and program turnbacks are likely to improve management efficiency in operating the grants, but also to pave the way for eventual elimination of much of the spending now being financed by the programs. However, the effects are less startling than might be imagined, because most of the grants scheduled to be turned back have already been consolidated or proposed for consolidation, so that spending under the categorical grants has perhaps already been eliminated. The devolution of AFDC and food stamps is more questionable: if national welfare standards are not mandated, these transfers seem almost certain to lower AFDC benefits and widen the state disparities in benefits. A logical alternative, suggested by many groups, is to turn back to the states the forty-four grants but not AFDC and food stamps.

Another potential improvement would be to turn back only grants now going to state governments and thus avoid the short- and long-run problems of assuring that sufficient funds are made available to local governments. A further improvement would be not to have the trust fund financing the turned-back grants wither away, since an adverse redistribution of fiscal resources across states will take place if it does.

The sharp cuts in grants are likely to cause problems for states already suffering from recession and high interest rates. As yet, no serious fiscal difficulties are apparent at the state-local level, but the worst dangers may be yet to come. Responses to the cutbacks in grants are also likely to be complicated by the spread of state tax limitation amendments that severely constrain state and local fiscal choices in an era of fiscal adversity. The obvious remedy would be to reduce the cutbacks in grants, and perhaps even to maintain current federal grant levels.

Finally, the chapter suggests another option for resolving the twin problems facing grants: categorical grants involve too much regulation and paperwork, and block grants involve too many risks that desirable federally financed spending will be eliminated. The alternative is simply to lower federal matching shares so that states have more incentive to limit their own spending even on programs financed by federal grants. This change will decentralize management decisions on federal grants in a way that will not throw out the baby with the bath water, as present block grant consolidations could do.

# CHAPTER SIX

# Long-Term Budget Strategies

CHARLES L. SCHULTZE

EARLIER chapters in this book have examined various aspects of the president's budget recommendations for fiscal 1983, described the economic and budgetary setting in which the budget will operate, and discussed some of the main issues in both the defense and civilian budgets that will confront Congress in its deliberations. This chapter examines the long-term budget alternatives that appear to be available and their economic consequences.

Last year's sweeping series of tax and budgetary measures, enacted by Congress largely in the form proposed by the incoming Reagan administration, has radically altered for the foreseeable future both the shape of the federal budget and the relationship between its revenues and expenditures. Because of last year's multiphased tax reduction, including the scheduled indexing of individual income taxes, federal revenues are now projected to decline as a share of the gross national product over the next three to five years for the first time in recent memory. Similarly, recent changes in authorization laws and appropriations have set the course of civilian spending on a downward trend in relation to national income and output for the first time in postwar history. Outside of social security, medicare, and several other transfer programs, the civilian activities of the federal government are to

I thank Robert W. Hartman, Barry P. Bosworth, and George L. Perry for their constructive advice. Stephen L. Garbacz provided research assistance, and Anita G. Whitlock typed the manuscript.

be significantly curtailed. Defense spending, on the other hand, has been set on a rapid upward course, and is now scheduled to grow much faster than GNP over the next five years.

In the past, deficits could be gradually eliminated, at least in theory, by holding the line on new spending and letting economic growth generate the needed additional revenues. This is no longer the case. The future losses in federal revenue from the 1981 Economic Recovery Tax Act and the scheduled rise in defense spending are very large relative to the cuts enacted in civilian spending programs. Without further action by Congress to reduce spending or raise taxes sharply, the federal deficit—already likely to exceed $100 billion in fiscal 1982—would grow rapidly over subsequent years, even if a reasonably optimistic path of economic recovery is assumed. The deficit would approach $170 billion by 1985, according to the administration's estimate (and a much larger amount, $230 billion, according to estimates developed below).

Last year the administration foresaw that its economic and budgetary programs would lead to a potential budget deficit of only $40 billion by 1985, to be eliminated by additional budget cuts that it promised to identify in its fiscal 1983 budget message. Early this year, faced with the prospect of vastly larger budget deficits than it had originally estimated—rising rather than falling over time—the administration proposed a threefold response. First, it strongly urged a continuation at unaltered levels of two major elements in its program—the scheduled tax reductions and the defense spending increase; second, while sparing the social security program, it recommended a broad array of civilian program cuts and administrative measures and some modest tax increases to reduce the budget deficit; and third, it accepted the inevitability of the remaining budget deficits, amounting by administration estimates to $92 billion in fiscal 1983 and falling slowly to $72 billion by fiscal 1985. (The alternative estimates presented below suggest that full acceptance of these administration proposals would yield budget deficits of $111 billion in 1983 and $115 billion in 1985.)

The economic, social, and political premises underlying the administration's budget proposals may be summarized as follows. The fiscal 1983 budget proposes large cuts in civilian spending programs; these cuts are at the margin of political, if not substantive, feasibility. Defense requirements are so urgent that the rapid buildup in military spending must not be slowed. The only remaining way to close the admittedly large long-run deficit gap is by a major tax increase, and the economic damage to private incentives from that reversal of basic policy would be greater than the gain from reducing the deficit.

While no budgetary actions are completely irrevocable, Congress will be setting the basic course of budgetary policy and significantly affecting the course of the economy for a number of years to come as it decides whether to accept the administration's strategic approach or adopt an alternative. This chapter examines the choices available, asking three important questions:

1. Where is the federal budget headed between now and 1985 and what forces have shaped its direction?

2. What are the long-term economic effects of reducing or not reducing the projected budget deficits?

3. What are the major alternative ways to reduce the longer-term budget deficits, and what are the consequences?

## The Forces Shaping the Federal Budget

As explained in chapter 2, the administration and the Congressional Budget Office (CBO) have issued widely divergent sets of estimates of the likely course of budget outlays, revenues, and deficits over the next five years, even though both used the same assumptions about budget policy. These estimates differ because of alternative economic assumptions and technical estimates. The CBO economic assumptions are roughly similar to those of most private forecasters. The administration's are more optimistic, with higher economic growth, less inflation, and lower interest rates. An examination of areas in which there are large technical differences—such as farm price supports and revenues from offshore oil leases—suggests that the CBO estimates are closer to what might be expected on the basis of past relationships. To avoid complicating the examination of long-term strategy with two sets of data at each point in the discussion, this chapter uses projections of budget revenues and expenditures that are an average of the administration and CBO estimates, with two-thirds

190                                                    Charles L. Schultze

**Table 6-1.** Baseline Budget Trends before Enactment of the 1981 Tax and Expenditure Measures, Fiscal Years 1981, 1983, and 1985[a]
Amounts in billions of dollars

|  | Amount | | | Percent of GNP | | |
|---|---|---|---|---|---|---|
| Item | 1981 | 1983 | 1985 | 1981 | 1983 | 1985 |
| Expenditures | 657 | 821 | 945 | 23.0 | 24.0 | 22.7 |
| Defense | 160 | 192 | 233 | 5.6 | 5.6 | 5.6 |
| Payments to individuals | 317 | 395 | 452 | 11.1 | 11.5 | 10.9 |
| Net interest | 69 | 97 | 99 | 2.4 | 2.8 | 2.4 |
| All other | 112 | 138 | 161 | 3.9 | 4.0 | 3.9 |
| Receipts | 599 | 743 | 950 | 21.0 | 21.7 | 22.8 |
| Deficit | −58 | −78 | 5 | −2.0 | −2.3 | 0.1 |

Sources: *Budget of the United States Government, Fiscal Year 1983;* Congressional Budget Office, *An Analysis of the President's Budgetary Proposals for Fiscal Year 1983* (Government Printing Office, 1982); and author's estimates. Figures are rounded.
a. Based on a weighted average of CBO and administration estimates (see text). CBO and administration estimates of nondefense outlays and revenues under the administration's 1983 budget program were adjusted to eliminate the spending and tax reductions under 1981 legislation and the proposed tax increases and spending cuts proposed in the 1983 budget. Net interest payments were adjusted to reflect the resulting changes in the public debt. The baseline defense budget was projected by holding constant its 1981 ratio to GNP (5.6 percent).

weight given to the CBO estimates and one-third to those of the administration. The resulting budget projections reflect an optimistic set of assumptions about economic activity: economic growth averaging 4 percent a year in the next three years and inflation falling to 6 percent, unemployment to 7 percent, and interest rates on short-term Treasury bills to 9 percent.

Table 6-1 represents an effort to project budget trends to 1985 on the basis of laws and policies in effect before President Reagan took office, but with the economic outlook that is now in prospect. It sets a baseline against which the subsequent changes in tax and expenditure policy can be measured. In this baseline projection, defense spending was assumed to maintain a constant share of GNP and to grow about 3 percent a year faster than inflation.

In the twenty years before 1981 total federal spending grew somewhat faster than the rest of the economy. Federal expenditures as a share of GNP rose from 19.2 percent in 1961 to 20.3 percent in 1971 and 23.0 percent in 1981. Within this total, however, defense outlays as a share of GNP declined while nondefense spending rose sharply:

|  | 1961 | 1971 | 1981 |
|---|---|---|---|
| Defense | 9.2 | 7.3 | 5.6 |
| Nondefense | 10.0 | 13.0 | 17.4 |

As table 6-1 shows, federal budget outlays under policies and programs in effect before President Reagan took office would have grown about in line with GNP between 1982 and 1985. The share of spending in GNP would have risen a bit in the first half of this period because of rising interest payments, but would then have fallen back to the starting point.

Because of bracket creep, federal revenues—under tax laws in effect before last year's Economic Recovery Tax Act—would have continued to rise sharply as a share of GNP. Marginal tax rates for middle- and upper-income groups would have risen even faster. After four years, the rising revenue share would have eliminated the budget deficit, given the assumed economic recovery and a "hold-the-line" approach to new spending programs and policies. In order to achieve a balanced budget by 1985, any tax reductions would have had to be offset by expenditure cuts. If, on the other hand, a deficit of, say, 1 percent of GNP were thought to be tolerable in 1985, taxes could have been cut by about $47 billion more than expenditures.

*The Outlook in 1981*

Table 6-2 shows the long-term results, for fiscal 1985, of the first stage of the administration's budget program, as enacted in 1981. (Throughout this chapter fiscal 1985 results are used to represent the long-term budget outcomes.) In both billions of dollars and percentage of GNP, the table first repeats the baseline, pre-Reagan, budget outlook. The next two columns then show how that outlook was changed by the actions taken last year. The Economic Recovery Tax Act of 1981 will cut prospective federal tax revenues some $185 billion below the baseline projections.[1] The three-stage reduction in individual income tax rates, the accelerated depreciation allowances, and the scheduled introduction of inflation indexing account for the bulk of the loss. The buildup in defense spending, launched earlier by the Carter administration and substantially speeded up by the incoming Reagan administration, will add some $60 billion to the baseline

---

1. The CBO estimates the fiscal 1985 revenue loss from the Economic Recovery Tax Act to be some $12 billion greater than does the administration. Congressional Budget Office, *An Analysis of the President's Budgetary Proposals for Fiscal Year 1983* (Government Printing Office, 1982), p. 4. The estimates in table 6-2 give two-thirds weight to the CBO estimates and one-third to those of the administration.

**Table 6-2. Reagan Administration Budget Program, Stage 1: Effect of 1981 Actions on Fiscal 1985 Budget**[a]

Amounts in billions of dollars

| | Amount | | | Percent of GNP | | |
|---|---|---|---|---|---|---|
| Item | Baseline | Stage 1 | Change | Baseline | Stage 1 | Change |
| Expenditures | 945 | 996[b] | 51 | 22.7 | 23.9 | 1.2 |
| Defense | 233 | 293 | 60 | 5.6 | 7.0 | 1.4 |
| Payments to individuals | 452 | 440 | −12 | 10.9 | 10.6 | −0.3 |
| Net interest | 99 | 138[b] | 39 | 2.4 | 3.3 | 0.9 |
| All other | 161 | 125 | −36 | 3.9 | 3.0 | −0.9 |
| Revenues | 950 | 765 | −185 | 22.8 | 18.4 | −4.4 |
| Deficit | 5 | −232[b] | −237 | 0.1 | −5.6 | −5.7 |

Sources: Same as table 6-1. Figures are rounded.
a. See text for explanation of stage 1.
b. The large deficits in stage 1, cumulated over the 1983–85 period, substantially increase the size of the public debt, and hence sharply raise net interest, total expenditures, and the deficit itself.

projections of federal outlays, more than offsetting the $48 billion in civilian budget cuts incorporated in the 1981 reconciliation bill and other legislation. The large budget deficits resulting from these revenue losses and spending increases, cumulated over the 1983–85 period, would then swell the national debt and, at the relatively high interest rates likely to prevail over the period, substantially raise the level of interest payments, thus adding still further to the deficit.

Only last summer the administration's midyear budget review projected that the tax cuts and defense buildup could be undertaken and the budget deficit eliminated by 1984. By now, less than a year later, the 1984 and 1985 budget deficits are almost sure to exceed $200 billion if no further action is taken to reduce them (see table 6-2). What led to this huge change in the perceived budgetary consequences of last year's tax and expenditure actions? First, the earlier budget projections had always assumed the need to find another $44 billion in civilian spending cuts in order to produce budget balances in 1984 and 1985. Second, the recession of 1981 intervened; even a forecast of relatively vigorous recovery starting this year leaves the 1985 economy substantially weaker than the earlier economic scenarios had predicted, which causes the 1985 deficit to increase by over $50 billion in the administration estimates (and by more than that according to the economic assumptions underlying table 6-2). Third, as noted earlier, because the higher deficits projected for 1982 and subsequent years add substantially to the national debt, they raise interest payments and further worsen the budgetary outlook. Fourth, the long-term outlook for interest rates has worsened even in the administration's forecasts, which further increases interest payments on the debt.[2] Fifth, the civilian spending cuts enacted by Congress in 1981 will produce substantially less budgetary savings by 1985 than was assumed in the administration's earlier budget plans.

*The Changes Proposed in 1982*

The administration's response to the changed economic circumstances and budgetary realities—which threaten to turn the promised budget balance in 1985 into a massive deficit—was spelled out in its 1983 budget. It was designed to preserve the key elements of the president's economic and budgetary strategy: the multiphase tax reductions of 1981 were to be preserved and major new taxes would not be enacted; the social security program would not be touched; and the defense buildup would proceed on course. What the administration did propose in its 1983 budget, as stage 2 of its long-run budget program, was a series of further substantial cuts in civilian spending programs, several management initiatives and sales of public assets designed to reduce the measured total of federal spending, and some modest tax increases. The budgetary results, should these proposals be fully enacted, are shown in table 6-3, projected to 1985. With social security and defense exempted from budget cuts (and with the size of potential cuts in several other major programs, such as medicare and veterans' compensation, severely limited by practical political considerations), even draconian reductions in other spending and exceedingly optimistic estimates of asset sales and related management initiatives would still leave the budget substantially in deficit, by over $100 billion in 1983 and $115 billion in 1985.[3] Further deficit

2. In July 1981 the administration estimated that the interest rate on three-month Treasury bills would fall to 6 percent by 1985; this year's budget message projects those rates at 8.5 percent; and the CBO projects them at 9.4 percent. With over $1 trillion of federal debt in the hands of the public by 1983, each 1 percent increase in the average interest rate paid on the federal debt adds $10 billion per year to budget outlays.

3. Even if Congress approved 80 percent of the outlay cuts and tax increases proposed by the administration and as much as one-half of the estimated management savings were effected, the deficit would be $125 billion in 1983 and almost $145 billion in 1985 (see table 2-9).

Charles L. Schultze

**Table 6-3. Reagan Administration Budget Program, Stage 2: Effect of 1982 Proposals on Fiscal 1985 Budget**[a]

Amounts in billions of dollars

| Item | Amount | | | Percent of GNP | | |
|---|---|---|---|---|---|---|
| | Stage 1 | Stage 2 | Change | Stage 1 | Stage 2 | Change |
| Expenditures | 996 | 898 | −98 | 23.9 | 21.6 | −2.4 |
| Defense | 293 | 293 | 0 | 7.0 | 7.0 | 0.0 |
| Payments to individuals | 440 | 417 | −23 | 10.6 | 10.0 | −0.6 |
| Net interest | 138 | 118 | −20 | 3.3 | 2.8 | −0.5 |
| All other | 125 | 70 | −55 | 3.0 | 1.7 | −1.3 |
| Revenues | 765 | 783 | 18 | 18.4 | 18.8 | 0.4 |
| Deficit | −232 | −115 | 117 | −5.6 | −2.8 | 2.8 |

Sources: Same as table 6-1. Figures are rounded.
a. See text for explanation of stage 2.

reductions would have required the administration to modify its basic strategy by slowing the defense buildup and postponing some of the scheduled tax cuts. Rather than do so, it accepted the persistence of substantial deficits, arguing in its budget and economic report that their magnitude was not such as to do serious economic damage, and that the costs of reducing them further by large tax increases would be greater than the benefits.

Because they are concentrated in a relatively narrow part of the total budget, the spending reductions proposed by the administration, coming on top of last year's cuts, would require quite dramatic reductions in many federal activities. As shown in table 6-4, for example, federal expenditures on all civilian programs, other than net interest and payments to individuals, would be cut almost in half between 1980 and 1985 when measured in inflation-adjusted terms. As a share of GNP, these federal programs— covering such diverse activities as support of education and training, research and development, maintenance of the national parks, the expenses of the FBI, and construction of federal-aid highways—would fall to levels below any reached in the last forty years. Table 6-5 illustrates the magnitude of the reductions for a number of particular federal programs. While the federal government would remain a major force in channeling payments for medical care between taxpayers and various beneficiaries, its role in delivering or supporting state and local delivery of public services would be radically reduced. But the service support and

Table 6-4. Proposed Expenditures for Payments to Individuals and All Other Federal
Civilian Programs, Selected Fiscal Years, 1940–85

| Expenditure | 1940 | 1950 | 1960 | 1970 | 1980 | 1983 (pro- posed) | 1985 (pro- posed) |
|---|---|---|---|---|---|---|---|
| *Billions of constant 1981 dollars* | | | | | | | |
| Payments to individuals[a] | 9.9 | 46.1 | 63.1 | 132.8 | 295.3 | 319.7 | 326.5 |
| All other programs[b] | 47.5 | 60.1 | 60.1 | 98.8 | 142.0 | 88.8 | 75.6 |
| *Percent of GNP* | | | | | | | |
| Payments to individuals[a] | 1.7 | 5.2 | 4.7 | 6.5 | 10.6 | 10.7 | 9.8 |
| All other programs[b] | 5.9 | 4.7 | 3.5 | 4.4 | 5.0 | 3.0 | 2.3 |

Sources: Office of Management and Budget, *Federal Government Finances* (GPO, 1982); *The Budget of the United States Government*, selected years; and author's calculations based on administration estimates.
  a. All programs labeled in the budget category "payments to individuals" except military retirement (included in "defense"). Its major components are: civilian retirement and insurance programs, medicare and medicaid, welfare (aid to families with dependent children, supplemental security income, and food stamps), student loans, housing assistance, and veterans' pensions and compensation.
  b. The "all other" program category shown in the budget document nets out several major categories of offsetting receipts, which are treated as negative expenditures—receipts from offshore oil leases, sale of federal land (from 1983 on), and the federal contribution to civil service retirement. The "all other" category in this table is *gross* of these items.

delivery role of the federal government, measured in dollars, is so
small compared with its role in providing defense and making
transfer payments that even radical reductions in this role fail by
a wide margin to eliminate the swelling budget deficit.

Because the potential budget deficit is so large, there is no way
to avoid making strategic choices this year that will strongly affect
the course of the recovery and the structure of the federal budget

Table 6-5. Percentage Reduction in Outlays for Selected Programs,
Fiscal Years 1981–85

| Program | Percent change |
|---|---|
| Criminal justice assistance | −90 |
| Training and job programs | −75 |
| Energy research and development | −62 |
| Education | −57 |
| Recreational resources | −43 |
| Environmental Protection Agency, regulatory enforcement and research programs | −42 |
| Social services | −41 |
| Transportation | −35 |
| Area and regional development | −35 |
| Management of national forests | −29 |

Sources: Based on administration budget estimates, deflated by the implicit deflator for "all other programs" in table 22, p. 9-61 of *Budget of the United States Government, Fiscal Year 1983*.

for years to come. Even inaction would have major consequences, since it would commit the nation to a growing budget deficit of unprecedented magnitude. The actual results of budgetary deliberations will—as always—reflect a series of incremental adjustments through compromise among sharply divergent interests, motivated by a blend of political, ideological, and social considerations. But witting or unwitting, the final decisions will embody a set of strategic choices about long-run economic and social policy of the federal government.

### The Economics of the Budget Deficit

The last part of chapter 2 discusses the interaction between monetary and fiscal policy over the past several years. It points out that monetary and fiscal policies were not significantly in conflict during those years, but are likely to move into conflict in the period ahead, as a continuing policy of slow money growth collides with a budget deficit growing steadily larger despite an assumed economic recovery. The chapter also emphasizes the difference between a policy that simply calls for lower budget deficits (yielding more *total* restraint on demand and a lower growth of GNP) and a policy that simultaneously eases monetary policy as budget deficits are reduced (yielding a different *mix* of GNP within an unchanged total). This chapter continues that discussion in the context of the longer-term strategic choices now facing Congress.

Before these choices are discussed, a preliminary comment is in order. The United States, along with almost every major industrial country, is currently engaged in the very difficult and costly task of trying to reduce a high and stubborn inflation through economic policies that restrict the growth of demand and spending. Modern industrial economies, which have done so well at most other economic tasks during the postwar period, have not discovered how to reduce inflation without substantially retarding the growth of output and employment. Even in the face of idle capacity and large unemployment, business firms and workers moderate their price and wage increases only very slowly (except in those firms where the situation gets so bad that bankruptcies and plant closings are imminent). Because prices and wages retreat so stubbornly, it is output and employment that suffer heavily when monetary and fiscal policies restrict the growth of demand. Gradually inflation subsides, but the cost of achieving that result through restrictive monetary and fiscal policy is large.

No set of monetary and fiscal policies can simultaneously produce a reduction in inflation and the trend of growth in employment and output the nation would like to have.[4] This chapter does suggest ways of improving the long-term outlook through changes in monetary and fiscal policy. But even if achieved, those improvements would not inaugurate a period in which a rapid growth in output and employment could be simultaneously pursued along with a continued reduction in inflation.

*The Effects of a Budget Deficit*

The existence of a large and continuing federal budget deficit affects the economy in two important ways. In the first place, borrowing to finance that deficit absorbs private savings that would otherwise be available for investment in housing or business plant and equipment. Reducing the deficit, therefore, frees up private saving to support investment. To look at the same phenomenon another way, the tax increases or government spending cuts that lower the deficit tend to reduce expenditures by consumers and government, leaving more resources available to produce factory buildings, machinery, or houses. Cutting the deficit thus tends to increase both the real and the financial resources available for investment purposes, while actions that swell the deficit shrink the resources available for investment. (To the extent that the proceeds of tax cuts are saved and not spent on consumer goods, this conclusion must be modified. That fraction of a deficit-creating tax cut which is saved does not reduce the financial or real resources available for investment.)

Second, budget deficits influence the level of GNP. While a reduction in the federal budget deficit increases the real and financial resources *available* for private investment, it does not itself generate that additional investment. Lower deficits do tend

---

4. Some people, including the author, believe that an incomes policy, especially a tax-based one, would improve matters. But for such policies to be effective it would still be necessary to pursue a restrictive monetary and fiscal stance. What incomes policies can primarily do is help restrictive demand policies bring inflation down faster, thereby shortening the period during which the lost output and employment must be suffered.

to produce some decline in interest rates, but there is no presumption that the decline will be large enough to induce the requisite additional investment. Taken by itself, therefore, a reduction (increase) in the deficit will lower (raise) the overall level of spending in the economy. To maintain the level of total spending and GNP, if that is desired, a reduction in the deficit must be accompanied by an easing of monetary policy to produce interest rates low enough to generate the additional private investment.

Conventional analysis, on which the preceding discussion was based, does not take into account what a long period of extremely high interest rates produced by the combination of tight money and huge budget deficits might do to the financial viability of American business. There is little postwar experience on which to base a forecast of the potential damage to financial structures. Continuation of today's interest rates could destroy parts of the thrift industry. And for nonfinancial businesses, the threat of bankruptcy, potential inability to cover debt service, and deteriorating creditworthiness could give rise to a phenomenon that has been avoided in the postwar period—a financially induced recession of substantial depth and long duration. The interest rate reduction accompanying a large cut in the $200 billion-plus deficits that are now in prospect for the mid-1980s could mitigate this threat. The fact that deficit reduction could be important in preventing such damage does not imply, however, that the resulting path of economic growth would necessarily be the desirable one. On this point, the conventional analysis is still relevant— ensuring the appropriate level of GNP may require some contribution from monetary policy.

Thus two different sets of considerations are relevant in deciding the appropriate size of the federal budget deficit:

—Reducing the deficit can change the *mix* of GNP; out of a given GNP, a larger share becomes available for private investment.

—Reducing the deficit, with no offsetting change in monetary policy, will lower the *level* of demand, employment, and GNP; to the extent that the government wants to place additional restraints on total demand and employment as a means of putting further downward pressure on inflation, reducing the deficit is a way to do so. But to the extent that only a change in mix is desired, the depressing effect of a deficit reduction would have to be offset by an easing of monetary policy. To design a reasonable long-term strategy for dealing with the prospective budget deficits that now face the country, it is therefore necessary to make decisions about both the level and the composition of economic activity. And that decision in turn involves considerations of both fiscal and monetary policy.

## The Question of Mix

Table 6-6 summarizes postwar trends in the share of GNP flowing into private saving and the availability of those savings for private investment. In order to assess the longer-term implications of sustaining large budget deficits, it also projects the saving ratio and investment availability to 1985 under two different assumptions about the size of the deficit that will have to be financed.

**Table 6-6. Private Saving and Its Uses, 1951–80, and Projections to 1985**
Percent of GNP

| | | | | 1985 | |
|---|---|---|---|---|---|
| | | | | Case A ($230 billion deficit) | Case B ($80 billion deficit) |
| Component and use | 1951–60 | 1961–70 | 1971–80 | | |
| **Total private saving** | **16.0** | **16.9** | **17.7** | **19.3** | **18.7** |
| Personal | 4.7 | 4.7 | 4.8[a] | 4.8 | 4.4 |
| Business | 11.3 | 11.7 | 12.0 | 13.2 | 13.0 |
| State and local pension funds[b] | . . . | 0.5 | 0.9 | 1.3 | 1.3 |
| **Total uses of saving** | **16.1** | **16.9** | **17.9** | **19.3** | **18.7** |
| Less: financing the federal deficit | 0.2 | 0.5 | 1.9 | 5.5 | 1.9 |
| Less: financing state and local deficits | . . . | 0.5 | −0.1 | 0.0 | 0.0 |
| Less: net foreign investment | 0.3 | 0.5 | 0.1 | −0.3 | 0.0 |
| **Amount available for private investment** | **15.6** | **15.4** | **16.0** | **14.1** | **16.8** |

Sources: U.S. Department of Commerce, *The National Income and Product Accounts of the United States* (selected issues), and author's estimates. Figures are rounded. Sources and uses of saving were estimated independently; a small statistical discrepancy shows up in the historical series.
a. In the last half of the 1970s (1976–80), personal saving fell to 3.9 percent of GNP.
b. The flow of savings into pension funds of private firms is included in personal saving. The net flow of funds into pension funds for state and local government employees is exactly the same in character and thus classified under "private saving" here.

Private saving is made up of two main components: personal saving and the gross retained earnings of business firms (profits after taxes and dividends plus depreciation allowances). As the table shows, the nation has modestly increased the share of income going to private saving in each of the last two decades. All this gain has been in the form of business saving and an increased accumulation in state and local pension funds—the personal saving share did not rise (and indeed in the last half of the 1970s it declined substantially). All the rise in the private saving ratio from the 1950s to the 1970s was absorbed by an increase in the size of the federal deficit that had to be financed. But the effect of this on the availability of financial and real resources for private investment was moderated by a swing from a deficit to a small surplus on the part of state and local governments and by the decline of net investment abroad by Americans. Despite the rather large rise in the amount of saving required to finance the federal deficit, therefore, a slight increase in the availability of funds for private investment did take place.

To show the magnitude of the current problem, the 1985 projection labeled ''case A'' in table 6-6 incorporates the $230 billion federal deficit that would be forthcoming by then if no actions are taken to reduce it. The ''case B'' projection assumes that the deficit is reduced by $150 billion to a level of $80 billion.[5]

The estimate of private saving in the case A projection assumes optimistically that individual and corporate tax reductions in the Economic Recovery Tax Act of 1981 will significantly raise private saving. While the act does substantially lower effective tax rates from what they otherwise would be, the average and marginal effective tax rates for most individual taxpayers in the middle-income brackets are reduced only to the levels of the mid-1970s. Part of the tax reduction simply offsets bracket creep that otherwise would have occurred. The more generous treatment of savings in the form of individual retirement accounts and Keogh plans for the self-employed should result in some increase in saving. The projection very optimistically assumes that the personal saving rate out of disposable income would rise from the 5.7

5. Because actions to reduce the annual deficits between now and 1985 would lower the public debt, and hence interest payments, a deficit reduction program of about $50, $90, and $130 billion in fiscal years 1983 through 1985 would produce a deficit reduction of approximately $150 billion in 1985.

percent average of the last half of the 1970s to 7.0 percent in 1985. Business saving as a share of GNP was assumed to continue on its modest upward trend and was then raised further by an amount equal to 60 percent of the corporate tax cut (the other 40 percent going to dividends).

State and local governments in the aggregate were assumed to run a balanced budget (although the combination of cuts in federal grants in aid and the aftermath of events like California's Proposition 13 could put them in deficit). The accumulation in state and local pension funds has continued to grow beyond the average of the 1970s, and further growth is projected to 1985. It was assumed that some part of the needed financing would come from abroad in the form of a U.S. current account deficit, but the magnitude of this relief is limited. Foreigners would be unwilling to finance a huge U.S. current account deficit, and exchange rate movements (a depreciation of the dollar) would limit financing from this source.

As shown in the last line of table 6-6, failure to reduce the federal deficit very substantially below the levels now in prospect would sharply lower the availability of funds for private investment, even with a highly optimistic assessment of the behavior of private saving. The 14 percent of GNP that would be available for investment is well below postwar experience. Housing construction would necessarily fall even lower than it is now. The crowding out of private investment would take place through the mechanism of very high interest rates maintained over a long period of time. Since the nation has no experience with such a situation, there is little basis on which to predict the consequences. But it is conceivable that severe financial strains would develop, leading to a major credit crunch and a subsequent recession longer and deeper than any in the postwar period.

Relatively optimistic assumptions show it would take a reduction in the 1985 deficit of at least $150 billion to make available for private investment a share of resources slightly larger than that which prevailed in the 1970s. It is probably reasonable to assume that housing investment would not return fully to the same share of GNP it had in the 1970s, partly because mortgage interest rates are likely in the best of circumstances to remain well above historical levels. Consequently, case B does make room for a rise somewhat above the average of the 1970s in the share of GNP going to business investment. But even with the large deficit reduction program that underlies case B, the room for a rise in investment is modest, especially in view of the nation's poor productivity performance and its need for a sharp increase in investment. A year ago, Secretary of the Treasury Donald T. Regan projected a rise in the private investment share of GNP of some 4 percentage points between 1981 and 1986.[6] It will now take a massive deficit reduction effort to make room for only a small fraction of that increase.

So far, the discussion has assumed a particular size for the total GNP and concentrated on the question of how the size of the federal deficit affects how much of the assumed GNP would be available for investment. But to reduce the deficit, as in case B, large spending cuts and tax increases must be enacted. An additional question must therefore be posed: will the resulting fiscal policy, combined with the present monetary policy, make it possible to achieve the projected path for GNP growth? That is, will investment be forthcoming in sufficient volume to absorb the real and financial resources available? If not, GNP would rise by less than the projections assume.

### The Question of Level

There is a two-way relationship between the budget and the level of economic activity. Budget policy, through changes in taxes and spending programs, affects the level of demand and output. But changes in demand and output lead to changes in private taxable income, which in turn changes budget revenues, federal outlays for unemployment compensation, and therefore the deficit. A traditional way of trying to isolate the magnitude of changes in budget policy itself, uncontaminated by the feedback effects of fluctuations in economic activity, is to calculate what the budget revenues, expenditures, and deficit would be over several years along a stable path of economic growth. That path is conventionally defined as one that keeps the rate of unemployment constant at some relatively low level. Such a "high-employment" calculation (assuming a constant 6 percent level of unemployment) is shown in table 6-7 for two assumptions: first, that no

6. Press release, U.S. Department of the Treasury, March 20, 1981.

Table 6-7. Deficits in the High-Employment Budget[a] under Two Policy Assumptions, Selected Fiscal Years, 1981–85

| Policy assumption | Deficit | | | |
|---|---|---|---|---|
| | 1981 | 1982 | 1983 | 1985 |
| No actions to reduce the stage 1 deficit | | | | |
| Billions of dollars | − 27 | − 53 | − 108 | − 202 |
| Percent of GNP | 0.9 | 1.7 | 3.1 | 4.8 |
| Actions to reduce 1985 deficit by $150 billion | | | | |
| Billions of dollars | − 27 | − 53 | − 58 | − 52[b] |
| Percent of GNP | 0.9 | 1.7 | 1.7 | 1.2 |

Sources: Same as table 6-1.
a. Assuming a constant 6 percent unemployment rate.
b. The *actual* budget deficit under the second assumption would be $80 billion, since unemployment in 1985 is projected to be more than 6 percent. This $80 billion budget, or 2.0 percent of GNP, is shown in the last column in table 6-6, which deals with the actual, not the high-employment, budget.

actions are taken to reduce the stage 1 budget deficit; and second, that actions are taken that achieve budget reductions starting at $50 billion in 1983 and rising to $150 billion by 1985 (including the effect of deficit-reducing actions on the public debt and hence on interest payments).

In the period immediately ahead, as the economy tries to struggle out of a recession, some budgetary stimulus may well be desirable. But there is no peacetime precedent for the high-employment deficit to continue rising to 5 percent of GNP. The stimulative effect of such a deficit on the demand for goods and services, especially in the consumer goods and defense industries, would be very great. While budget policy without correction would be stimulative to an unprecedented degree over the next three to four years, monetary policy has been set on an equally unprecedented course of restraint. Earlier this year, even before the second phase of the scheduled tax cut took place, and in the midst of a recession, long-term interest rates (both absolutely and in relation to inflation) reached postwar peaks, partly in expectation of the conflict between slow money growth and huge budget deficits.

Since there is no precedent for either the stimulative magnitude of the prospective deficits or the restrictiveness of the announced monetary policy, it is exceedingly difficult to analyze the ramifications of the conflict. Conventional analysis, looking to historical relationships between money, interest rates, deficits, and private demand for goods and services, suggests an outcome in which the large tax cuts, the rapid defense buildup, and other elements adding to the deficit would generate enough growth in the non-interest-sensitive parts of the economy to offset the effects of monetary policy, but perhaps not enough to launch major new inflationary pressures. On average, real interest rates would continue over the foreseeable future to equal or exceed the unprecedented levels of the last six months, but both interest rates and economic activity would fluctuate erratically. Interest-sensitive industries—autos, housing, inventory goods—would continue at very depressed levels.[7] In addition, as discussed earlier, continuation of very high interest rates over a long period could weaken the financial structure of many business firms enough to induce a serious and long-lived overall recession.

Large tax increases and spending cuts sufficient to reduce the budget deficit by the $150 billion shown in case B of table 6-6 would reduce interest rates below the levels that would prevail with the higher budget deficits. Moreover, to the extent that the level of today's long-term interest rates reflects an anticipation of the consequences of future large budget deficits, a credible series of actions to lower those future deficits could affect current interest rates even before any changes had occurred in the deficits themselves. The question is, how far would rates fall and what would be the likely growth of GNP and employment in a world with current monetary policy and a substantially reduced deficit? Would growth be lower than necessary to promote a continued decline in inflation? If not, then there is no reason to accompany the deficit reduction with a change in monetary policy. But if so, some easing of monetary policy would be desirable as an accompaniment to the deficit reduction.

Typically, during their first several years economic recoveries after the early 1950s produced an average annual growth rate in the neighborhood of 5 percent. While recoveries differed, real long-term interest rates (corporate Aaa rates less the inflation rate) usually ranged between 1 and 3 percent.[8] With the partial

7. With today's tight money, unchecked budget deficits of the magnitude shown in case A of table 6-6 would guarantee a highly erratic and unbalanced economy. With easier money, those deficits would guarantee a renewal of inflation.

8. The average of the current and prior three years' rate of increase in the GNP deflator (less the direct impact of farm and oil price changes in 1973–75 and 1979–81) was used to calculate real interest rates. The aborted recovery of 1959 was excluded as being atypical.

exception of 1972–73 and 1976–77, these recoveries were not driven by stimulative budget policies. If that same low level of real interest rates would now prevail, and the high-employment deficit were kept a roughly constant share of GNP, there is no reason to believe that the forces now making for recovery would be any weaker than the postwar average. But with the money supply now scheduled to grow at only 4 to 4.5 percent a year, while inflation is projected to average some 6 percent over the next three years, even a major deficit reduction plan is likely to leave real interest rates well above the range that characterized earlier postwar recoveries. Economic growth would probably not proceed at a pace sufficient to keep the average rate of unemployment much below 8.5 percent over the next three years. Or to say it another way, only a very large rise in the velocity of circulation would make it possible to have a significant growth in real GNP, given the slow growth of money and the gradual decline in inflation projected for the next several years. But in turn the interest rates needed to generate that rise in velocity would themselves be too high to sustain a growth in real GNP sufficient to pull unemployment down very far.[9]

A policy mix that raises taxes and cuts spending enough to lower the 1985 deficit by $150 billion, while maintaining the present course of monetary policy, would intensify the restraints on national spending and gradually exert still greater downward pressure on inflation. Ultimately the lower inflation would itself ease the growth-restraining effect of 4 percent money growth. If that is the desired outcome, then a major deficit reduction program need not be accompanied by an easing of monetary policy.

A policy that keeps unemployment near 8.5 percent for the next three years, however, is more rigorous than necessary to maintain some progress in reducing inflation. With a truly large deficit reduction program in place, it would be possible to ease monetary policy cautiously without abandoning the fight against inflation, and aim perhaps for an average growth of real GNP during the 1982–85 period in the neighborhood of 4 percent. Conceivably, of course, continued tight money and unprecedented levels of interest rates would stimulate the public to invent innovative ways to

9. For a discussion of the very high velocity growth implicit in the economic forecasts of the administration and the CBO, see CBO, *An Analysis of the President's Budgetary Proposals for Fiscal Year 1983*, pp. 40–42.

conserve their holdings of cash balances, so that the Federal Reserve Board's current money targets would permit lower interest rates and higher growth. But this would be easier money achieved by sheer good luck rather than design, and surely such a development cannot be counted on.

The above analysis assumes that the underlying inflation rate will decline over the next three years, but only gradually, reaching a level of 5 to 6 percent by 1985. Such an outcome would be within the general range of private forecasts. If, contrary to expectations, inflation should collapse much more rapidly, however, even slow money growth could finance a more satisfactory rate of economic growth. (A lower price level is equivalent to an increase in the money supply.) In that improbable but not impossible case, no easing of monetary policy would be called for.

### Measures for Reducing the Long-Term Deficit

As the magnitude of the long-term deficit projections has become known, it has also become apparent that previously suggested alternative strategies—cutting here or there, postponing tax cuts, closing loopholes—will not suffice. In order to produce a budget reduction program of anything like the $150 billion suggested above, Congress will have to adopt a much different approach. First, there can be no major untouchable elements in the budget. The social and political consensus required to take actions of the magnitude that is called for will not be forthcoming if any important sector of the budget or of society is exempt. In particular, the program must include cuts in defense[10] and social security and must require some sacrifice from those who received the bulk of the benefits of last year's individual tax cuts. Second, rather than being able to emphasize one set of alternatives over another, Congress will have to use many different sources of deficit reduction. Substantive criteria will remain relevant; for example, business investment incentives should be reduced as little as possible, and further reductions in programs for the poor and near-poor should be made only if the case is

10. If maintaining the present rapid pace of the defense buildup were clearly essential to national security, an exemption might be feasible. But as argued in chapter 3, this is by no means the case and, equally important, may not be perceived in Congress to be the case.

particularly strong. More than is usually true, however, the package will have to be put together with an eye to maximizing political acceptability. A potential reduction that is itself politically acceptable or that helps secure enactment of some other difficult budget reductions enters the contest with substantial marks in its favor.

It was estimated earlier that deficit reductions starting at $50 billion in 1983 and building up to about $150 billion by 1985 would be necessary to maintain the high-employment deficit roughly constant in the neighborhood of 1.5 percent of GNP (see table 6-7). After such reductions, the 1985 budget would show a high-employment deficit of $52 billion and—since unemployment in 1985 is projected to be somewhat higher than 6 percent—an actual deficit of $80 billion. There is, of course, no principle, economic or otherwise, that suggests that reducing the federal deficit to approximately its 1982 high-employment level is precisely the appropriate course to follow. But a reduction of at least that much seems desirable. Achieving that goal would avert a situation in which federal deficits would significantly crowd out private investment and it would in fact make available the resources for a small increase in the investment share of GNP. It would contribute toward lowering the excessive level of interest rates. To the extent that the specific consequences of economic policy can be foreseen several years in advance, the resulting fiscal stance, in combination with some easing of monetary policy, would make possible a pace of economic growth large enough to yield gradual reductions in today's high unemployment but modest enough to maintain downward pressure on inflation. And because it would require $150 billion of deficit reduction, it is an ambitious goal.

Budget actions that provide substantial reductions in the deficit over several years bring an added bonus; because they slow the growth of the public debt, they lower expenditures for interest payments.[11] Hence a combination of tax increases and spending cuts starting at $50 billion in 1983 and growing to $130 billion in

11. The lower deficits would also bring somewhat lower interest rates, even without a change in monetary policy. However, the economic assumptions used in the CBO and administration projections already incorporate a substantial fall in real interest rates, a development that would be feasible only after a large drop in the budget deficit. A further reduction seems unwarranted.

1985 would make possible the target deficit reduction of $150 billion in 1985.

Earlier this year, the administration proposed a deficit reduction program that by its estimates would amount to some $100 billion by 1985.[12] As noted earlier, that deficit reduction program seeks to maintain intact the basic thrust of the administration's 1981 economic and budgetary program. The bulk of the budget cuts would be concentrated in the same broad area as were last year's spending cuts—that is, in the one-quarter of the federal budget excluding defense, interest, and transfer payments.

There are two main reasons that other areas of the budget should incur reductions, however. First, apart from the questions it raises on substantive grounds, concentrating budget reductions in the very narrow area proposed by the administration would make it impossible to secure the social and political consensus needed to reduce the deficit by the needed amount. And second, even complete enactment of the administration's program would still leave an additional $30 billion to $40 billion in budget reductions to be found by 1985.

Alternative ways to reduce the deficit are identified and discussed very briefly in the sections that follow.

### Tax Increases or Deferrals of Tax Reductions

There are three major approaches to raising taxes by substantial amounts: general income tax increases; general or specific taxes on consumption; and closing loopholes.

GENERAL INCOME TAX INCREASES. While there are numerous ways to provide a general income tax increase, two have recently been suggested: an indefinite delay in the third (10 percent) increment of last year's tax cut, due to take effect in July 1983, and a delay in the introduction of inflation indexing, scheduled to begin in 1985. The third stage of the individual tax cut accounts for about 40 percent of the tax rate reduction enacted last year.

12. See *Budget of the United States, Fiscal Year 1983*, p. 3-8. However, as a recent analysis by the CBO has pointed out, several of the proposed savings are highly questionable, especially the $5 billion additional revenue from offshore oil receipts, the $4 billion in extra sales of public land and other property, and $4 billion in savings from lower growth in the nation's medical care costs (CBO, *An Analysis of the President's Budgetary Proposals for Fiscal Year 1983*). Even if Congress enacted all of its proposed cuts, the administration's estimate of $100 billion of savings should be discounted by perhaps $10 billion.

An alternative that would be quite similar in its effect on individual taxpayers would be the temporary imposition of an income tax surcharge; each taxpayer would calculate his tax and then add a specified percentage (the surcharge) to that tax. Since the top-bracket rate was reduced from 70 to 50 percent in the first round of last year's tax cut, postponement of the third stage of the tax cut would have only a slight effect on taxpayers with very high incomes. The surcharge, on the other hand, would impose the same proportional increase on all taxpayers, and thus might be a more acceptable alternative. A 12 percent surcharge would yield the same revenue gain in 1985 as postponement of the third stage of the individual income tax cut.

The table below shows the revenue gains from these three alternatives for 1983 and 1985. It does not include a surcharge or other increase for corporate taxes. Substantial criticism can indeed be leveled at the particular structure of business investment incentives included in last year's Economic Recovery Tax Act.[13] Nevertheless, enactment of structural changes in those incentives is highly unlikely this year, and it would be unwise at the present time simply to lower the overall level of incentives provided by last year's act.

|  | 1983 (billions of dollars) | 1985 (billions of dollars) |
|---|---|---|
| Delay third stage of tax reduction under the Economic Recovery Tax Act of 1981 | 9 | 40 |
| Impose 12 percent surcharge on individual income tax | 36 | 41 |
| Delay indexing | 0 | 12 |

All the proposals suggested above would raise marginal tax rates, especially for middle- and upper-middle-income taxpayers, higher than those that will exist when the Economic Recovery Tax Act is fully in effect. But the rates would not be much different from what they are now. Under the Economic Recovery Tax Act,

13. See, for example, the vastly different effects on rates of return for investment in various types of plant and equipment as shown in the 1982 *Economic Report of the President*, p. 123.

the tax cuts for individuals would amount to some $128 billion by 1985. According to the CBO, between October 1981 and 1985, bracket creep due to inflation would have raised taxes by $71 billion. Deferral of the third stage of the act or a 12 percent surcharge, plus postponement of indexing, would still leave the value of the act's tax cut at $74 billion—which would almost exactly offset bracket creep. Individual taxpayers would fare differently, with lower- and middle-income taxpayers being better off under the surcharge. On balance, however, neither approach would make the tax burdens on individuals significantly worse than in 1981, although the potential improvement under the full implementation of the 1981 tax act would not be forthcoming.

TAXES ON CONSUMPTION. A substantially different approach would impose taxes on consumption, either generally or on specific items. Table 6-8 provides estimates of the revenue gain from various proposals of this kind.

Adopting a national value-added tax or a sales tax could provide substantial additional revenues. Even with liberal exemptions— for food, medical care, education expenditures, and the like—a 4 percent value-added tax could yield some $50 billion a year by

**Table 6-8. Projected Revenue Gains from Taxes on Consumption, Fiscal Years 1983 and 1985**

Billions of dollars

| Consumption tax | 1983 | 1985 |
|---|---|---|
| 4 percent value-added tax with liberal exemptions[a] | 40 | 49 |
| Deregulation of natural gas with windfall tax[b] | 5–15 | c |
| Gasoline tax increase | | |
| Increase in the current 4-cent tax to 13 cents | 10 | 10 |
| Conversion of current tax to a 15 percent ad valorem tax | 17 | 18 |
| Doubled excise taxes on alcohol and tobacco | 6 | 7 |
| $5 a barrel oil import fee | 15–20 | 15–20 |

Sources: Author's estimates, calculated from Department of Commerce, *The National Income and Product Accounts of the United States,* selected issues; data provided by Federal Highway Administration, Division of Highway Statistics; Congressional Budget Office, *Reducing the Federal Deficit: Strategies and Options* (GPO, 1982), p. 201.

a. Exemptions for food, medical care, educational expenses, and other worthy purposes equal to about one-half of consumer expenditures. See Charles E. McLure, Jr., in Felicity Skidmore, ed., "VAT Versus the Payroll Tax," *Social Security Financing* (MIT Press, 1981), p. 138.

b. If the adjustment of natural gas prices to market levels after decontrol is a gradual one, and decontrol does not occur until late in 1982, substantial windfall tax receipts might not occur until fiscal 1984. Since partial decontrol will occur in 1985 in any event, the additional revenues available in that year from a windfall tax enacted several years earlier may shrink.

c. Assessing the likely revenue gain in later years is particularly difficult, and thus a numerical estimate for 1985 is not given.

1985. Proposing a value-added or sales tax as the principal means of reducing the current deficit has some notable disadvantages, however. Most important, such a tax would come on top of the cuts in federal programs providing benefits to lower- and lower-middle-income people and after a big reduction in taxes weighted heavily toward upper-income groups. Whatever its long-run merits or faults, an attempt to enact it as part of a broad deficit reduction package would almost surely make that package politically intolerable. From an economic standpoint, the tax has the added disadvantage that it would raise the consumer price index by about 2 percentage points the year it was introduced. And to the extent it caused an upward adjustment in wages, it would add still further to the CPI in later periods. Seeking to gain revenues by imposing additional taxes on alcohol and tobacco faces the same kind of difficulties.

Currently natural gas prices are being held well below market levels. Under current law, in 1985 prices for some categories of natural gas will be decontrolled, while others will not. When that occurs, very substantial distortions will occur in the natural gas market.[14] Those disruptions, together with the more general inefficiencies that occur when natural gas prices are kept substantially below the market price, provide a reason to decontrol natural gas immediately. Such decontrol would provide large windfall profits to owners of "old" gas. Enactment of a windfall tax would capture part of those revenues, and, together with the increase in corporate profits tax collected from gas producers that would occur, could provide substantial additional revenues. Unfortunately, alternative decontrol plans and economic assumptions yield different conclusions about the size of the price increase that would follow decontrol. Instability in the world oil market has increased the uncertainty. Hence there is a wide range shown in table 6-8 for the revenue yield of this tax. Moreover, since partial decontrol will in any event occur in 1985, the incremental revenues from earlier decontrol will not be permanent.

Against the clear gain in national efficiency and the additional

14. Gas sold under "old" contracts will remain under control. Different regions of the country have quite different proportions of their gas consumption under those old contracts, and, because of the way natural gas is priced at retail, will have very different capabilities of bidding for the uncontrolled gas.

budget revenues from gas decontrol must be placed the resulting price increase. According to a recent study by the Department of Energy, complete deregulation of old and new gas would cause the GNP deflator to rise between 1.4 and 2.5 percent in the year after it occurred. (But this estimate was made before the recent softness in world oil prices. Presumably the price effects of decontrol would be somewhat less at the present time.) Subsequently, however, the inflation rate would fall below its projected path, since the partial decontrol scheduled for 1985 would have occurred sooner.[15]

The tax on gasoline has remained at four cents a gallon since 1959. As inflation has occurred, the real value of the tax has fallen. Raising the gasoline tax to thirteen cents would simply restore it to the same real value as that of a four-cent tax in the 1950s. The revenue yield would be slightly less than $10 billion in both 1983 and 1985. An argument could also be made for raising the tax still further. The United States has by far the lowest gasoline taxes of any major oil-importing country. There is much to be said for a deficit-reducing tax that penalizes the consumption of an import that should be discouraged on national security and other grounds. One argument sometimes made for an increase in the gasoline tax is that it would help prevent the lower real price of gasoline, caused by the current temporary glut, from eroding the progress in gasoline conservation that has been made in recent years. Converting the current four-cent tax to a 15 percent ad valorem tax would both raise the level of the tax and automatically keep it in line with changes in the price of gasoline. The revenue from this action would be substantial—$17 billion in 1983 and $18 billion in 1985. The gasoline tax increase shares the same problem as the decontrol of natural gas: the 15 percent ad valorem tax would add about 0.7 percent to the CPI in the year after it was first imposed.

An alternative to increasing the gasoline tax would be the imposition of a fee on imported oil. An oil import fee would raise the price of both imported and domestic oil, and the direct revenue from the fee would be supplemented by higher revenues from the

15. U.S. Department of Energy, "A Study of Alternatives to the Natural Gas Policy Act of 1978," November 1981, p. 28. See also James R. Capra and David C. Beek, "Combining Decontrol of Natural Gas with a New Tax on Producer Revenues," *Federal Reserve Bank of New York Quarterly Review,* vol. 6 (Winter 1981–82), pp. 63–67.

existing windfall tax on domestic oil producers. A $5 import fee ought to produce between $15 billion and $20 billion in revenues, the specific amount depending in part on the ability of oil-using business firms to pass along the higher prices to their customers. Compared with an increase in the gasoline tax, an oil import fee has the advantage of providing incentives for conserving all uses of oil, not just gasoline. Since only part of the additional revenues received by domestic oil producers would be taxed away, their profits would be improved. (Imposing an excise tax on both domestic and imported oil would be administratively more complex, but would channel all the proceeds from higher oil prices to the government.) Like a gasoline tax increase, an oil import fee or oil excise tax would increase the CPI and other price indexes in the year it was made effective. It would also impose a special competitive disadvantage on those American exports that used oil importantly as a raw material (for example, chemicals).

To the extent that these consumption taxes raise the level of prices, and the Federal Reserve does not "accommodate" the price rise with an expanded supply of money, the interest rates associated with any given recovery path would be increased.

CLOSING LOOPHOLES. Table 6-9 identifies some major possibilities for raising revenues through reforms in the tax structure. An even more comprehensive list has been identified by the CBO.[16] The administration's proposals to raise taxes by closing loopholes total almost $16 billion by 1985. They are explained in the 1983 budget document.

There are several other reforms that are particularly relevant to the treatment of current economic and budgetary problems, because they would reward savings, provide incentives to hold down prices, or address, on the tax side, some of the problems of entitlement programs (see table 6-9).

One such change, for example, would be to place a limit on the deductibility of employer contributions to medical care plans ($120 has often been suggested as a reasonable monthly limit). The availability of untaxed insurance as part of employer-paid fringe benefits discourages competition among health providers to deliver health care more efficiently. (Taking $100 in the form of

16. In CBO, *Reducing the Federal Deficit: Strategies and Options* (GPO, 1982).

**Table 6-9. Projected Revenue Gains from Selected Tax Reforms, Fiscal Years 1983 and 1985**

Billions of dollars

| Tax reform | 1983 | 1985 |
|---|---|---|
| **Administration proposals** | **10.5** | **15.8** |
| Primarily business firms | 8.7 | 13.3 |
| Primarily individuals | 1.8 | 2.5 |
| **Reforms that stimulate savings and/or reduce cost increases** | **3.7** | **12.5** |
| Limit tax-free employer contributions for health plans to $120 a month | 2.5 | 4.4 |
| Terminate deductibility of consumer interest payments | 1.2 | 8.1 |
| **Reforms in tax treatment of entitlement programs** | **3.5** | **4.0** |
| Tax all unemployment insurance benefits | 1.9 | 1.7 |
| Tax half of retirement benefits for social security recipients with income above $20,000–$25,000 | 1.6 | 2.3 |
| **Total** | **17.7** | **32.3** |

Sources: *Budget of the United States Government, Fiscal Year 1983*, p. 4-16; and CBO, *Reducing the Federal Deficit*, app. B.

a wage increase is taxable; taking $100 in the form of a more generous medical plan is tax free.) As a consequence, the medical care system of the nation continually evolves in the direction of removing incentives for more efficient and lower-cost medical care.

Eliminating the deductibility of interest on consumer installment debt would remove an anomaly in the U.S. tax code that subsidizes consumer borrowing and penalizes saving. Consideration of the present plight of the automobile industry suggests, however, that this particular reform might be best postponed or phased in gradually.

There are several tax reforms that would improve the fairness of entitlement programs—taxing fully the benefits from unemployment compensation and taxing one-half the retirement benefits for social security recipients with total income above some level, say $25,000 for couples and $20,000 for single individuals.

As is always the case, these reforms are politically difficult. They offend either a very large number of voting beneficiaries or a small number of contributing beneficiaries. But in the context of an across-the-board effort to put together a deficit reduction program, and with the backing of the administration, some of these reforms would appear to be good candidates for incorporation in the package.

*Expenditure Reductions*

It will be convenient to examine the possibilities for expenditure reduction under three broad categories: defense, entitlements, and "all other" programs.

DEFENSE. Chapter 3 of this book examines the five-year defense plans of the Reagan administration, which embody a very large annual increase in defense spending—about 9 percent a year over and above inflation between now and 1985. It provides an estimate of the annual costs of investing in and maintaining in combat readiness the "baseline" armed forces of the United States. It then analyzes for each of the major components of the armed forces—strategic nuclear, tactical nuclear, and conventional—the plans of the Reagan administration to invest much more heavily in the existing baseline forces and to expand certain aspects of those forces on a very rapid timetable.

The analysis in chapter 3 suggests that the baseline forces were significantly underfunded in the years 1972–80, and that real expansion of defense outlays would be necessary to compensate for that underfunding in the years ahead. But the chapter also concludes that a number of measures could be taken to moderate both the pace and the magnitude of the defense buildup while still providing a major strengthening of the armed forces, as is widely agreed to be necessary. The table below summarizes the intermediate reductions in defense outlays that would achieve this result. In fiscal 1984 and 1985, between $25 and $30 billion a year in budget savings could be realized.

|  | *1983* (billions of dollars) | *1984* (billions of dollars) | *1985* (billions of dollars) |
|---|---|---|---|
| Strategic nuclear forces | 3.5 | 8.9 | 9.2 |
| Tactical nuclear forces | 0.3 | 0.3 | 0.3 |
| Conventional forces | 7.3 | 18.6 | 19.6 |
| Total | 11.1 | 27.8 | 29.1 |

ENTITLEMENT PROGRAMS. There are two major ways to secure reductions in spending on entitlement programs. One is to propose structural changes in them, including permanent changes in their indexing provisions. Another approach (which does not foreclose the adoption of reforms) is to reduce or suspend temporarily some or all of the prospective indexing increases explicitly to lower the current budget deficit.

There are two cogent arguments for incorporating the latter approach in a comprehensive budget reduction program. First, if it can be shown that every major element of society will participate in reducing the deficit, it may be possible to secure reasonable reductions in programs like social security that sometimes appear to be politically untouchable. Second, in the period 1977–80 the CPI overstated the "true" rise in the cost of living by some 5 to 6 percent and exceeded the growth of wages by some 8 percent. While those who have just come on the beneficiary rolls did not receive this particularly generous increase, a one-time reduction of indexing to recoup these "extra" payments can be defended as still leaving most beneficiaries fully protected against recent inflation, or (if the larger 8 percent reduction is applied) at least as well protected as the working population.

The table below shows the reduction in budget outlays that would be forthcoming in 1983 and 1985 by reductions of 2.5 percent and 4 percent in the cost-of-living increases of all indexed programs in 1983 and 1984. The estimates do not reduce indexing for supplemental security income and food stamps on the grounds that the poor have already been relatively hard hit and that the food price index in the 1977–81 period did not overstate the true rise in food costs.

|  | 1983 (billions of dollars) | 1985 (billions of dollars) |
|---|---|---|
| Indexing reduced by 5 percent (2.5 percent a year in 1983 and 1984) | 6 | 13 |
| Indexing reduced by 8 percent (4 percent a year in 1983 and 1984) | 10 | 21 |

Both the administration and the CBO have put forth a number of suggestions for structural changes in the various entitlement programs.[17] Those are summarized in table 6-10, where entitle-

17. See Office of Management and Budget, *Major Themes and Additional Budget Details, Fiscal Year 1983* (GPO, 1982); CBO, *Reducing the Federal Deficit*.

**Table 6-10. Reductions in Entitlement Programs Identified by the Administration and the Congressional Budget Office, Fiscal Year 1985**
Billions of dollars

| Program | Congressional Budget Office[a] | Administration[b] |
|---|---|---|
| **Middle-class retirement, social insurance, and related programs** | **7.9** | **6.9** |
| | (2.3)[c] | (2.0)[c] |
| Social security (OASDI) | 2.0 | 0.0 |
| Medicare | 2.4 | 3.7 |
| Federal retirement | 0.5 | 1.5 |
| Child nutrition[d] | 1.4 | 0.5 |
| Other | 1.6 | 1.1 |
| **Means-tested programs for the poor and near-poor** | **1.5** | **10.0** |
| | (1.8)[c] | (12.9)[c] |
| Medicaid | 0.9 | 3.7 |
| Food stamps | 0.0 | 2.9 |
| Student loans | 0.5 | 1.4 |
| SSI and AFDC | 0.1 | 1.8 |
| Other | 0.0 | 0.2 |

Sources: Same as table 6-9.

a. The CBO also identified a number of options to reduce or defer indexing of some entitlement programs.

b. The administration also claimed savings of $4 billion in medicare as a result of reductions in medical care expenses to be achieved through legislation that will be submitted to Congress later.

c. Numbers in parentheses represent the size of the proposed reduction as a percentage of baseline program outlays.

d. Some child nutrition programs are means-tested and some of the benefits go to the poor. But the largest dollar amounts are for the school lunch and special milk programs, the bulk of whose benefits do not go to the poor.

ment programs are separated into two main categories: middle-class retirement and insurance programs and means-tested programs for the poor and near-poor.

The two key questions to be answered in considering basic structural measures to reduce spending on entitlement programs are whether structural reforms in the highly sensitive social security program should be attempted, and to what extent benefit programs for the poor and near-poor should be further cut.

With respect to the first question, it could be argued on both substantive and political grounds that the newly constituted National Commission on Social Security should be allowed to complete its work before any structural reforms are undertaken. This argument takes an even greater force if consensus can be secured to make a one-time reduction in the indexing of social security benefits.

With respect to the second question, it is likely that much of any further reductions in benefits for the poor under means-tested programs would come in benefits going to the working poor. While reforms in program administration or in illogical benefit structures should always be given consideration, a further erosion of work incentives for the poor who can and do work should be avoided.

ALL OTHER PROGRAMS. The bulk of the administration's budget reductions are concentrated in the 25 percent of the budget represented by the programs exclusive of defense, interest, and transfer payments. The administration's reductions would amount to about $50 billion by 1985—on top of $36 billion in cuts enacted last year. As noted earlier, the two series of reductions would cut inflation-adjusted outlays in this sector of the budget by almost 50 percent between 1981 and 1985. The CBO has also identified a series of possible budget cuts in this area, amounting in total to $18 billion by 1985.

While cuts in this sector of the budget have already been large, a perusal of the administration and CBO lists suggests that some further reductions could be made. A review of the potential reductions also suggests, however, that deeply felt value judgments and the arguments of interest groups will make it very difficult to secure consensus on a specific set of measures. One item on the CBO list, for example, is a reduction in the federal share of support for local investment in mass transit facilities from the current 80 percent to 50 percent. The saving would be substantial—$560 million a year by 1985. Another item on the CBO list is the termination of the direct loan program of the Small Business Administration, for a $505 million 1985 savings. The CBO also identifies $3.1 billion worth of possible reductions in farm programs. These are not extreme, but typical items. The difficulties involved can be inferred simply from a description of the proposals.

The central conclusion to be drawn from an examination of the various proposals for budget reductions in this area is that while further cuts can and should be made, they cannot be relied upon to form the main part of a deficit reduction program of the magnitude set forth earlier.

## Obstacles to Change

The preceding discussion emphasizes two themes: a large reduction in the longer-term budget deficit, combined with a cautious easing of monetary policy, would improve the nation's economic prospects; and only a relatively comprehensive deficit reduction program involving all the major elements of the budget is likely to succeed.

While a reduction in the fiscal 1983 budget deficit would be a desirable component of an overall economic program, Congress needs to pay particular attention to measures that yield large deficit reductions in 1984, 1985, and later years. It is not the recession-generated budget deficits of the moment that are the danger. What poses the threat to the economy is the prospect of budget deficits that would continue to swell to unprecedented heights even as recovery proceeded.

There are several major problems that must be overcome before a policy can be put in place that involves both tighter budgets and easier money. For several years now, a large number of people, including many financial executives, have come to equate the reduction of inflation with a steady reduction in the growth of the money supply. The toughness and credibility of the Federal Reserve are judged by many vocal and influential critics in terms of how firmly the Federal Reserve refrains from raising its monetary targets in the face of growing strains and how successful it is in meeting those targets—annually, quarterly, and, according to some critics, even monthly. Hence the Federal Reserve probably faces (and certainly believes it faces) the problem of worsened expectations in the event that it proceeds on its own to either raise its targets for money growth or overrun the existing ones. It is widely believed that participants in financial markets would interpret such action as a weakening of anti-inflationary resolve, which might cause long-term interest rates to rise rather than fall. Only with a large and credible set of actions to reduce the deficit, agreed upon by the political actors and virtually assured of enactment, could the Federal Reserve take some steps to ease monetary policy without incurring the expectational consequences that might well accompany unilateral action.

A quite different problem arises for Congress in trying to put into place an integrated approach that substantially reduces the deficit while moderately easing monetary policy. The president and the leaders of both parties in Congress—all independent actors—must come into broad agreement to enact a comprehensive deficit reduction package. Without an explicit agreement, each of them will find it difficult to act, for quite different reasons. If, for example, either the president or one of the parties in Congress threatens to make political capital in the 1982 election out of efforts by the other two to cut defense spending or scale back cost-of-living allowances in social security, it will be very unattractive for any one of them to take the lead. It is also possible that the prospect of some easing in monetary policy, to follow upon a deficit reduction package, would make it more feasible for some members of Congress to vote for the measures that make up the package.

Under these circumstances, it may be necessary to have some sort of agreement, however general, among all the parties on the broad outlines of an approach before any one of them feels free to act. This is surely true in the case of the president and the leaders of both parties in Congress with respect to the deficit reduction package. In the case of monetary policy, it would be very difficult to devise a highly specific contingent agreement. The Federal Reserve, for example, would have to remain free to deal in good faith with economic surprises without being accused of violating the agreement. But surely, if the basic willingness were there, representatives of each group—the executive, the congressional party leaders, and the Federal Reserve—could, after discussion, come to agreement on some broad guidelines or principles that would support each group in doing what it could not do alone.

CHAPTER SEVEN

# Making Budget Decisions

ROBERT W. HARTMAN

FEDERAL BUDGET decisions not only reflect views about fiscal and social policy, but also are substantially shaped by electoral politics and by the processes of government. Breaking a budget stalemate appears to require that a compromise between quite divergent views be worked out by the president and the two houses of Congress in this election year using a still-evolving budget process. It will not be easy. Moreover, in the past year such actions as reconciliation and closing the government for a day have left the public more confused than ever at a time when calm judgment is needed to deal with the serious substantive issues raised by this year's budget.

This chapter tries to provide a background for understanding some of the procedural developments of the past and alternatives for the future. It first discusses legislative developments through President Reagan's first year in office, then examines prospects for avoiding a stalemate this year, and concludes with a look at alternative future budgetary procedures, ranging from relatively weak budget controls to a constitutional amendment to balance the budget.

The author thanks Henry J. Aaron, Arthur M. Hauptman, Darwin G. Johnson, and Robert D. Reischauer for helpful comments, Allan M. Rivlin for research assistance, and Jane R. Taylor for secretarial assistance.

### Evolution of Budget Reform

"The president proposes and the Congress disposes" is short-hand for the American system of handling federal laws, including the budget. While budgetary procedures of the executive branch changed little in the 1970s, those of the Congress underwent significant change.

*The Executive Branch*

The preparation of the president's budget proposal each January has been more or less the same for the last twenty-five years. In the spring preceding the budget's submission, the Office of Management and Budget conducts a spring preview, a series of meetings and presentations involving OMB and agency officials, in an attempt to identify the issues likely to have a major impact on the upcoming budget. These reviews may lead to further study, to directives to agencies to prepare specific proposals, and to the development of planning ceilings for the agencies. By the fall, the OMB's attention turns more directly to the budget. Ordinarily the OMB director holds meetings to review all parts of the budget. Decisions are made on the administration's economic assumptions and overall fiscal policy. These are translated into firm budget guidance to each government agency. As the calendar year draws to a close, there is a series of exchanges of budget submissions between the OMB and the agencies, culminating in final negotiations between the White House and the agency heads. Various presidents have involved themselves in the process in greater or lesser detail, but the president is always the final arbiter.

When a new president comes to office, the transition imposes a need for supplementing procedures in the executive branch. At the start of both the Carter and Reagan presidencies in 1977 and 1981, budget amendments were hurriedly put together for delivery to the Congress by March to meet the congressional budget calendar. Obviously, the telescoped amending process cannot involve as much agency consultation or give-and-take as there is in the ordinary budget deliberations. In 1981 there was almost none, in part because OMB Director David Stockman was knowledgeable and had a comprehensive program and in part because in early 1981 there was little expert opposition either in the White House or in the agencies. Thus President Reagan's first-stage budget proposal in 1981 was conceived and born in the OMB. The fiscal 1983 budget, which had a full year to develop, was not an all-OMB product. Stockman's power had been eroded by his candid observations in a magazine article,[1] and several forceful cabinet officials had developed power and influence with the president. Thus the 1983 budget was more a joint product of the agencies and the OMB, although in some important respects (most notably the new federalism proposals discussed in chapter 5) the proposals were crafted with little agency involvement.

The OMB's main role usually ends with the submission of the president's budget to Congress. Although the OMB monitors the budget's progress and clears officials' testimony, the brunt of the responsibility for defending the president's proposals falls to agency chiefs. While the appearance of unswerving loyalty to the president is always maintained by agency officials who want to keep their jobs, deals that depart from the president's proposals are often cut between agency heads, who may be acting on behalf of outside interest groups, and committee chairmen. There was little evidence that this "iron triangle" of interest group, agency, and congressional committee exerted influence in 1981, in part because the OMB took a much stronger interest than customary in the budget's progress through Congress. Indeed, because most of the key budget legislation was encompassed in a single bill, the Omnibus Budget Reconciliation Act of 1981, the iron triangle would have had to be designed by a computer. Stockman was able to exert full control over President Reagan's spending plans because the OMB played a large part in drafting the "bipartisan" Gramm-Latta proposals that later became law.[2] The interdependence of the parts of the fiscal 1983 presidential budget proposal or a possible compromise package makes it likely that the OMB will continue to play a central role in negotiations with Congress.

### Congressional Budgetary Procedures

Before 1974 the Congress did not deal with the president's budget submission in a systematic or well-coordinated manner.

1. See William Greider, "The Education of David Stockman," *Atlantic Monthly,* December 1981, pp. 27–54.
2. Dale Tate, "Reconciliation's Long Term Consequences in Question as Reagan Signs Massive Bill," *Congressional Quarterly Weekly Report,* vol. 39 (August 15, 1981), pp. 1463–66.

The legislative proposals in the president's budget were simply parceled out to the various committees in each house.[3] Proposed *appropriations* (which set dollar limits, usually called *budget authority*, on the commitment of funds for any particular government activity) were sent to the Appropriations Committee in each house, which then allocated the requests to its subcommittees. Proposed *authorizations* (which establish the legal basis for the federal government to engage in an activity, such as the Vocational Education Act, and set an upper limit on appropriations for that activity, usually over several years) were sent to the pertinent authorizing committee (for example, the Senate Labor and Human Resources Committee) for consideration. Tax change proposals went to the House Ways and Means Committee and later to the Senate Finance Committee. Each committee worked at its own pace, and after each piece of legislation cleared both houses and a conference committee to reconcile differences, it was sent to the president for signature. The "budget" that emerged was the uncoordinated sum of the spending consequences of all these laws.[4]

No committee of Congress was in charge of the budget as a whole. Although the Ways and Means and Finance Committees were in command of the laws governing taxes, they acted independently, and often in ignorance, of actions taken by the spending committees. The Appropriations Committees did give some overall guidance to their subcommittees and usually cut spending below the president's request. Authorizing committees were totally uncoordinated and often circumvented the Appropriations Committees by establishing and liberalizing *entitlements*. Entitlements are authorizing laws that establish a beneficiary's claim to a government payment (for example, food stamps), thereby making the subsequent appropriation an *uncontrollable* item in the sense that the Appropriations Committees had no discretion over it. Aside from the lack of coordination and of a central accountable entity, this congressional process lacked timeliness. Some appro-

3. The budget document itself is not a proposed law. It is accompanied by proposed laws that are very specific. There is no single law that can be called "the budget." See the discussion in the text of budget resolutions.
4. And of laws passed earlier which established "permanent appropriations" (such as for interest on the national debt) that do not require annual legislation.

priations became law before the start of the fiscal year; others did not. When a regular appropriation had not been passed, an agency would be financed under a *continuing resolution,* a stopgap measure that left much to be desired.

## The Congressional Budget and Impoundment Control Act of 1974

Most of these procedures remain intact today, but the Congressional Budget and Impoundment Control Act of 1974 made several important changes in budgetary procedures while building on the existing structure of legislative activity. The act created a Committee on the Budget in each house to coordinate budget policy and a Congressional Budget Office to provide staff expertise. The coordinating role of the Budget Committees can best be understood through the procedural calendar also established by the 1974 act. Under the new procedures the proposed laws implementing the president's budget are still parceled out to the authorization, appropriation, and tax committees, but action on the floor of Congress is not permitted until certain milestones are passed. The cycle begins in mid-March, when each committee sends a report to the Budget Committee containing its recommendations for budgetary action in its domain of expertise.

The Budget Committees draft and report out by April 15 a *first concurrent resolution on the budget.* This resolution specifies aggregate targets for budget authority, outlays, revenues, and deficits, as well as for the cumulative debt subject to statutory limit.[5] The resolution also sets forth targets for budget authority and outlays in each function (national defense, health, and so forth). Budget Committee staff translates them into targets for

---

5. The debt subject to statutory limit includes virtually all Treasury debt whether owned by the public or by federal agencies. The unified budget deficit ("the deficit" in everyday parlance), on the other hand, nets out the annual surplus of federal trust funds (almost always held in the form of Treasury securities), and it does not include the deficit of off-budget entities, which are financed by the issue of Treasury debt. Thus the annual increase in the debt subject to statutory limit (except for small adjustments relating to cash accounts) equals the unified budget deficit plus the trust fund surplus plus the deficit of off-budget entities. The debt subject to statutory limit will rise even if the budget, as conventionally defined, is balanced; it will cease rising only if there is a surplus on non-trust fund accounts ("federal funds") equal to or greater than the deficit of off-budget entities. See *Budget of the United States Government, Fiscal Year 1983, Special Analysis E: Borrowing and Debt.*

each committee that has jurisdiction over some part of the budget. Once a common first concurrent resolution has passed each house, scheduled for May 15, the authorizing and appropriating committees, acting under the guidance of the first resolution, may bring bills to the floor.[6] All the while, the Congressional Budget Office keeps track of the progress of legislation and aids the Budget Committees in informing members if the targets in the resolution are likely to be breached. Thus during the summer, when most spending legislation is being enacted, the committees of Congress are under only one (nonbinding) constraint—the target for spending or taxing allocated to them as a result of the first concurrent resolution.

The congressional budgetary process culminates in September, just before the start of the fiscal year, which was shifted to October by the 1974 act. The act requires Congress to pass a *second concurrent resolution* in September and, if necessary, to revise the limits contained in the first resolution. The estimates for spending and taxing in the second resolution are ''binding'' in this sense: once the resolution has been passed, any member can kill legislation that raises the outlays and budget authority above their ceiling or reduces revenues below the revenue floor by objecting to its consideration. Before any such legislation can be passed, a *third concurrent resolution* is required to change the limits. Thus the final binding budget under the new procedures constrains only *legislative action*; it does not limit the budgetary outcomes themselves. Indeed, the budget resolutions are only a set of rules for Congress; they are not signed by the president and have no status as laws. Also, if at the time the second concurrent resolution is adopted the previous actions of any committee are found to be inconsistent with the dollar limits of the second resolution, the situation would be rectified by the *reconciliation process*. In the second resolution itself, committees would receive reconciliation instructions that directed them to amend or to rescind appropriations or other spending legislation or to change the tax laws. The legislation drafted by the committees given these directives would be packaged (without change) by the Budget Committees into a

---

6. The 1974 act required that authorizing legislation be reported by committees no later than May 15, but numerous waivers of procedure have weakened this constraint.

single *budget reconciliation act.* The budget reconciliation act must clear Congress by September 25, to give the president time to sign it before the fiscal year begins.[7]

## How the Process Worked

These procedures operated pretty much as the legislation intended between 1976 (when the new procedures were first fully implemented) and 1978 (covering the budgets for fiscal years 1977–79). As shown in table 7-1, the budget calendar was adhered to in that period, and the first resolution outlay targets were not breached by either committee legislative activity or subsequent events. Revenues were slightly overestimated in fiscal 1977 but underestimated in 1978 and 1979, and the actual budget deficit came in well under initial estimates.

This propitious start for a new procedure was facilitated by the state of the economy and the reaction to it in Congress. In 1977 and 1978 recovery from the recession of the mid-1970s was the central economic preoccupation of the country. President Carter's first budgetary actions, amending the 1978 budget, were explicitly designed to stimulate the economy. The substantive committees of Congress supported him, and the Budget Committees made little challenge, thus establishing their place in the legislature without disturbing continuing power relationships.

Fiscal 1979 represented a transition for the economy and for budget policy. When President Carter first proposed his budget for that year in January 1978, the centerpiece was a tax cut intended to maintain the growth of the economy. As time passed, however, it became clear that the economy was improving significantly and that inflation was worsening. The president narrowed the proposed tax cut, and these lower limits were incorporated in the second concurrent resolution passed in September. In October, when the tax bill reached the floor of the Senate, several proposals to deepen the tax cut beyond the limits of the second resolution were defeated when Senator Edmund S. Muskie, Budget Committee chairman, objected and was upheld by the Senate.

---

7. See Allen Schick, *Reconciliation and the Congressional Budget Process* (American Enterprise Institute for Public Policy Research, 1981).

**Table 7-1. Outlays and Revenues under Congressional Budget Resolutions and Actual Outcomes, Fiscal Years 1977–82**

Billions of dollars

| Item | Date of conference agreement | Out-lays[a] | Reve-nues[a] | Deficit |
|---|---|---|---|---|
| *Fiscal 1977* | | | | |
| First resolution | 5/13/76 | 413.3 | 362.5 | 50.8 |
| Second resolution | 9/16/76 | 413.1 | 362.5 | 50.6 |
| Actual | . . . | 401.9 | 356.9 | 45.0 |
| Overrun or shortfall[b] ( − ) | . . . | − 11.4 | − 5.6 | − 5.8 |
| *Fiscal 1978* | | | | |
| First resolution | 5/17/77 | 461.0 | 396.3 | 64.7 |
| Second resolution | 9/15/77 | 458.3 | 397.0 | 61.3 |
| Actual | . . . | 449.9 | 401.1 | 48.8 |
| Overrun or shortfall[b] ( − ) | . . . | − 11.1 | 4.8 | − 15.9 |
| *Fiscal 1979* | | | | |
| First resolution | 5/17/78 | 498.8 | 447.9 | 50.9 |
| Second resolution | 9/23/78 | 487.5 | 448.7 | 38.8 |
| Actual | . . . | 493.7 | 465.9 | 27.7 |
| Overrun or shortfall[b] ( − ) | . . . | − 5.1 | 18.0 | − 23.2 |
| *Fiscal 1980* | | | | |
| First resolution | 5/24/79 | 532.0 | 509.0 | 23.0 |
| Second resolution | 11/28/79 | 547.6 | 517.8 | 29.8 |
| Actual | . . . | 579.6 | 520.0 | 59.6 |
| Overrun or shortfall[b] ( − ) | . . . | 47.6 | 11.0 | 36.6 |
| *Fiscal 1981* | | | | |
| First resolution | 6/12/80 | 613.6 | 613.8 | 0.2[c] |
| Second resolution | 11/20/80 | 632.4 | 605.0 | 27.4 |
| Actual | . . . | 657.2 | 599.3 | 57.9 |
| Overrun or shortfall[b] ( − ) | . . . | 43.6 | − 14.5 | 58.1 |
| *Fiscal 1982* | | | | |
| First resolution | 5/21/81 | 695.5 | 657.8 | 37.7 |
| Second resolution | 11/19/81 | 695.5 | 657.8 | 37.7 |
| Actual[d] | . . . | 725.3 | 626.8 | 98.6 |

Source: Congressional Budget Office.

a. Actual outlays and revenues in each year use the definitions in force at the time. In fiscal 1982 the actual reflects new definitions adopted after the budget resolutions for that year were voted.

b. From first resolution.

c. Surplus.

d. Estimated in *Budget of the United States Government, Fiscal Year 1983*, p. 2-14.

Beginning with the 1980 budget, attention turned to fighting inflation, and budgetary difficulties began to develop. The 1980 budget proposed by President Carter in January 1979 was billed as an austerity budget. It included what seemed then to be unusually large spending cuts, and the deficit was limited to under $30 billion, a figure Carter had promised in the fall of 1978. For the first time the new budgetary procedures had to deal with unpleasant choices, and the results were not encouraging. Because President Carter had proposed a $30 billion deficit and because inflation was raging in early 1979, the Budget Committees felt obliged to issue a first concurrent resolution with a deficit no larger than the president had proposed. The first resolution therefore assumed that certain savings, amounting to about $5.6 billion, would be made by authorizing committees. These were referred to in the conference report on the first resolution but not in the resolution itself. As the summer wore on these legislative savings failed to materialize in committee actions, and a deep division developed between the two houses.[8] For the second concurrent resolution, the Senate Budget Committee decided to carry out the reconciliation procedures and called for $4 billion in mandatory savings, and the full Senate agreed. The House Budget Committee could not agree to implement reconciliation, and after a protracted delay in conference the second budget resolution passed in late November 1979 with no reconciliation. This resolution still projected a fiscal 1980 deficit of under $30 billion, even though all indications were that such a level could not be reached without further deficit-reducing legislation. The failure to implement reconciliation meant that such legislation would not be enacted. The Budget Committees were becoming convinced that the weak mechanism for enforcing legislative savings assumed in the first concurrent resolution needed strengthening.

## The Budget Prelude of Fiscal 1981

The procedural developments in the 1981 budgetary process were a turning point. In January 1980 President Carter sent Congress his budget proposal, tailored to election-year politics.

8. The legislative savings were supported by the Carter administration, but its influence with Congress was low in mid-1979, the period in which the president went on a solitary retreat and then fired several members of the cabinet.

It dropped the austerity theme and tried to offend no important constituency. Perhaps because of the public's awareness that the second budget resolution for fiscal 1980 was phony in the sense that its assumptions were not likely to be realized, a sharp eye was cast on Carter's January proposal. The reaction was skepticism, and this contributed to plummeting financial markets early in 1980. Interest rates on three-month Treasury bills rose from 12 to 15.5 percent between January and March. Bond and stock prices fell precipitously.

President Carter withdrew his budget seven weeks after it was submitted and began an extensive series of conferences with members of Congress on an acceptable alternative. The chairmen and members of the Budget Committees played a major role along with the leadership of Congress in these negotiations. After President Carter submitted his revised budget in March, the Budget Committees took advantage of this enhanced role and supported a first concurrent resolution that included reconciliation instructions directing eight House and ten Senate authorizing committees to report legislation reducing outlays by over $6 billion in 1981. Tax committees were instructed to raise more than $4 billion in revenues. These actions were only a small part of those needed to balance the budget as promised in the resolution.[9] The committees were instructed to report legislation within a few weeks of the first resolution, which passed in June 1980.

The move to cut spending stalled in the middle of 1980. The recession coupled with an election led to a stalemate. The Senate passed a reconciliation bill in July and the House passed its quite different bill in September. The conference committee, which numbered over one hundred, repeatedly deadlocked and did not pass the reconciliation act until early December after the long-delayed second budget resolution was voted.

The Omnibus Budget Reconciliation Act of 1980 was a disappointing piece of legislation. Since the reconciliation instructions included in the first concurrent resolution specified savings targets for fiscal 1981 only, a number of committees "complied" by drafting changes in law that shifted expenditures from 1981 to

9. Further savings were assumed to be made on appropriations. As a safeguard, the first resolution called for delaying the transmittal to the president of appropriations bills that exceeded the resolution targets until a second resolution had been approved.

future years. Other committees included legislation that actually raised spending in some programs to partly offset cuts made. A reduction in cost-of-living adjustments for federal civilian and military retirees that passed the Senate was dropped by the conference. In all, the Omnibus Budget Reconciliation Act provided $4.6 billion in outlay reductions and $3.6 billion in new taxes, for a total deficit-reduction package of about $8 billion, well under the action needed to balance the budget as originally intended.

Two additional innovations in the fiscal 1981 congressional budgetary process are worth noting. First, both houses of Congress made a start on multiyear budgeting. The budget resolutions incorporated budget targets for the out-years fiscal 1982 and 1983 as well as for the budget year 1981, but each house set different targets for future years. Second, for the first time levels of federal credit activity were specified. This "credit budget" attempted to curb the total volume of both new direct loans and guaranteed loan commitments of federal agencies by requesting that appropriation limitations be extended to all federal credit activity. Such actions were intended to increase control since many federal credit activities are subject to weak limits imposed by authorizing legislation that sets the terms of loans, by executive discretion, or even by market demand. As in the early years of the new budgetary process, however, these "credit limits" were revised during fiscal 1981 to conform to what was happening to federal credit, rather than the other way around.

### The Reagan Revolution

In many ways the stage had been set for President Reagan's entrance. Over time, the Budget Committees had increasingly extended their roles in and influence over budgeting outcomes. A major procedural breakthrough had been made in 1980 when reconciliation instructions were incorporated in the first concurrent resolution. And yet the Stockman-directed progress of President Reagan's budgetary legislation through the summer of 1981 is regarded by many as a revolution because of the size and scope of the changes made and the threat they pose to hallowed congressional procedures.

Within about seven weeks of taking office, President Reagan

sent Congress a full-blown set of budget revisions for fiscal 1982 and beyond. The most controversial proposals were an increase in spending for national defense, a reduction in business and personal taxes, and a huge cut in federal nondefense spending. The administration, with the support of the Republican-controlled Senate Budget Committee, sought to carry out as much of the spending reduction program as possible in the form of reconciliation action. The Senate in late March (just a few days after the president's budget revisions were submitted) passed a resolution instructing its committees to make major budget cuts.

These instructions were incorporated in the Senate's first concurrent resolution (which passed in May). The House proceeded along a more conventional track. The Budget Committee reported a first concurrent resolution that included reconciliation instructions. This resolution, which bore the stamp of Chairman James R. Jones, was challenged on the floor of the House by a substitute resolution cosponsored by Delbert L. Latta (the ranking Republican on the House Budget Committee) and Phil Gramm (a Democratic member of the committee and a leader of a group of conservative Democrats called "Boll Weevils"). Gramm-Latta I, as the budget resolution became known, passed the House in late May, after an apparently effective presidential television plea for it. The Senate passed an equivalent resolution the next day.

Gramm-Latta was monumental in a number of respects. First, it contained instructions for budget reductions addressed to fifteen House committees and fourteen Senate committees. The instructions specified amounts to be saved for fiscal years 1982, 1983, and 1984. This multiyear focus was designed to avoid the temporary cosmetic cuts of the previous year's legislation and to complement the administration's multiyear tax-cutting plan. Second, the outlay reductions totaled $36 billion, $47 billion, and $56 billion for the three fiscal years, over 8 percent of nondefense, noninterest outlays. These sums were several times larger than previous reconciliation actions. Third, the reconciliation savings were to be made in two types of authorizing legislation: entitlements and discretionary programs. For entitlement spending, a reconciliation directive to the authorizing committee is recognized as the only way to impose restraint since subsequent appropriations are perfunctory. But spending for other programs (for example, grants to states for education programs) can be limited either by proposing limits on annual appropriations or by the much stronger measure of directing the committee that authorized the program to lower the authorization ceiling over several years. The latter arrangement was a feature of Gramm-Latta (and was not part of the Jones proposal that was defeated).

The congressional committees responded to the reconciliation instructions by submitting legislation affecting 250 different federal programs.[10] Arguing that some of the changes proposed in the House showed a "clear danger of Congressional backsliding and a return to spending as usual,"[11] the administration quickly fashioned an alternative reconciliation bill, called Gramm-Latta II, to replace the work of several committees. Gramm-Latta II, like its predecessor, narrowly passed the House, after gaining support from the Boll Weevils and a group of moderate Republicans called "Gypsy Moths" who demanded and received certain concessions from the administration. After an efficiently run conference, the president in August signed the Omnibus Budget Reconciliation Act of 1981, an inch-thick compendium of twenty separate titles covering a range from Agriculture and Forestry to Health Professions. The law changed entitlement program eligibility rules (for example, for food stamps), limited the amounts authorized in scores of programs for 1982–84, rewrote major parts of substantive law having little effect on the budget (for example, for radio and TV broadcasting), and probably did a few other things that have not been discovered yet.

This extraordinary law was debated on the floor of the House for two days. There were no hearings at all on some sections of the law. The possibility of amending the bill was strictly limited, and it was voted on in a single vote, not section by section.

The reconciliation act's companion legislation, the Economic Recovery Tax Act of 1981, was meanwhile wending its way through the Senate Finance Committee and the House Ways and

10. One committee, the House Energy and Commerce Committee, could not agree on a response. Its chairman forwarded Democratic proposals to the House Budget Committee. It is not clear what sanctions can be taken against a committee that refuses to comply— other than the Budget Committee writing its own legislation.

11. Ronald Reagan, "The President's News Conference of June 16, 1981," *Weekly Compilation of Presidential Documents*, vol. 17 (June 22, 1981), p. 632.

Means Committee. The first concurrent resolution had set targets for tax cuts for 1982–84. A period of negotiation between the White House and the Democratic chairman of the Ways and Means Committee, Congressman Dan Rostenkowski, had produced no agreement, especially on the size and phasing-in of a personal income tax. Accordingly, the administration decided to attract enough Boll Weevil votes to its side to command a majority in the House by offering to include tax changes that would appeal to them. Rostenkowski countered with additional lures to keep the Boll Weevils in the fold. OMB Director Stockman characterized the resulting scramble as: "The hogs were really feeding. The greed level, the level of opportunism, just got out of control." [12] Despite this, the Economic Recovery Tax Act complied with the revenue reduction limits in the first concurrent resolution, although the act's tax cut for 1985 (which was deepened by adding indexation of the individual income tax in that year) probably went beyond what the supporters of the concurrent resolution had envisioned.

*Aftermath*

Congress adjourned in August. The members heard from constituents about high interest rates, and they had time to think about what had transpired in the first half year of budget policy under President Reagan. Congress prides itself on being a deliberative body. The helter-skelter of enacting reconciliation and the tax bill was the opposite of a careful legislative process. The modus operandi of the Congress had for a long time been: the work is done by committees that share power. In 1981 the Senate had ceded full control to the Budget Committee, and in the House the committee proposals for reconciliation had been thrown out. The main function of Appropriations Committee members had been as watchdog on the Treasury. But the reconciliation process had given the play to the Budget Committees and the authorizing committees, leaving Appropriations a cipher. Members of Congress like to show their expertise and independence by sponsoring amendments and the like, but the whole legislative show in 1981

12. As quoted in Greider, "Education of David Stockman," p. 51.

had boiled down to two votes for or against President Reagan's entire program. These concerns, as well as uneasiness about the economy, presaged trouble ahead.

The president's initial budget plan had contemplated program cuts to be made in areas not covered by reconciliation. So had the first concurrent resolution on the 1982 budget. The exact size of these cuts was a matter of confusion, in part because the president's cuts were measured from a baseline different from that used in reconciliation. Moreover, some of the members of Congress who had been lured into the administration's camp for the reconciliation thought they had been promised some relenting in the pursuit of further cuts.

Against this backdrop came the Reagan administration's fall offensive. A new package of budget cuts encompassing entitlement reductions, appropriations reductions, and even some "revenue enhancement" was announced by the administration on September 24 (incidentally making it absolutely impossible to meet the deadlines set by the 1974 act). The program was not well received by Congress. The entitlement package was never even formally introduced and the tax enhancers were withdrawn. The administration decided, however, to make yet another fight over its proposed across-the-board (with some exceptions) reductions in appropriations.

When the fiscal year began on October 1, no appropriations bills had been signed into law.[13] As a result, the entire government was being funded under a continuing appropriation law. The first continuing appropriation resolution, signed into law on September 30, is a relatively short document setting limits on the commitment of funds for the first part of the year. Instead of specifying appropriations on a line-by-line basis as in ordinary appropriations laws, the resolution sets spending limits by mechanical rules. Thus the limit on spending for each program is as follows: if both houses have passed an appropriation for that program, it may operate at the lesser of the two appropriated amounts; if only one house has passed an appropriation, spending may continue at the lesser of the appropriated amount or the "current rate." The

13. The legislative branch appropriation was incorporated into the first continuing appropriation resolution.

**Table 7-2. Status of Fiscal Year 1982 Appropriations, as of March 15, 1982**

Budget authority in billions of dollars

| Title of appropriation | Date enacted | September administration request | House bill | Senate bill | Final action | Difference between final action and administration request |
|---|---|---|---|---|---|---|
| Agriculture and related agencies | 12/23/81 | 22.3 | 22.7 | 22.9 | 22.6 | +0.3 |
| Defense Department | 12/29/81 | 200.9 | 197.4 | 203.7 | 199.9 | −1.0 |
| District of Columbia | 12/4/81 | 0.6 | 0.5 | 0.6 | 0.6 | * |
| Energy and Water Development | 12/4/81 | 12.1 | 13.2 | 12.8 | 12.5 | +0.4 |
| Foreign Aid | 12/29/81 | 7.8 | 7.4 | 7.3 | 7.5 | −0.3 |
| HUD, Veterans, NASA | 12/23/81 | 58.7 | 62.6 | 60.5 | 60.4 | +1.7 |
| Interior and related agencies | 12/23/81 | 6.4 | 11.1 | 7.4 | 7.2 | +0.8 |
| Legislative Branch | 10/1/81 | 1.4 | 1.1[a] | 0.9[a] | 1.3 | −0.1 |
| Military Construction | 12/23/81 | 7.3 | 6.9 | 7.3 | 7.1 | −0.2 |
| Transportation and related agencies | 12/23/81 | 9.8 | 11.1 | 10.4 | 10.1 | +0.3 |
| Subtotal | | 327.3 | 334.0 | 333.8 | 329.2 | +1.9 |
| Labor, HHS, Education | ⋯ | 82.5 | 85.2 | 84.8[b] | ⋯ | ⋯ |
| State, Justice, Commerce, Judiciary | ⋯ | 8.2 | 8.7 | 8.6[b] | ⋯ | ⋯ |
| Treasury, Postal Service, General Government | ⋯ | 9.1 | 9.7 | 9.4[b] | ⋯ | ⋯ |

Sources: *Congressional Quarterly Weekly Report*, vol. 40 (January 16, 1982), p. 103; and *Weekly Compilation of Presidential Documents*, vol. 17, nos. 43–53 (October 26, 1981–January 4, 1982).

* Less than $100 million.

a. House bill excludes cost of Senate operation and vice versa.

b. Committee approved amount.

current rate generally means the rate of the previous fiscal year.[14] The first continuing appropriation set an expiration date of November 20, 1981, in the expectation that regular appropriations laws, which supersede continuing appropriations, would be on the books by that time.

As it turned out, very few appropriations—and none of the major ones—had been passed by Friday, November 20, because of the continuing controversy over the administration's fall-offensive cuts, and a second continuing appropriation was needed. The Congress agreed on such a bill at the final hour and sent it to President Reagan. Over the weekend of November 21–22, President Reagan decided to veto the continuing resolution and did so on Monday, November 23. As a result, federal offices throughout the country closed that day, nonessential workers were sent home, and President Reagan and members of Congress (who stayed on the job—their appropriation had passed) got together that same day on a compromise extension of the continuing resolution until December 15. On December 15, with few appropriations yet enacted, still another continuing appropriation was passed until February 15, 1982.

By the end of December 1981 most appropriations laws (though not the biggest nondefense one, for the Departments of Labor, Health and Human Services, and Education) had been signed into law. As indicated in table 7-2, the administration was forced to accept some increases over its fall proposals in the appropriations that passed. In defense and foreign aid, appropriations were below the administration's request; but the Agriculture, Interior, and combined Housing and Urban Development, Veterans Administration, and National Aeronautics and Space Administration appropriations exceeded the administration's request. So far, total appropriations for fiscal 1982 are about $1.9 billion above the administration's fall proposals. For the major appropriations not passed at the time of this writing, it appears that another $3 billion will probably be added. (These comparisons are for budget au-

14. Even so, "current rate" is an ambiguous term because "the" rate of the previous fiscal year may be quite different rates for each quarter (which is generally the period over which the OMB apportions appropriations to agencies) and the final quarter of the fiscal year may not reflect what the Appropriations Committee intends as the limit for the next period.

thority; differences in outlays would be smaller.) While it is probably true that these discretionary appropriations would have been even higher if the administration had not waged a fall offensive, it is clear that President Reagan's total mastery over budgeting began to erode in the appropriations process. It is also evident that the patent disregard for the Appropriations Committees' prerogatives in the reconciliation process stiffened these committees' resistance to further cuts.

It is universally agreed that operating a large part of the government under continuing appropriations is a most unsatisfactory way of doing the public's business. First, because the continuing resolution is simply a set of general rules to limit spending, it tends to perpetuate spending patterns that conform to no one's preferences and it can lead to unintended consequences. For example, if one house of Congress passes a low appropriation for a particular program, quite conceivably as a result of a vendetta by one member of the Appropriations Committee, that low appropriation governs the program no matter how high the other house sets it. On a regular appropriation, matters such as this as well as simple mistakes are taken care of in conference before a final bill is approved. Second, continuing appropriations lead to even greater managerial inefficiency than is customary in government activities. When an agency manager does not know what level of funds will be available for the whole fiscal year, the inevitable tendency is to be cautious in committing funds. Contracts are not let early in the year, to ensure that funds will be available later in the year. Then when the full appropriation is finally voted, there is frantic activity to commit funds before they expire. On some accounts, particularly those pertaining to salaries and expenses of employees, the tendency is to be optimistic: don't fire anybody until it is absolutely necessary. If the optimism proves to have been false when the full appropriation becomes law, the agency may have to fire too many people or furlough (put on unpaid leave) an entire staff. There is ample evidence that this kind of behavior was developing as fiscal 1982 unfolded.

The legislative history of the 1982 budget ended on a sour note. In November, in the midst of the dispute over the administration's reductions in appropriations and well after it had become evident that economic events had transformed the projected budget outcomes of the first concurrent resolution, both houses passed a second concurrent resolution. Instead of acknowledging the sharply changed economic circumstances and reaching some decision on appropriations still outstanding, the second concurrent resolution simply rubber-stamped the outdated first resolution. In effect, Congress decided to put over into calendar 1982 any further decisions on the budget.

## Retrospective

The six years that the new congressional budget has been in effect cover a rough period in the nation's economic history, encompassing a recovery from the worst recession since the 1930s, the onset of high and highly variable inflation and interest rates, and the beginning of a period of retrenchment in federal spending. The congressional budgetary process has emerged from this period with some scars, but with the solid achievement of having proved resilient to changing needs. Stimulating the economy called for accommodative Budget Committees, but as the economic and political trend moved toward spending restraint, the control mechanism was strengthened. When a president needed support in making a credible budget, the budgetary process provided an opportunity for joint action with the Congress, but it also provided room for a confrontation when the parties differed sharply. Such resilience could be interpreted as a lack of discipline, a process with no firm direction. But a more accurate lesson to be learned is that economic and political circumstances do change and a flexible procedure is needed to allow changes in direction.

### Prospects for Peaceful Reform

The budgetary history of the last few years raises two kinds of questions for the future. First, how will budget procedures affect the decisions to be made in the coming year? Second, what modifications in budgetary processes should be made in the longer term?

## Stalemate and Its Alternatives, 1983

Congressional action on President Reagan's 1983 budget is uncommonly difficult to forecast. The public and Congress seem to agree that the projected deficits (especially if adjusted to more realistic economic assumptions than those of the administration) are too high, but there is little evidence of a consensus on how to lower them. The major disagreements are over whether to raise revenues or lower outlays and which types of spending and taxing should bear the brunt of the burden. The prospects for a repeat performance by President Reagan in securing substantially complete acceptance of his budget seem remote. On the other hand, expecting Congress to fashion a budget entirely on its own is unrealistic. Any group in Congress that takes the lead on formulating a package—which would necessarily involve both higher taxes and major program cuts—would face the attendant political danger of being blamed (possibly by the president) for being the enemy of the elderly or the taxpayer, among others. It is hard to imagine that many congressmen would relish that role, and it is nearly inconceivable that the Democratic chairmen of the House Budget Committee and the Ways and Means Committee, who lost out to President Reagan in 1981, would voluntarily take that chance again.

Another possibility is that the president and Congress will agree to compromise. A bipartisan coalition in the Congress and the president would concur on a set of budgetary actions perceived as being built on the president's plan but with significant modifications. The agreed-upon package would almost certainly require a single vote since the individual parts of it could not pass in an election year; accordingly, such a package would probably take the form either of firm reconciliation instructions or even of specific legislation attached to some other bill, such as an impending act to raise the limit on the public debt. These shortcuts would further erode the conventional way of doing business in Congress; thus opposition should be expected not only on substantive and partisan political grounds but also on procedural ones. This is a substantial number of hurdles to get over.

If an agreement is not reached, a stalemate is possible. Unlike other legislative action, a budgetary stalemate does not mean that nothing happens. In this case it would probably mean passing a first concurrent resolution on the budget that did not contain mandatory instructions to authorizing committees to come up with budget-saving legislation, and it might mean passing some appropriations that would greatly exceed the president's proposals, which would then be vetoed. (Or the Appropriations Committees could fail to act at all.) By October 1 a continuing resolution covering spending for most of the agencies and extending through the November election would be needed. Essentially stalemate means that the difficult budget decisions of early 1982 would be pushed ahead to a postelection session of Congress, where a clearer consensus might emerge. This scenario appears to be fraught with great risks to the economy as the uncertainty about the budget stretches out over months, and it greatly increases the possibility of a radical reaction to what will be perceived as an intractable budget mess. One such radical solution—a constitutional amendment to balance the budget—is discussed below.

It is important to end this account with the reminder that, if there were a solution to the budgetary impasse that commanded strong popular support, the budgetary process in the Congress would not stand in its way. Even with presidential opposition, one can imagine the congressional leadership riding the crest of a popular wave to beat back whatever fragmentary congressional opposition to a popular outcome developed. The Congressional Budget and Impoundment Control Act is proof that Congress, acting alone, can undertake changes that roil customary legislative relationships. Only when an attempt is made to preempt traditional legislative procedures with legislation that does not enjoy wide popular support does the system seem to fail. Should stalemate ensue in 1982, the blame should rest more on the failure to reach a consensus than on a shortcoming of the budgetary process. Indeed, the only hope of a better outcome lies in the budgetary process forcing all parties to attempt to reach such an agreement.

### Longer-Run Reforms

When the current budget crisis subsides, attention will turn to reexamination of the procedures by which Congress tackles the budget. Many members of Congress object to the steps taken in recent years as being an effort to make the Budget Committees all-powerful, thereby challenging the shared-power tradition and even raising questions about the role of party leadership in Congress. These members would like to curb the Budget Committees and make them responsive to the views and actions of other committees.

Such a reversion to past procedures makes the most sense if future Congresses are uninterested in budgetary control but are mainly concerned with retuning priorities in a growing budget. In that case, enhancing the power of specialized committees would build on their strength in conducting full reviews of existing and proposed programs, considering legislative alternatives in detail, ascertaining the views of interest groups, and building constituent coalitions for government programs. These are functions that a budget committee, no matter how hard-working, cannot accomplish as effectively. The Budget Committees' role in this more traditional congressional arrangement would be to set fiscal policy and dollar limits on broad priorities; this primary function of coordination probably implies some revision of the congressional calendar (to allow time for a sensible debate on priorities), some consideration of the process of setting economic assumptions (so that the fiscal plans of each Budget Committee and the president's proposal are not being measured differently), and some better system for reducing each committee's incentives to get as much of the budget pie as it can. These changes would be marginal; the budgetary process could revert to what it was in 1976–79.

Procedural changes directed toward strengthening budget control, on the other hand, make the most sense if one envisions the environment of the future as one of heightened attention to slowing expenditure growth and cutting deficits. The crucial procedural innovation of the last few years—reconciliation early in the budget decision process—seems essential to any move to strengthen control. Because the predominant message for the congressional committees in this austerity scenario is that spending be cut and taxes raised, it is unrealistic to expect such measures to be put into effect unless committees are forced to act. This is the primary function of reconciliation: it allows Congress as a whole to order its committees to take actions.

Early reconciliation does not have to follow the pattern set by David Stockman in 1981. The coverage of reconciliation instructions, in particular, may have gone overboard in that year. To control entitlement programs, there is general agreement that early reconciliation is a must. Authorizing committees are the only agents that can effect restraint by rewriting the laws, and they need external direction and adequate time. For the parts of federal spending that are not governed by entitlements, the most direct avenue of control is appropriations, not underlying laws, as in the 1981 reconciliation. Efforts to control appropriations by reconciling them in the second concurrent budget resolution at the end of a budget cycle are futile. Effective control of appropriations would mean that mandatory limits would have to be moved up to the first concurrent resolution. Since current budgetary procedures already contain a mechanism for providing dollar guidance to the Appropriations Committees,[15] all that would have to be done is to make such guidance mandatory, probably by moving the dollar limits into the budget resolution and stating them as instructions rather than guidance. Naturally, this procedural reform would not solve the problem of the Appropriations Committees shifting funds out of one budget year into the next; the simplest solution would be to move toward two-year appropriation bills (and two-year mandatory instructions in the first budget resolution) in pertinent parts of the budget.

Early reconciliation and early mandatory limits on appropriations would strengthen budgetary procedures, but they might create new problems that required further adjustments in the process. One of these is the timing of the first budget resolution. If the first resolution is to be the vehicle for mandatory spending cuts and tax increases, a case can be made for pushing the deadline for the resolution beyond May to give the budget committees time to digest the views of the president and of the committees. A case can also be made that the resolution should be issued before May to give working committees time to hold hearings, consult experts, and deliberate before writing the laws. No one wants to repeat the haste of legislation in 1981. Since the length of a year is immutable, both of these timing changes cannot be made.[16] One school of thought holds that the solution is a biennial budget. The first year would be devoted to events leading up to a first concurrent

15. The mechanism is the allocation of dollar limits by committee under section 302 of the Congressional Budget and Impoundment Control Act.

16. Starting the new fiscal year in January rather than October to lengthen the decision period is regarded as out of the question, if only because economic forecasts would have to be made so far in advance that they would be less credible than they are now

resolution and the second to carrying out that resolution by issuing two-year appropriations. This idea has some obvious problems relating to economic forecasts (see footnote 16) and to the timing of elections and presidential transitions.[17]

Another aspect of budget reform intended to strengthen existing procedures relates to the coverage of the budget and the scope of its control. The most obvious, though not widely recognized, weakness here is that current budgetary procedures are asymmetrically weak in dealing with taxation. Budget resolutions spell out spending limits by function while the only tax guidance offered is a single number for the amount revenues are to be raised or lowered. While there is a legislative-structure reason for this imbalance[18] and the tax committees' hegemony inspires awe, stronger budget control implies greater detail in the budget resolution on the kind of tax changes it seeks. This could be accomplished by specifying broad targets by tax type (for example, income tax or excise tax) or by functional breakdown of tax expenditures (for example, to eliminate subsidies that the tax system gives to health and to housing). Along the same lines, centralized budget control could be strengthened by tighter controls on federal credit activities. For example, Congressmen Norman Y. Mineta and Edwin R. Bethune, Jr. (and 150 cosponsors) have suggested in House bill 2372 that targets for new direct loan obligations and loan guarantee commitments be incorporated in the first budget resolution and that the second resolution set binding limits on legislative activity pertaining to loans. The Mineta-Bethune bill would also require extensive reports on the status of federal credit activity and its relation to monetary policy from the Treasury and the Federal Reserve Board. Of equally serious concern for control are off-budget entities, but here the major activity is that of one organization, the Federal Financing

17. If a two-year cycle commenced in October of even-numbered years, President Reagan's first budget proposal made with the help of a full staff would be for the two years starting in October 1984, only a few months before his term expires. Starting in an odd year interposes a congressional election in the middle of the two-year deliberative process.

18. A single spending number could not be allocated among the various committees, but the functional breakdown in the budget resolutions makes this feasible. However, there is only one tax committee in each house, so a single revenue target can be allocated to its proper committee.

Bank, and it can be dealt with in a number of ways that do not entail revamping budgetary procedures.[19]

The long list of reforms considered under this heading of strengthening budgetary procedures requires two cautionary notes. First, if all the reforms were implemented, the process might fall from its own weight. The work load from existing procedures is already heavy, and a new calendar, stronger directions, broader coverage, and so on could bring sheer confusion and weaken the whole structure. Second, it seems ludicrous to fortify congressional procedures for pinpointing fiscal policy decisions and fine-tuning federal credit activities without giving serious consideration to how these decisions interact with monetary policy. As chapters 2 and 6 of this book illustrate, setting standards for fiscal policy requires some understanding of, and presumably influence over, general monetary and credit conditions. There are now only weak links between Federal Reserve decisions and the budgetary process—mostly consisting of the central bank informing Congress of its goals and accomplishments—and no forum for arriving at the appropriate policy mix. This of course stems from a long tradition, but since we are breaking with the past in so many other ways, maybe it is time for a review of congressional control over money and credit.

### A Constitutional Amendment to Balance the Budget

The most radical approach to changing budgetary procedures would be replacing the annual assessment of fiscal alternatives with a fixed external rule, such as a constitutional requirement that the budget be balanced each year. This approach is generally favored by those who feel that the present system is biased toward excessive growth of government and deficit financing of public expenditures. The adoption of a constitutional amendment to balance the budget would considerably change existing budgetary procedures and other aspects of running the government.

One version of a constitutional amendment has passed the

---

19. See Congressional Budget Office, *The Federal Financing Bank and the Budgetary Treatment of Federal Credit Activities* (CBO, 1982); and Andrew S. Carron, "Fiscal Activities outside the Budget," in Joseph A. Pechman, ed., *Setting National Priorities: The 1982 Budget* (Brookings Institution, 1981), pp. 261–69.

Senate Committee on the Judiciary and seems to gain momentum each time a budgetary target is missed or a deadline is not met. The amendment also seems to have election-year appeal because it offers members of Congress a chance to vote for the popular balanced budget without having to cut programs or raise taxes. Senate Joint Resolution 58 provides for a balanced budget by requiring Congress to adopt before the start of each fiscal year a "statement" (budget) in which planned outlays are no greater than total receipts. It also requires that the planned receipts of the budget grow no faster than national income grew in the previous (calendar) year. The final control is that "the Congress and the President shall ensure that actual outlays do not exceed the outlays set forth" in the budget statement. The amendment would allow a simple majority of each house of Congress to waive the receipts-growth clause, while a 60 percent vote in each house would be needed to approve a planned deficit.[20]

Obviously many facets of such a balanced budget amendment warrant extended discussion. Several criticisms can be listed. Eliminating discretionary fiscal policy might spur undue reliance on other aggregate control measures. Strict control of spending could shift attention to regulation as an alternative or to credit activities unless control over them was strengthened. The amendment's weak guidance for the rate of growth of receipts could make estimating receipts an even more political exercise than it is now. The case for the amendment boils down to a belief that history demonstrates that nothing less will bring about a balanced budget.[21]

One aspect of Senate Joint Resolution 58 directly impinges on budgetary procedures. The stipulation that the president and Congress ensure that actual outlays do not exceed planned outlays would seem to require a whole new set of budget-policing proce-

20. There is also a specific waiver for a declaration of war and a section forbidding Congress to require states to "engage in additional activities" unless the federal government puts up all the necessary funds. See *Balanced Budget–Tax Limitation Constitutional Amendment*, S. Rept. 97-151, 97 Cong. 1 sess. (Government Printing Office, 1981), p. 2.

21. For a fuller discussion of the pro's and con's of a balanced budget amendment, see Bruce K. MacLaury, "Proposals to Limit Federal Spending and Balance the Budget," in Joseph A. Pechman, ed., *Setting National Priorities: The 1980 Budget* (Brookings Institution, 1979), pp. 213–23; and Alvin Rabushka and William Craig Stubblebine, eds., *Constraining Federal Taxing and Spending* (Hoover Institution, forthcoming).

dures. Currently the entire budgetary process is based on guiding legislation (authorizations or appropriations) that set upper limits on the commitment of funds over a certain period. The actual amount spent as a result of such commitments—outlays—is not directly controlled by existing procedures. Actual outlays either for a particular program or in the aggregate may exceed planned outlays for any number of reasons: an unforeseen economic or natural event, unexpectedly rapid completion of contracts, incorrect projections of case loads, prices, or interest rates, and so on. These factors would still exist under a constitutional amendment, so there would have to be an enforcement mechanism to ensure that if a preponderance of the uncontrolled items were overrunning the planned outlay level, some underruns would be available for offset. In practice, this would almost certainly mean that Congress would have to delegate to the president the power to make such adjustments.[22] If Congress made such a delegation with no constraints, this would give a president broad license to impound (not spend appropriated) funds, which ironically was the "abuse of power" (by President Nixon) that brought on budget reform in the first place. Giving the president a line-item veto, a measure favored by President Reagan, would have a similar effect. An alternative possibility would be for Congress to delegate the power to impound subject to limits on how much any particular program could be cut. This, in turn, is the equivalent of agencies living under an insecurity similar to that of a continuing resolution: not knowing in advance how much they will have to spend.[23]

A constitutional amendment would greatly change federal budgeting. It would inevitably shift more power to the executive branch and would focus more attention on matters such as the budget being on target (just as public attention now focuses on money supply growth being on target) and less attention on broad

22. Congress could assign a committee the power to ensure that actual outlays stayed on target or it could regularly appropriate so little that an overrun could not occur. Neither approach would last long: committees have no executive power, which is necessary to control outlays, and sham outlay estimates are sitting ducks for frustrated spending committees.

23. It is actually a greater insecurity because a continuing resolution creates uncertainties about the level of funds an agency can *commit* while the balanced budget amendment creates uncertainty about *spending*, something that most agencies have much less ability to control.

budget policy goals. For more than just the obvious reasons a constitutional amendment would therefore open a new chapter on how the federal government conducts its operations.[24]

## Conclusion

The preoccupation of this chapter with budgetary decisionmaking processes should not divert attention from the real issues behind the policy crisis. Government officials are seeking to find a noninflationary way to move massive amounts of resources from consumer industries to investment and defense industries, from the public to the private sector, from Washington to the state capitals, from the dole to wages and dividends, from the current standard of living to the nation's future well-being. Under the best of circumstances, these changes would be hard to bring off. The fact that we are attempting to move very fast only heightens the dislocations that change always brings. Add in a partisan political environment and a Hippocratic ethic for politicians ("Do no harm") and you have a recipe for stalemate or a hypocritical compromise ("Do no electoral damage").

No budgetary process or external imperative can make tough decisions easy. The present procedures have proved flexible enough in the past to accommodate a variety of economic circumstances. As economic and political changes have made a shift to greater restraint in public spending seem desirable, budgetary control procedures have been strengthened and the shift has been carried out. The budgetary process would help any grand compromise reached in 1982 between the president and Congress by providing a legislative vehicle that forced all parties to such an agreement to join. And the process can be strengthened for future years by formally incorporating early reconciliation and increasing the scope of budget resolutions. Or it can be put back to the guidance procedures of budget reform's early years. The choice will depend on the expected need for tightness of budgetary control.

24. If two-thirds of both houses of Congress approved an amendment like Senate Joint Resolution 58, it would then have to be ratified by three-quarters of the state legislatures and would take effect in the second fiscal year after ratification. Since the amendment takes spending and taxing for the preceding year as a base, budgeting up to the effective date would probably be very divisive.

A constitutional amendment to balance the budget at bottom expresses a lack of faith that Congress can achieve budgetary control and a strong belief in the importance of such an achievement. The difficulties of reaching a budget compromise in 1982 have apparently created a climate where voting for a constitutional amendment to balance the budget is an easy vote for an esteemed goal. In reality, such an amendment would bring about profound changes in the government, not all of which are intended by its proponents.

# Individual Income Tax Provisions of the 1981 Tax Act

JOHN KARL SCHOLZ

THE Economic Recovery Tax Act of 1981 provided the largest income tax cut in America's history. The act dramatically reduced tax rates, provided new tax incentives for saving, and added numerous other special deductions. The purpose of this appendix is to provide estimates of the magnitude and distribution of the tax cuts for the years 1982–84. This is done by comparing the revenues generated under the new law with those that would have been generated under the previous law. The analysis is devoted exclusively to the individual income tax provisions of the act.

The data for this analysis come from an income tax file developed by the Internal Revenue Service, which contains all the tax information from a random stratified sample of 155,212 tax returns filed for the year 1977. The file was projected to later years on the basis of published tax return data for 1979 and changes in incomes and prices assumed in the budget for fiscal 1982 and later years. The calculations were computed by using a tax calculator developed by the Brookings Tax Project, which reads information from tax returns and computes adjusted gross income, taxable income, and taxes after credits. The provisions of the 1981 tax act were incorporated into the tax calculator program on the basis of several assumptions that are described in detail at the end of this appendix.

## Aggregate Estimates

Estimates of total income tax liabilities under the old and new tax laws for calendar years 1982–84 are given in table A-1. The tax cut amounts to an estimated $41 billion in 1982, $85 billion in 1983, and $116 billion in 1984, or, as a percentage of the total income tax liability under the 1980 law, 12.7 percent in 1982, 22.0 percent in 1983, and 26.1 percent in 1984. However, a significant portion of this tax cut merely offsets the effect of the creep upward in the tax brackets resulting from inflation. When compared with what tax liabilities would have been under the 1980 tax law adjusted for inflation (at rates projected in the 1982 budget), the tax cuts average only 2.6 percent in 1982, 9.2 percent in 1983, and 11.0 percent in 1984. In other words, about 80 percent of the 1982 cut and over 50 percent of the 1983 and 1984 cuts offset the increase in effective tax rates that would have occurred because of continuing inflation during this period.

### Estimates by Income Class

Table A-2 compares the effective tax rates under the 1982, 1983, and 1984 laws with the effective rates generated by the 1980 law

**Table A-1. Total Adjusted Gross Income and Total Individual Income Tax Liabilities under the 1980 Law and the Economic Recovery Tax Act of 1981, Calendar Years 1982–84**

Billions of dollars unless otherwise indicated

| | | Tax liability | | | Tax reduction | |
| | Adjusted gross | | | | Percent of adjusted gross | Percent of tax under |
| Year | income[a] | 1980 law | 1981 law | Amount | income[a] | 1980 law |
|---|---|---|---|---|---|---|
| | | 1981 law compared with the 1980 law | | | | |
| 1982 | 1,968 | 325 | 284 | 41 | 2.1 | 12.7 |
| 1983 | 2,227 | 390 | 305 | 85 | 3.9 | 22.0 |
| 1984 | 2,432 | 446 | 330 | 116 | 4.8 | 26.1 |
| | | 1981 law compared with the indexed 1980 law | | | | |
| 1982 | 1,968 | 291 | 284 | 8 | 0.4 | 2.6 |
| 1983 | 2,227 | 335 | 305 | 31 | 1.4 | 9.2 |
| 1984 | 2,432 | 371 | 330 | 41 | 1.7 | 11.0 |

Source: Calculations based on the Brookings 1977 income tax file projected to 1982–84. Figures are rounded.
a. As defined in the 1980 law.

**Table A-2.** Individual Income Tax Liabilities under the 1980 Law
and the Economic Recovery Tax Act of 1981, Calendar Years 1982–84

| Adjusted gross income class (dollars)[a] | Effective tax rate (percent) | | | Tax reduction | |
|---|---|---|---|---|---|
| | 1980 law | 1981 law | Percent of tax | Percent of adjusted gross income before tax | Percent of adjusted gross income after tax |
| **1982** | | | | | |
| 0–5,000 | 1.2 | 1.1 | 10.7 | 0.1 | 0.1 |
| 5,000–10,000 | 6.5 | 5.8 | 11.4 | 0.7 | 0.8 |
| 10,000–15,000 | 10.0 | 8.9 | 11.2 | 1.1 | 1.2 |
| 15,000–20,000 | 12.3 | 10.9 | 11.2 | 1.4 | 1.6 |
| 20,000–25,000 | 13.5 | 11.9 | 11.5 | 1.5 | 1.8 |
| 25,000–50,000 | 15.8 | 13.8 | 12.4 | 1.9 | 2.3 |
| 50,000–100,000 | 23.4 | 20.3 | 13.3 | 3.1 | 4.1 |
| 100,000–200,000 | 33.3 | 28.9 | 13.2 | 4.4 | 6.6 |
| 200,000–500,000 | 40.8 | 34.4 | 15.8 | 6.4 | 10.9 |
| 500,000–1,000,000 | 44.6 | 36.9 | 19.2 | 8.6 | 15.5 |
| 1,000,000 and over | 47.3 | 36.9 | 22.0 | 10.4 | 19.7 |
| All classes[b] | 16.5 | 14.4 | 12.7 | 2.1 | 2.5 |
| **1983** | | | | | |
| 0–5,000 | 1.2 | 1.0 | 21.8 | 0.3 | 0.3 |
| 5,000–10,000 | 6.8 | 5.4 | 20.5 | 1.4 | 1.5 |
| 10,000–15,000 | 10.2 | 8.1 | 20.6 | 2.1 | 2.4 |
| 15,000–20,000 | 12.5 | 9.9 | 20.8 | 2.6 | 3.0 |
| 20,000–25,000 | 14.0 | 11.0 | 21.4 | 3.0 | 3.5 |
| 25,000–50,000 | 16.1 | 12.4 | 22.9 | 3.7 | 4.4 |
| 50,000–100,000 | 23.5 | 18.1 | 22.8 | 5.4 | 7.0 |
| 100,000–200,000 | 33.4 | 26.5 | 20.5 | 6.8 | 10.3 |
| 200,000–500,000 | 40.8 | 33.2 | 18.8 | 7.7 | 13.0 |
| 500,000–1,000,000 | 44.8 | 35.8 | 20.0 | 9.0 | 16.2 |
| 1,000,000 and over | 47.3 | 36.8 | 22.2 | 10.5 | 19.9 |
| All classes[b] | 17.5 | 13.7 | 22.0 | 3.9 | 4.7 |
| **1984** | | | | | |
| 0–5,000 | 1.3 | 1.0 | 25.3 | 0.3 | 0.3 |
| 5,000–10,000 | 6.9 | 5.3 | 24.1 | 1.7 | 1.8 |
| 10,000–15,000 | 10.5 | 7.9 | 24.4 | 2.6 | 2.9 |
| 15,000–20,000 | 12.8 | 9.6 | 24.9 | 3.2 | 3.6 |
| 20,000–25,000 | 14.3 | 10.6 | 25.5 | 3.6 | 4.2 |
| 25,000–50,000 | 16.4 | 12.0 | 26.6 | 4.3 | 5.2 |
| 50,000–100,000 | 23.4 | 17.3 | 26.0 | 6.1 | 8.0 |
| 100,000–200,000 | 33.7 | 24.3 | 27.1 | 9.0 | 13.6 |
| 200,000–500,000 | 40.8 | 30.9 | 24.3 | 9.9 | 16.8 |
| 500,000–1,000,000 | 44.9 | 33.4 | 25.8 | 11.6 | 21.0 |
| 1,000,000 and over | 47.2 | 33.5 | 29.1 | 13.8 | 26.1 |
| All classes[b] | 18.3 | 13.6 | 26.1 | 4.8 | 5.9 |

Source: Calculations based on the Brookings 1977 income tax file projected to 1982–84. Figures are rounded.
a. As defined in the 1980 law.
b. Includes negative adjusted gross income.

projected to those years. The returns are classified by their adjusted gross income under the 1980 law. Effective tax rates under the old and new laws were calculated by dividing taxes after credits by adjusted gross income.

The Economic Recovery Tax Act of 1981 was billed as an "across-the-board" tax cut—it reduces taxes proportionately for all income classes. As table A-2 illustrates, this is roughly the case. The tax reduction for 1984, which averages 26.1 percent, varies between 24 and 27 percent for all income classes except for that over $1 million, where the tax reduction averages 29 percent. The higher percentage cut in the top brackets is attributable to the cut in the top-bracket rate on unearned income from 70 percent to 50 percent, the reduction in the top capital gains rate from 28 percent to 20 percent, and new saving provisions, the benefits of which will be concentrated in the top part of the income distribution.

One consequence of a uniform reduction in tax rates is that the change in disposable income is not uniform. Because the tax burden rises with income, a uniform reduction in tax rates increases disposable income relatively more in the higher tax brackets than in lower brackets. This is illustrated by the last column of table A-2. In 1984 the change in disposable income resulting from the tax cut increases steadily from a low of 0.3 percent for those receiving less than $5,000 to a high of 26 percent for those with incomes of more than $1 million.

A great deal of the debate before the 1981 tax cuts were enacted was concerned with whether the new tax law would reduce tax liabilities enough to offset the tax-raising effect of inflation as a result of bracket creep in various income classes. In table A-3, the taxes to be paid in 1982–84 are compared with the tax that would have been paid had the 1980 law been indexed. To obtain the indexed 1980 law, the personal exemptions were raised, the zero bracket amount was increased, and the rate tables were adjusted by the projected inflation rates.

As shown in table A-3, the tax cuts for the lower-income classes (those earning below $15,000 adjusted gross income) will not compensate for the effect of inflation. For those earning more than $15,000 a year, there is a "real" reduction in the percentage change in effective rates. For 1984, these reductions increase from 4.3 percent at $15,000 to 28.6 percent in the highest income class.

Table A-3. Individual Income Tax Liabilities under the 1980 Law Indexed for Inflation
and the Economic Recovery Tax Act of 1981, Calendar Years 1982–84

| Adjusted gross income class (dollars)[a] | Effective tax rate (percent) | | Percent of tax | Tax reduction | |
|---|---|---|---|---|---|
| | 1980 law indexed | 1981 law | | Percent of adjusted gross income before tax | Percent of adjusted gross income after tax |
| **1982** | | | | | |
| 0–5,000 | 0.5 | 1.1 | −112.3 | −0.6 | −0.6 |
| 5,000–10,000 | 5.0 | 5.8 | −15.3 | −0.8 | −0.8 |
| 10,000–15,000 | 8.4 | 8.8 | −4.9 | −0.4 | −0.4 |
| 15,000–20,000 | 10.7 | 10.9 | −1.5 | −0.2 | −0.2 |
| 20,000–25,000 | 12.0 | 11.9 | 1.0 | 0.1 | 0.1 |
| 25,000–50,000 | 14.1 | 13.8 | 1.9 | 0.3 | 0.3 |
| 50,000–100,000 | 20.9 | 20.3 | 2.9 | 0.6 | 0.8 |
| 100,000–200,000 | 31.2 | 28.9 | 7.3 | 2.3 | 3.3 |
| 200,000–500,000 | 39.4 | 34.3 | 12.9 | 5.1 | 8.4 |
| 500,000–1,000,000 | 44.1 | 36.0 | 18.2 | 8.0 | 14.3 |
| 1,000,000 and over | 47.1 | 36.9 | 21.6 | 10.2 | 19.3 |
| All classes[b] | 14.8 | 14.4 | 2.6 | 0.4 | 0.5 |
| **1983** | | | | | |
| 0–5,000 | 0.3 | 1.0 | −203.9 | −0.7 | −0.7 |
| 5,000–10,000 | 4.6 | 5.4 | −16.5 | −0.8 | −0.8 |
| 10,000–15,000 | 8.1 | 8.1 | −0.6 | −0.1 | −0.1 |
| 15,000–20,000 | 10.3 | 9.9 | 3.9 | 0.4 | 0.4 |
| 20,000–25,000 | 11.9 | 11.0 | 7.9 | 0.9 | 1.1 |
| 25,000–50,000 | 13.8 | 12.4 | 9.9 | 1.4 | 1.6 |
| 50,000–100,000 | 19.9 | 18.1 | 9.1 | 1.8 | 2.3 |
| 100,000–200,000 | 30.3 | 26.5 | 12.5 | 3.8 | 5.4 |
| 200,000–500,000 | 38.9 | 33.2 | 14.7 | 5.7 | 9.4 |
| 500,000–1,000,000 | 43.9 | 35.8 | 18.5 | 8.1 | 14.5 |
| 1,000,000 and over | 47.0 | 36.8 | 21.7 | 10.2 | 19.3 |
| All classes[b] | 15.1 | 13.7 | 9.2 | 1.4 | 1.6 |
| **1984** | | | | | |
| 0–5,000 | 0.2 | 1.0 | −392.1 | −0.8 | −0.8 |
| 5,000–10,000 | 4.3 | 5.3 | −23.8 | −1.0 | −1.1 |
| 10,000–15,000 | 7.8 | 7.9 | −2.0 | −0.2 | −0.2 |
| 15,000–20,000 | 10.0 | 9.6 | 4.3 | 0.4 | 0.5 |
| 20,000–25,000 | 11.7 | 10.6 | 9.0 | 1.1 | 1.2 |
| 25,000–50,000 | 13.6 | 12.0 | 11.5 | 1.6 | 1.8 |
| 50,000–100,000 | 19.1 | 17.3 | 9.1 | 1.7 | 2.2 |
| 100,000–200,000 | 29.4 | 24.3 | 17.4 | 5.1 | 7.3 |
| 200,000–500,000 | 38.3 | 30.9 | 19.4 | 7.5 | 12.1 |
| 500,000–1,000,000 | 43.8 | 33.4 | 23.9 | 10.5 | 18.6 |
| 1,000,000 and over | 46.8 | 33.5 | 28.6 | 13.4 | 25.2 |
| All classes[b] | 15.2 | 13.6 | 11.0 | 1.7 | 2.0 |

Source: Calculations based on the Brookings 1977 income tax file projected to 1982–84. Figures are rounded.
Minus sign indicates tax increase.
a. As defined in the 1980 law.
b. Includes negative adjusted gross income.

**Detailed Estimates of Individual Provisions**

Table A-4 presents detailed estimates of the tax reductions resulting from the major provisions of the 1981 act by income classes for 1982, 1983, and 1984.

*Rate Cuts*

The cornerstone of the 1981 individual income tax cut is a set of cumulative across-the-board rate reductions of 10 percent in 1982, 19 percent in 1983, and 23 percent in 1984. These rate changes are by far the most significant individual income tax reductions of the 1981 act. As shown in table A-4, revenues will be reduced by an estimated $104.8 billion in 1984 as a consequence of the rate reductions. As is suggested by the term *across-the-board,* all income classes will get substantial reductions in tax liability.

*Savings Incentives*

A stated objective of the 1981 tax act was to provide incentives for people to increase their savings. In addition to rate cuts, these incentives take three forms. The provisions for individual retirement accounts (IRAs) and self-employed pension plans (Keoghs) were liberalized, and interest from certain specific savings certificates (all savers) was excluded from taxation.

Major changes were made in the law with respect to individual retirement accounts. The deductible contribution by an employed person to an IRA was increased from $1,500 to $2,000 and, in the case of spousal IRAs, from $1,750 to $2,250. In addition, an individual who is already participating in a qualified employer retirement plan will be allowed to establish an IRA.

As shown in table A-5, the estimated revenue loss from IRA deductions is $2.9 billion in 1984. Though taxpayers in all income classes will benefit from the new IRAs, the reduction in tax burdens in the $50,000 to $100,000 income class accounts for 45.5 percent of the $2.9 billion estimated reduction in tax revenues.

The 1981 law increased the maximum contribution to Keogh plans established by self-employed persons from $7,500 to $15,000. This provision, which will reduce tax revenues by $360 million in 1984 (see table A-5), will have virtually no impact on those with adjusted gross incomes of less than $50,000: most of the benefit will go to those with adjusted gross incomes of more than $100,000.

The all savers provision allows an individual a once-in-a-lifetime exclusion of up to $1,000 ($2,000 on joint returns) for interest earned on an investment in a special qualified savings certificate issued by saving and loan associations, banks, and credit unions in the period October 1, 1981, to December 31, 1982. In 1982, $2.4 billion in revenue will be lost as a consequence of the all savers legislation. As with the new IRA provisions, the all savers legislation will reduce tax liabilities in all income classes, but 54 percent of the benefit will go to those with adjusted gross incomes between $50,000 and $200,000.

To recover some of the revenue lost from the new savings provisions, the $200 exclusion for interest and dividend income ($400 on joint returns), which applied only to the years 1981 and 1982, was repealed for 1982. This repeal, which reinstates the $100 dividend exclusion ($200 on joint returns), will increase tax revenues $3 billion in 1982. In 1985 and subsequent years, individuals will be allowed to deduct 15 percent of net interest up to $3,000 ($6,000 on joint returns). This new provision will reduce revenues $1.9 billion in 1985.

### Child Care Credit, Charitable Contributions Deduction

Two provisions of the Economic Recovery Tax Act of 1981 affect those in lower-income classes proportionately more than those in upper-income classes. These provisions allow nonitemizers to deduct a portion of their charitable contributions and will allow lower- and moderate-income people to take a larger child and dependent care credit. As shown in table A-4, these two provisions reduce tax revenues by $640 million in 1984.

### Deduction for Two-Earner Couples

Another major provision of the 1981 act is the deduction for two-earner married couples, which was intended to moderate the so-called marriage penalty resulting from the income-splitting provision and the special rate schedule for single persons. The deduction will be 5 percent of the earned income of the spouse with lower earnings (up to $30,000) in 1982 and 10 percent in 1983 and later years.

Table A-4. Income Tax Reductions Resulting from the Major Provisions of the Economic Recovery Tax Act of 1981, Calendar Years 1982–84
Millions of dollars unless otherwise indicated

| Adjusted gross income (dollars)[a] | Rate cuts | | Two-earner deduction | | Savings incentives[b] | | Charity and child care credit | | Total | |
|---|---|---|---|---|---|---|---|---|---|---|
| | Amount | Percent[c] | Amount | Percent[c] | Amount | Percent[c] | Amount | Percent[c] | Amount | Percent[c] |
| **1982** | | | | | | | | | | |
| 0–5,000 | 173.9 | 0.2 | * | * | −24.3 | −0.1 | 9.3 | * | 158.9 | 0.1 |
| 5,000–10,000 | 953.2 | 0.8 | 10.1 | * | −132.6 | −0.1 | 42.9 | * | 873.6 | 0.7 |
| 10,000–15,000 | 1,950.1 | 1.1 | 60.2 | * | −179.7 | −0.1 | 67.5 | * | 1,898.1 | 1.1 |
| 15,000–20,000 | 2,621.8 | 1.4 | 146.3 | 0.1 | −168.8 | −0.1 | 63.0 | * | 2,662.3 | 1.4 |
| 20,000–25,000 | 3,099.6 | 1.4 | 278.5 | 0.1 | −69.7 | * | 46.5 | * | 3,354.9 | 1.5 |
| 25,000–50,000 | 13,208.7 | 1.6 | 2,191.7 | 0.3 | 408.7 | 0.1 | 51.5 | * | 15,860.6 | 1.9 |
| 50,000–100,000 | 6,523.7 | 2.3 | 624.8 | 0.2 | 1,529.3 | 0.5 | 7.8 | * | 8,685.6 | 3.1 |
| 100,000–200,000 | 3,151.7 | 3.6 | 143.5 | 0.2 | 572.3 | 0.7 | 1.0 | * | 3,868.5 | 4.4 |
| 200,000–500,000 | 2,339.3 | 6.0 | 35.2 | 0.1 | 141.7 | 0.4 | 0.1 | * | 2,516.3 | 6.4 |
| 500,000–1,000,000 | 773.0 | 8.4 | 3.1 | * | 13.4 | 0.1 | * | * | 789.5 | 8.6 |
| 1,000,000 and over | 897.9 | 10.3 | 0.7 | * | 3.7 | * | * | * | 902.3 | 10.4 |
| All classes[d] | 35,592.8 | 1.8 | 3,494.2 | 0.2 | 2,093.7 | 0.1 | 289.7 | * | 41,470.4 | 2.1 |
| **1983** | | | | | | | | | | |
| 0–5,000 | 105.4 | 0.2 | * | * | 0.8 | * | 8.0 | * | 114.2 | 0.3 |
| 5,000–10,000 | 1,451.2 | 1.3 | 16.9 | * | 43.8 | * | 36.7 | * | 1,548.6 | 1.4 |
| 10,000–15,000 | 3,267.0 | 2.0 | 96.5 | 0.1 | 61.0 | * | 59.8 | * | 3,484.3 | 2.1 |
| 15,000–20,000 | 4,569.3 | 2.4 | 228.0 | 0.1 | 73.2 | * | 61.9 | * | 4,932.4 | 2.6 |
| 20,000–25,000 | 5,738.6 | 2.7 | 436.3 | 0.2 | 146.2 | 0.1 | 42.6 | * | 6,363.7 | 3.0 |

| | | | | | | | | | |
|---|---|---|---|---|---|---|---|---|---|
| 25,000–50,000 | 28,786.5 | 3.1 | 4,437.4 | 0.5 | 1,379.8 | 0.1 | 69.0 | * | 34,672.7 | 3.7 |
| 50,000–100,000 | 17,095.1 | 4.4 | 1,585.3 | 0.4 | 2,204.9 | 0.6 | 11.6 | * | 20,896.9 | 5.4 |
| 100,000–200,000 | 6,583.4 | 5.9 | 358.8 | 0.3 | 759.5 | 0.7 | 1.6 | * | 7,703.3 | 6.8 |
| 200,000–500,000 | 3,587.4 | 7.1 | 89.6 | 0.2 | 200.4 | 0.4 | 0.2 | * | 3,877.6 | 7.7 |
| 500,000–1,000,000 | 1,032.6 | 8.7 | 8.2 | 0.1 | 18.7 | 0.2 | * | * | 1,059.5 | 9.0 |
| 1,000,000 and over | 1,118.7 | 10.4 | 2.0 | * | 4.7 | * | * | * | 1,125.4 | 10.5 |
| All classes^d | 73,335.1 | 3.3 | 7,259.1 | 0.3 | 4,892.9 | 0.2 | 291.4 | * | 85,778.5 | 3.9 |
| **1984** | | | | | | | | | | |
| 0–5,000 | 108.5 | 0.3 | * | * | 0.1 | * | 22.8 | 0.1 | 131.4 | 0.3 |
| 5,000–10,000 | 1,647.5 | 1.6 | 13.3 | * | 17.8 | * | 85.8 | 0.1 | 1,764.4 | 1.7 |
| 10,000–15,000 | 3,929.1 | 2.4 | 77.8 | * | 42.8 | * | 117.5 | 0.1 | 4,167.2 | 2.6 |
| 15,000–20,000 | 5,602.7 | 3.0 | 189.5 | 0.1 | 54.5 | * | 119.1 | 0.1 | 5,965.8 | 3.2 |
| 20,000–25,000 | 6,938.7 | 3.4 | 388.0 | 0.2 | 96.5 | * | 86.4 | * | 7,509.6 | 3.6 |
| 25,000–50,000 | 38,554.5 | 3.8 | 4,415.5 | 0.4 | 915.1 | 0.1 | 174.9 | * | 44,060.0 | 4.3 |
| 50,000–100,000 | 27,438.3 | 5.4 | 1,939.8 | 0.4 | 1,411.4 | 0.3 | 31.1 | * | 30,820.6 | 6.1 |
| 100,000–200,000 | 11,353.6 | 8.3 | 421.9 | 0.3 | 544.1 | 0.4 | 2.6 | * | 12,322.2 | 9.0 |
| 200,000–500,000 | 5,859.6 | 9.5 | 107.6 | 0.2 | 157.9 | 0.3 | 0.3 | * | 6,125.4 | 9.9 |
| 500,000–1,000,000 | 1,644.5 | 11.4 | 10.4 | 0.1 | 14.3 | 0.1 | * | * | 1,669.2 | 11.6 |
| 1,000,000 and over | 1,738.4 | 13.7 | 2.3 | * | 3.4 | * | * | * | 1,744.1 | 13.8 |
| All classes^d | 104,815.4 | 4.3 | 7,566.0 | 0.3 | 3,257.8 | 0.1 | 640.4 | * | 116,279.6 | 4.8 |

Source: Calculations based on the Brookings 1977 income tax file projected to 1982–84. Figures are rounded.
*Less than 0.05.
a. As defined in the 1980 law.
b. Savings incentives include individual retirement accounts, all savers certificates, Keogh plans, and interest and dividend exclusions. Minus signs indicate tax increases.
c. Percentage of adjusted gross income.
d. Includes negative adjusted gross income.

**Table A-5. Income Tax Reductions Resulting from the Savings Incentives of the Economic Recovery Tax Act of 1981, Calendar Years 1982–84**

Millions of dollars

| Adjusted gross income (dollars)[a] | IRAs | Keoghs | All savers certificates[b] | Interest and dividend exclusion[c] |
|---|---|---|---|---|
| **1982** | | | | |
| 0–5,000 | 0.3 | 0.0 | 2.3 | −27.0 |
| 5,000–10,000 | 22.5 | 0.0 | 22.1 | −177.3 |
| 10,000–15,000 | 41.6 | 0.0 | 25.4 | −246.7 |
| 15,000–20,000 | 65.3 | 0.0 | 28.2 | −262.3 |
| 20,000–25,000 | 169.4 | 0.0 | 51.2 | −290.3 |
| 25,000–50,000 | 964.0 | 0.8 | 744.7 | −1,300.8 |
| 50,000–100,000 | 949.4 | 93.6 | 1,077.1 | −590.7 |
| 100,000–200,000 | 252.1 | 111.6 | 325.7 | −117.1 |
| 200,000–500,000 | 59.2 | 26.8 | 79.5 | −23.8 |
| 500,000–1,000,000 | 5.7 | 2.1 | 7.7 | −2.1 |
| 1,000,000 and over | 1.6 | 0.5 | 2.1 | −0.6 |
| All classes[d] | 2,531.3 | 235.4 | 2,366.1 | −3,039.1 |
| **1983** | | | | |
| 0–5,000 | 0.0 | 0.0 | 0.8 | . . . |
| 5,000–10,000 | 21.3 | 0.0 | 22.5 | . . . |
| 10,000–15,000 | 27.5 | 0.0 | 33.5 | . . . |
| 15,000–20,000 | 39.0 | 0.0 | 34.2 | . . . |
| 20,000–25,000 | 113.5 | 0.0 | 32.8 | . . . |
| 25,000–50,000 | 978.2 | 0.9 | 400.7 | . . . |
| 50,000–100,000 | 1,132.1 | 97.6 | 975.2 | . . . |
| 100,000–200,000 | 302.0 | 163.5 | 294.0 | . . . |
| 200,000–500,000 | 77.0 | 45.9 | 77.5 | . . . |
| 500,000–1,000,000 | 7.6 | 3.6 | 7.5 | . . . |
| 1,000,000 and over | 2.1 | 0.8 | 1.8 | . . . |
| All classes[d] | 2,700.2 | 312.2 | 1,880.5 | . . . |
| **1984** | | | | |
| 0–5,000 | 0.1 | 0.0 | . . . | . . . |
| 5,000–10,000 | 17.8 | 0.0 | . . . | . . . |
| 10,000–15,000 | 42.8 | 0.0 | . . . | . . . |
| 15,000–20,000 | 54.5 | 0.0 | . . . | . . . |
| 20,000–25,000 | 96.5 | 0.0 | . . . | . . . |
| 25,000–50,000 | 914.5 | 0.6 | . . . | . . . |
| 50,000–100,000 | 1,320.9 | 90.5 | . . . | . . . |
| 100,000–200,000 | 345.3 | 198.9 | . . . | . . . |
| 200,000–500,000 | 94.3 | 63.8 | . . . | . . . |
| 500,000–1,000,000 | 9.3 | 4.9 | . . . | . . . |
| 1,000,000 and over | 2.3 | 1.0 | . . . | . . . |
| All classes[d] | 2,898.0 | 359.7 | . . . | . . . |

Source: Calculations based on the Brookings 1977 income tax file projected to 1982–84. Figures are rounded.

a. As defined in the 1980 law.

b. No figures are given for 1984 because this provision was limited to the period October 1, 1981, to December 31, 1982.

c. Minus signs for 1982 figures indicate tax increases. No figures are given for 1983 and 1984 because the dividend exclusion of $100 was reinstated effective in 1983.

d. Includes negative adjusted gross income.

The deduction for two-earner couples will reduce total tax revenues by $7.6 billion in 1984 (see table A-4). The major beneficiaries of this deduction are married couples reporting adjusted gross income between $25,000 and $50,000, who will receive 58 percent of the benefit from the deduction.

**Assumptions**

The most important assumptions made in developing the estimates for this appendix are as follows:

*Deduction for two-earner married couples.* The income tax file does not contain information on the distribution of earnings reported on joint returns. To estimate the income of each spouse, use was made of a Treasury Department matrix that gives, for each income class, a distribution of the earnings of spouses in two-earner couples.

*Charitable contributions deductions for nonitemizers.* Data on the contributions of nonitemizers are not available. It was assumed that nonitemizers are split into four groups of equal size, which give 100, 75, 50, or 25 percent of the maximum contribution ($100 in 1982 and 1983; $300 in 1984). As provided in the 1981 act, 25 percent of these amounts were allowed as deductions. (The allowable deduction is increased to 50 percent of contributions up to $300 in 1985 and 100 percent of contributions in 1986 and later years.) If it were assumed that all nonitemizers give the maximum amount each year, the annual revenue loss from the charitable contributions provision would increase about 60 percent.

*Child and dependent care credit.* The 1981 act increases outlays eligible for the credit from $2,000 to $2,400 for each of the first two dependents for all taxpayers and raises the rates of the credit from 20 percent to 30 percent for taxpayers with income of $10,000 or less, with a phaseout of the credit between $10,000 and $28,000. The increased credit was calculated directly from the amounts reported in the tax file.

*Individual retirement accounts.* It was assumed that, as incomes rise, the percentage of people participating in IRA plans will rise from 0 percent for those reporting less than $5,000 annual adjusted gross income to 40 percent of those reporting more than $50,000. For each participant the size of the IRA contribution was obtained from the following formula: IRA = 5 (dividend income + interest income − all savers) − 100. This formula assumes the participants will transfer assets to IRAs when interest and dividend income from those assets exceeds $100. The factor of five reflects both the estimated interest rate and expected utilization of the provision. The limit for any one individual earner was set at the statutory limit of $2,000. For joint returns, the IRA deduction for each spouse was estimated from the Treasury matrix used to calculate the effect of the new deduction for two-earner couples.

If it were assumed that as incomes rise the percentage of people participating in IRA plans would increase from 0 percent for those reporting less than $5,000 to 100 percent for those reporting more than $50,000, and if IRA contributions were increased to IRA = 10 (dividend income + interest income − all savers), the revenue loss from the IRA provision would triple.

*Self-employed pension plans.* The limit of the deduction for these plans was raised from $7,500 to $15,000.

*Tax-exempt savings certificates (all savers).* It was assumed that the pool of purchasers of all savers certificates would be 10 percent of all people below the 30 percent marginal tax bracket and all those above this level. For this pool, the amount of tax-exempt interest was calculated from the following equation: all savers interest = 0.6 (dividend income − 200) + 0.8 (interest income − 100). This equation assumes that people will transfer a portion of their interest- and dividend-bearing assets that yield more than $200 in dividend income and $100 in interest income. To allow for the statutory limit of the interest on all savers certificates to 70 percent of the one-year Treasury bill rates, the reduction in tax liabilities was limited to $2,857 ($2,000 divided by 0.7). One-eighth of the total deduction for all savers certificates was distributed to 1981, one-half to 1982, and the remaining three-eighths to 1983.

If it were assumed that all people who had sufficient interest and dividend income purchased all savers certificates, as defined by the equation, all savers interest = (dividend income − 200) + (interest income − 100), the revenue loss would double.

*Exclusion for interest and dividends.* The $200 deduction for interest and dividends ($400 on joint returns) was replaced by a dividend deduction of $100 ($200 on joint returns).

# APPENDIX B

# Tax Expenditures

JULIE A. CARR

TAX EXPENDITURES are departures from identical treatment of all types of income under the individual and corporation income taxes. The term was coined to emphasize the similarity between a direct government expenditure for a public purpose and a concession in the tax law designed to induce or subsidize private action toward the same end. The major difference between the two is that direct expenditures are shown in the budget as outlays, while tax expenditures reduce receipts. The Congressional Budget Act of 1974 requires listing tax expenditures in each budget and directs all congressional committees to identify any changes made in them by new legislation.

The 1974 act defines tax expenditures as "revenue losses attributable to provisions of the federal tax laws which allow a special exclusion, exemption, or deduction from gross income or which provide a special credit, a preferential rate of tax, or a deferral of tax liability." For this purpose, "gross income" is generally regarded as being as close to economic income as practical measurement permits. (Thus capital gains are included in full, but imputed incomes such as rental values of owned homes are not because they are difficult to measure.) The personal exemption, standard deduction, and rate schedules are considered part of the normal income tax structure and thus are not tax expenditures.

A tax provision generates a tax expenditure under this definition when two conditions are fulfilled: the provision must be special in that it applies to a narrow class of transactions or transactors; and there must be a general provision to which the special provision is a clear exception. A special provision implies a reference standard against which the exception can be compared. As in the past, this year's concept of tax expenditures uses the general provisions of the Internal Revenue Code as a reference standard, but the standard has been modified by the Reagan administration in three major respects: the accelerated cost recovery system (ACRS) enacted under the Economic Recovery Tax Act of 1981, the graduated rates of the corporation income tax, and the deduction for two-earner married couples were included in this reference standard. However, the tables in this appendix follow the standard used in previous years and thus include the excess of ACRS depreciation over economic depreciation, the cost of the graduated corporate rates, and the deduction for two-earner married couples.

In this year's budget, tax expenditures are estimated as outlay equivalents rather than revenue losses, as in previous budgets. This is done by measuring the tax expenditure as the amount of outlays that would be required to provide an equal after-tax income to the taxpayer. For many tax expenditures, the outlay equivalents are higher than the revenue losses as traditionally estimated, because taxpayers would have to pay taxes on the higher income derived from budget outlays. But the federal deficit is not changed by this methodology, because both outlays and receipts are raised by the higher amount.

Tax expenditures in fiscal 1983 are estimated at $317.1 billion. If they were replaced by direct expenditures of the same value to taxpayers, both outlays and receipts would be raised by $317.1 billion; thus current services outlays in 1983 would be $1,096.4 billion instead of the $779.3 billion reported in the budget, and receipts would be $970.4 billion, but the deficit would remain at $126.0 billion (table B-1).[1] (Total tax expenditures are the sum of the revenue effects of the individual items, each computed separately and assuming no other changes in the tax laws. They

1. Current services outlays and receipts are the amounts the government would spend and collect if all programs were continued at the January 1, 1982, level with no policy changes.

**Table B-1. Effect of Tax Expenditures on the Federal Current Services Budget, Fiscal Year 1983[a]**

Billions of dollars

| Item | Outlays | Receipts | Deficit |
|---|---|---|---|
| Current services budget | 779.3 | 653.3 | − 126.0 |
| Tax expenditures[b] | 317.1 | 317.1 | ... |
| Revised total | 1,096.4 | 970.4 | − 126.0 |

Sources: *Budget of the United States Government, Fiscal Year 1983, Special Analysis A: Current Services Estimates*, p. 14; *Special Analysis G: Tax Expenditures*, pp. 28–30; and *Estimates of Federal Tax Expenditures for Fiscal Years 1982–1987*, prepared for the Committee on Ways and Means and the Committee on Finance by the Staff of the Joint Committee on Taxation, 97 Cong. 2 sess. (Government Printing Office, 1982), pp. 13, 15.

a. Current services outlays and receipts are the amount the government would spend and collect if all programs were continued at the 1982 level with no policy changes.

b. See text for explanation.

probably understate the total revenue effects because individuals are pushed into higher brackets if all or a group of tax expenditures are removed simultaneously.)

The major tax expenditures are (1) personal deductions under the individual income tax (for state and local income, sales and property taxes, charitable contributions, medical expenses, and interest paid); (2) exclusions from taxable income (state and local government bond interest, employee benefits, and transfer payments such as social security, unemployment compensation, and welfare); (3) preferential treatment of long-term capital gains; and (4) tax credits and accelerated depreciation for investment. A list of the major tax expenditures is given in table B-2.

Tax expenditures have grown much faster than direct outlays over the past several years. This is largely because inflation has pushed taxpayers into higher marginal tax rate brackets; the cost of the tax expenditures is estimated as though the exclusions and deductions were abolished and the resulting additional taxable income were taxed at those higher rates. However, some tax expenditures have grown more rapidly because they are more widely used; an example is the exclusion of interest on state and local industrial development bonds, which more than tripled in revenue cost between 1979 and 1982.

The inclusion of estimates of tax expenditures in the budget encourages the administration and Congress to consider them in budget decisions. The total of tax expenditures is 39 percent as large as that of budget outlays before allowances for civilian

**Table B-2.  Outlay Equivalents for Major Tax Expenditures, Fiscal Year 1983**
Millions of dollars

| Tax expenditure | Amount |
|---|---|
| Deductibility of state and local nonbusiness taxes | 32,170 |
| Deductibility of charitable contributions | 10,390 |
| Deductibility of mortgage interest and interest on consumer debt | 35,120 |
| Deductibility of medical expenses | 4,210 |
| Deductibility of casualty losses | 1,165 |
| Deduction for two-earner married couples | 3,980 |
| Exemptions for elderly and blind and tax credit for the elderly | 2,535 |
| Exemptions for parents of students aged 19 and over | 1,020 |
| Exclusion of employer contributions to pension, health, and welfare plans[a] | 67,815 |
| Exclusion and deferral of interest payments[b] | 24,915 |
| Exclusion of benefits and allowances to armed forces personnel | 2,450 |
| Exclusion of transfer payments | 21,695 |
| Dividend exclusion | 650 |
| Earned income credit[c] | 500 |
| Residential, conservation, and new technology energy credits | 1,790 |
| Job credits | 200 |
| Credit for child and dependent care expenses | 2,020 |
| Tax credits or exclusions for income from abroad | 4,580 |
| Preferential treatment of capital gains[d] | 30,255 |
| Investment tax credit | 29,365 |
| Accelerated cost recovery system | 13,505 |
| Safe harbor leasing rules | 4,600 |
| Excess of percentage over cost depletion and expensing of exploration and development costs | 9,310 |
| Expensing of construction period interest and taxes | 615 |
| Credit for, and expensing of, research and development expenditures | −200 |
| Deferral of income of domestic international sales corporations and controlled foreign corporations | 2,775 |
| Excess bad debt reserves of financial institutions | 1,030 |
| Reduced rates on first $100,000 of corporate income | 7,125 |
| Other | 1,520 |
| Total | 317,105 |

Sources: *Special Analysis G*, pp. 28–30; and *Estimates of Federal Tax Expenditures for Fiscal Years 1982–1987*, pp. 13, 15.

a. Includes contributions to individual retirement accounts and prepaid legal services and plans for the self-employed.

b. Includes exclusion of interest on state and local government debt and life insurance savings and deferral of interest on federal savings bonds.

c. The figure in this table indicates the tax subsidies provided by the earned income tax credit. The credit also increases budget outlays by $1.2 billion.

d. Includes credit for rehabilitation of structures.

agency pay raises and offsetting receipts (see table B-3), and in recent years has grown faster. For some budget functions, tax expenditures (for example, aid for commerce and housing and aid to state and local governments) exceed direct outlays. The distributional effects of tax expenditures are often quite different from those of direct expenditures; for example, the deductibility of mortgage interest is of little benefit to the poor, whereas outlays for rent subsidies do help them.

**Table B-3. Federal Current Services Outlays and Tax Expenditures, by Function, Fiscal Year 1983[a]**

Billions of dollars unless otherwise indicated

| Budget function | Current services outlays | Tax expenditures Amount[b] | Tax expenditures Percent of outlays |
|---|---|---|---|
| National defense | 202.3 | 2.6 | 1.3 |
| International affairs | 11.7 | 4.9 | 41.9 |
| General science, space, and technology | 7.6 | − 0.2[c] | − 2.6[c] |
| Energy | 5.5 | 10.5 | 190.9 |
| Natural resources and environment | 10.7 | 3.0 | 28.0 |
| Agriculture | 4.5 | 0.6 | 13.3 |
| Commerce and housing credit | 3.6 | 142.7 | 3,963.9 |
| Transportation | 20.9 | 0.1 | 0.5 |
| Community and regional development | 7.3 | 0.4 | 5.5 |
| Education, training, employment, and social services | 26.7 | 19.3 | 72.3 |
| Health | 82.5 | 27.9 | 33.8 |
| Income security | 271.5 | 71.1 | 26.2 |
| Veterans' benefits and services | 24.9 | 1.6 | 6.4 |
| Administration of justice | 4.8 | . . . | . . . |
| Interest | 115.1 | 0.7 | 0.6 |
| General government | 4.8 | 0.1 | 2.1 |
| General purpose fiscal assistance to state and local government | 6.6 | 31.8 | 481.8 |
| Subtotal | 811.0 | 317.1 | 39.1 |
| Allowances for civilian agency pay raises | 1.5 | . . . | . . . |
| Undistributed offsetting receipts | − 33.4 | . . . | . . . |
| Total outlays | 779.1 | 317.1 | 40.7 |

Sources: *Special Analysis A*, p. 8; *Special Analysis G*, pp. 28–30; and *Estimates of Federal Tax Expenditures for Fiscal Years 1982–1987*, pp. 13, 15. Figures are rounded.
a. Current services outlays and receipts are the amounts the government would spend and collect if all programs were continued at the 1982 level with no policy changes.
b. Amounts obtained by addition of individual items in each category.
c. A transitional gain resulting from substitution of a credit for expensing.

There is a continual tug-of-war between the proponents of tax expenditures and budget and tax experts who resist the proliferation of special tax provisions because they complicate the tax laws and are frequently less efficient than direct expenditures. Congressional appropriations committees prefer direct outlays, and the tax committees prefer tax expenditures. The budget committees, recognizing both the similarities of and the differences between the two approaches, are trying to focus the attention of Congress on the merits of individual proposals rather than on the choice of the committee that originates the legislation. Budget decisions can be truly effective only when tax expenditures are recognized as being similar in many ways to direct expenditures.

Given the urgent need for revenue, increasing consideration is being given to the possibility of curbing wasteful and inefficient tax expenditures (see chapter 6). The Reagan administration has proposed the elimination of a number of tax expenditures and the introduction of new tax expenditures for enterprise zones, which would raise on balance an estimated $7.2 billion in fiscal 1983, $13.4 billion in 1984, and $13.0 billion in 1985 (see chapter 2 and table 2-6).